ENGLISH POETRY

Sussex Books

Sussex Publications Ltd.
85 Linden Gardens, London W2 4EU

Published in 1976 by Sussex Books

Library Edition (cloth) ISBN 0 - 905272 - 00 - 5
Paperback Edition ISBN 0 - 905272 - 01 - 3

Printed by Unwin Brothers Ltd., The Gresham Press, Old Woking, Surrey

CONTENTS

LIST OF CONTRIBUTORS

Elizabeth Salter is Professor of English at York University and author of *Piers Plowman: an Introduction* and *Chaucer: the Knight's Tale and the Clerk's Tale.*

Derek Pearsall is Reader in English at York University and author of *John Lydgate.*

Frank Kermode is Professor of English at Cambridge University. His many books include *Romantic Image, The Sense of an Ending* and *Shakespeare, Spenser, Donne.*

A.J. Smith is Professor of English at Keele University, author of *John Donne: the Songs and Sonets*, and editor of Donne's *Complete Poems* (Penguin).

John Broadbent is Professor of English at East Anglia University; he is author of *Some Graver Subject* and other books on Milton, and of *Poetic Love.*

Lorna Sage is Tutor at East Anglia University and an editor of Milton's *Odes, Pastorals and Masques.*

Ian Jack is Reader in English Poetry at Pembroke College, Cambridge. His publications include *Augustan Satire* and *Keats and the Mirror of Art.*

Richard Luckett is Lecturer in English at Cambridge University and Fellow of St Catherine's College.

Christopher Salvesen is Professor of English at Reading University and author of *The Landscape of Memory.*

William Walsh is Professor of Commonwealth Literature at Leeds University and author of *The Use of Imagination* and *Coleridge: the Work and the Relevance.*

John Dixon Hunt is Reader in English at York University, author of *The Pre-Raphaelite Imagination*, and editor of *Tennyson: In Memoriam, a Casebook.*

David Palmer is Senior Lecturer in English at Hull University, author of *The Rise of English Studies* and editor of *Writers and their Background: Tennyson.*

Richard Ellmann is Professor of English at Oxford University. His books include *Yeats: the Man and the Masks, The Identity of Yeats* and works on James Joyce.

Laurence Lerner is Professor of English at Sussex University. He has published novels and poetry (most recently *A.R.T.H.U.R., The Life and Opinions of a Digital Computer*), and the critical studies *The Truthtellers* and *The Uses of Nostalgia.*

M.L. Rosenthal is Professor of English at New York University and author of *A Primer of Ezra Pound, The New Poets* and *Poetry and the Common Life.*

Cyril Connolly was editor of the literary journal *Horizon* throughout the Forties and regular critic for *The Sunday Times* for more than twenty years until his death in 1974.

Stephen Spender is Professor of English at University College London. His books include *The Creative Element, The Struggle of the Modern* and *English and American Sensibilities*; he published his *Collected Poems* in 1955.

David Daiches is Professor of English at Sussex University. Among his many critical studies are *The Novel and the Modern World, Critical Approaches to Literature* and *A Critical History of English Literature.*

John Wain is Professor of Poetry at the University of Oxford. His novels include *Hurry on Down* and *A Winter in the Hills*; he has published several volumes of poetry and among his critical works are *Essays on Literature and Ideas* and *Samuel Johnson.*

Ted Walker is a teacher of languages. He has published five books of poems: *Those Other Growths, Fox on a Barn Door, The Solitaries, The Night Bathers* and *Gloves to the Hangman.*

Peter Hollindale is Lecturer in English and Education at the University of York and author of *Shakespeare's King Henry IV part II.* He is Editor for the original recordings.

Alan Sinfield is Lecturer in English at Sussex University and author of *The Language of Tennyson's "In Memoriam"*. He is the Editor of this book.

Acknowledgements. The publishers would like to thank the following for permission to reproduce extracts from their publications: George Allen and Unwin Ltd., Jonathan Cape Ltd., J.M.Dent and Sons Ltd., Faber and Faber Ltd., The Hogarth Press Ltd., Macmillan and Co. Ltd., Wolfe Publishing Ltd. We would also like to thank Catherine Nicolson for her work in preparing the text.

INTRODUCTION

In this book, none of which has appeared before in print, some of the most distinguished literary critics writing today consider the works of the major English poets. Their thoughts may serve as a general introduction, but they will be of most value to those who have read the better-known poems and made what sense they can of them for themselves, but now feel the need of further guidance and stimulation to help them in the development of their ideas and responses.

The unusual feature of this collection is that all the pieces in it are taken from recordings of unscripted talks. The ums and ers, the false starts and repetitions, have been edited out and I have tidied the quotations and references, but there remains a real sense of the speaking voice and of the mind revealed in the actual process of thought; the critic seems to be face to face with his reader rather than his typewriter.

This spontaneity is strongest and most rewarding in the chapters where there are two speakers. Students often find it difficult to appreciate that the interesting critical problems, largely because they hinge upon imaginative responses and artistic judgements, have no one clearly correct answer. In these dialogues we see experts respecting each other's opinions but nevertheless disagreeing, often about matters of emphasis but sometimes about fundamental issues; and these disagreements are conducted not in footnotes or in alternating letters to journals, but immediately, point by point across the table. Of course, one consequence is that the discussion does not always follow a straight line, but a misunderstanding, an abrupt change of direction or a question incompletely answered may often be more suggestive than a polished essay.

The talks, though they range widely, centre on traditionally important topics. In an opening conversation with Peter Wilson *I consider the resources of language at the poet's command and the critical terms we use to describe them.* Elizabeth Salter *and* Derek Pearsall *discuss the kinds of realism with which Chaucer endows his characters, in the process elucidating several of the* Canterbury Tales *and aspects of* Troilus and Criseyde. *The similarities and differences between the Metaphysical Poets are disputed with unrivalled scholarship and critical experience by* Frank Kermode *and* A.J. Smith. J.B. Broadbent *and* Lorna Sage *argue the roles of God and Satan in* Paradise Lost *and of chastity in* Comus, *opening up the whole issue of Milton's apparently unsympathetic attitudes.* Ian Jack *and* Richard Luckett *pick out the common features of Augustan poetry but also emphasize its lively diversity. Wordsworth's and Coleridge's notions of the imagination and the unprecedentedly natural tone they develop receive most attention from* Christopher Salvesen *and* William Walsh, *who finally disagree about the qualities of Keats' "To Autumn".* John Dixon Hunt *and* David Palmer *take up the claim that there is a split between the morbid young Tennyson and the magesterial Poet Laureate and re-evaluate* Idylls of the King.

All the speakers draw continually upon the detail of the poems to support their arguments, but this seems particularly helpful as an approach to twentieth-century poetry, which is often thought perplexing. The talks of Laurence Lerner *and* M.L. Rosenthal *illustrate the chief features of modern poetry by explaining their response to a few poems by Pound, Eliot, Yeats, Stevens and Auden.* Richard Ellmann, *whose books on Yeats' developing thought and style are classics, spends most of his time on three poems from different stages of Yeats' career.*

With recent writing the most interesting historical and critical perspective may be supplied by those who have been immediately involved. In the final chapters Cyril Connolly, Stephen Spender *and* David Daiches *consider the poetry and society of the Thirties both as they experienced them and with hindsight, and* John Wain *evaluates Dylan Thomas partly from the viewpoint of a poet who grew up under the influence of his writing.* Ted Walker *completes this merging of artist and critic with an account of his own creative methods which is also a radical and illuminating criticism.*

The pieces in this book do not pretend to establish a unified theory, either of critical principles or of the history of English poetry, but that is perhaps no great failing. The approach in each case is prompted by, not imposed upon, the poetry; there is no insistence upon the exclusive value of one kind of literary experience. The speakers all, I think, offer models of a sensitive, patient and informed engagement with poetry, eschewing the pursuit of the intricate or the abstruse for their own sakes. Surely Dryden, one of the first in England to reflect at length upon the matter, stated a proper and sufficient view of the role of critics: they should be "defenders of poets, and commentators on their works; to illustrate obscure beauties; to place some passages in a better light; to redeem others from malicious interpretations; to help out an author's modesty, who is not ostentatious of his wit".

Alan Sinfield
Brighton, 1975

I

THE LANGUAGE OF POETRY

Alan Sinfield, Lecturer in English at Sussex University
with **Peter Wilson** of the Bush Theatre, London

Introduction

What is poetry? The enthusiastic young Keats said it comes

sometimes like fearful claps of thunder,
Or the low rumblings earth's regions under;
And sometimes like a gentle whispering
Of all the secrets of some wond'rous thing
That breathes about us in the vacant air;
So that we look around with prying stare,
Perhaps to see shapes of light, aerial limning,
And catch soft floatings from a faint-heard hymning.

It may be all this but, looking at it more coolly, poetry is initially an exciting idea in the mind of the poet; then it becomes an exciting idea in the mind of the reader. In between, inescapably, it is words on a page. If we would have the poem, therefore, we must develop the fullest capacity for attending to the language of poetry, for appreciating the means the writer may use to achieve a huge power or a delicate nuance of expression.

Hence it seems right to have as a preliminary to chapters about the English poets an enquiry into the nature of poetic language. With Peter Wilson I consider how it differs from ordinary language and how it functions in its more important aspects, trying to establish a coherent theoretical perspective whilst maintaining a sense of the varying styles of different periods of literature.

THE LANGUAGE OF POETRY

Peter Wilson: Wordsworth asserts in the Preface to *Lyrical Ballads* that "there neither is, nor can be, any *essential* difference between the language of prose and metrical composition". Would you agree?

Alan Sinfield: That depends what you mean by "essential". What Wordsworth particularly disliked, surely, was eighteenth-century "poetic diction". He

Peter Wilson: Yes, he quotes Gray's sonnet—

> In vain to me the smiling mornings shine,
> And reddening Phoebus lifts his golden fire:
> The birds in vain their amorous descant join,
> Or cheerful fields assume their green attire.

Alan Sinfield: We use the phrase "poetic diction" to describe the way eighteenth-century poets adopted expressions translated out of Virgil's pastoral poems and transmitted through Milton—expressions like "finny flock" for fish, or the line you just quoted for the sun rising: "reddening Phoebus lifts his golden fire".

I think there are several reasons why this kind of poetic language was popular at that time. One of the most interesting—if we consider the example of "finny flock"—is that they weren't interested in individual fish or their specific fishiness, but in a more general notion of the relations between all created things. To point out that sheep when they get together aren't unlike fish when they get together is to imply a general statement about the relationship of all created things in a potentially perfect order, a great chain of being going from the Angels, to Man, to Animals, to Vegetables and then to rocks and the earth itself. This is the assumption about the world that "poetic diction" was intended to express.

They chose to use Virgil's language because they thought that the society of Augustus Caesar in which he wrote was the most harmoniously ordered that there had been and afforded the best opportunity for the full expression of human potential. Since Wordsworth's time we have increasingly doubted the possibility, perhaps even the desirability, of establishing the kind of order that "poetic diction" was supposed to represent. Modern poets very much object to the idea that any sort of diction might of itself be preferable or out of place in poetry.

Peter Wilson: And yet we think of the eighteenth century, or the early part at least, as an age of satire.

Alan Sinfield: The Augustans were well aware that if you have an ideal notion of what relations between people and the world should be like then in many cases you are going to be disappointed. "Poetic diction" is often most interesting to us when it is working contrastively, for instance in a "mock heroic" style, when high-flown language is applied to trivial things to expose their inadequacy.

Peter Wilson: Can we return to the original question, then: whether there is any essential difference between the language of poetry and ordinary language.

Alan Sinfield: The main point, which ought to subsume all the others, is that poetic language is more highly structured than ordinary language. It is more patterned, there are more significant, complex and orderly inter-relations between the various elements working within the structure of language. It is denser, more shapely, less random. Of course, ordinary language is structured too, otherwise we couldn't begin to understand each other. There is an infinite number of unspoken agreements amongst people within a language community as to what is happening when one person speaks or writes to another. These agreements fall into three groups.

First of all there is what is usually called the lexical or semantic level, the level of diction. It's concerned with individual word meanings which you could look up in the dictionary, but it's not only a matter of definitions. It is also all those much more precise and intimate understandings between people about the kinds of things you say in some instances and not in others—how slang is appropriate in some kinds of conversation, how you might suppress your regional accent slightly when you are in an interview or, for that matter, being recorded. Linguists often call this quantity "register".

The second group is syntax: the system by which we link words together in phrases and sentences so that we know, for instance, whether the man kicks the dog or the dog kicks the man. That's an example of the difference made by word order; the other main constituent of syntax is accidence—the use of auxiliaries and inflectional endings to indicate whether we're talking about one cup of tea or several, and whether we've had, are having, or are about to have them. These grammatical connectives are needed all the time if we are going to get any further than just a kind of muttering, or rather gasping, of single words.

The third kind of structuring in language is what we might call "the means of transmission"—mainly speaking or writing. Something like "a cup of tea" becomes a question if you say it with a rising inflection; in writing we have to find other methods, in this case a question mark.

Peter Wilson: So you're distinguishing three basic principles: first we have to understand the *meanings* of the words we use, then the rules for *combining* them, and then the *means of communication* through voice or writing. And people who learn languages have to pick up all three aspects of this analysis.

Alan Sinfield: The way you put it implies a sequence. In fact it all happens at once. Most babies begin with some kind of spluttering which their parents interpret as "Mama" or "Dada". The sound and the word go together. Combining them in sentences of increasing complexity develops very rapidly and many six-year-olds are capable of making all the sophisticated sentences you find in Milton or Shakespeare. Most of us use this fantastically complicated medium with ease and take it all for granted; we discover it with an unpleasant shock when we try to manage a foreign language. Even the simplest spontaneous utterance presupposes a structured choice between an enormous number of possibilities. But then there's also the possibility of more precise, more original, more striking, more exciting uses of language.

Peter Wilson: Like poetry?

Alan Sinfield: Exactly. Within the general structure of language we make our own structures, sentence by sentence, all the time. The poet does this with exceptional intensity, bringing all the elements into an even higher degree of inter-relatedness than occurs ordinarily.

Peter Wilson: Can we have an example, keeping to matters of diction for the moment?

Alan Sinfield: There is a passage in Book IX (line 214) of *Paradise Lost* where Eve is suggesting to Adam that they should split up for the morning and work separately. This is a crucial decision—perhaps anyone is more susceptible to temptation when alone, but certainly in Milton's world Eve is more vulnerable when she is not with Adam. This is what she says:

"Let us divide our labors, thou where choice
Leads thee, or where most needs, whether to wind
The woodbine round this arbor, or direct
The clasping ivy where to climb, while I
In yonder spring of roses intermixed
With myrtle, find what to redress till noon.
For while so near each other thus all day
Our task we choose, what wonder if so near
Looks intervene and smiles, or object new
Casual discourse draw on, which intermits
Our day's work, brought to little, though begun
Early, and th'hour of supper comes unearned."

There's such a quality of observation of character in this. We tend to think about Milton as the great bard—of the start of Book III where he is thundering on about sitting there in his blindness getting his inspiration. But here Eve is revealed very personally. In the first sentence she is quite wilfully assertive; she says in effect, "you can go where you like, Adam, *I'm* going over here". This implication is cunningly conveyed despite her apparent wish to be helpful. The second half of the passage is full of anticipations of the impending Fall. Eve says they find continual distractions when they are together, but she is going to be distracted by Satan; she says "Looks intervene and smiles" but the talking serpent is far more potent; certainly it will be an "object new", but it will draw on far more than "Casual discourse"; far more than the day's work will be intermitted and "brought to little"—their whole life in Paradise. And "th'hour of supper" in the last line makes us think of the crucial role of eating in the story.

Peter Wilson: All this is Milton's irony, isn't it? He says one thing and allows the reader to infer another as well.

Alan Sinfield: Yes, we have the outcome in mind as well as the immediate situation, because we know the story already. This is another kind of extra structuring beyond that in casual language. You do get irony in ordinary language, of course, but normally it is fairly clod-hopping and clear. Here the words interact in an unusually complex way in our minds; there are additional dimensions of inter-connection, not only within the passage but radiating out from it across the whole poem.

I think we should take one more instance which works in a

rather different way, the last stanza of Keats' poem "To Autumn". In the first two stanzas an extraordinary impression of the abundance and fruitfulness brought forth by nature and all ready for harvest in the autumn is built up. Then follows the third stanza:

Where are the songs of Spring? Ay, where are they?
    Think not of them, thou hast thy music too,—
While barred clouds bloom the soft-dying day,
    And touch the stubble-plains with rosy hue;
Then in a wailful choir the small gnats mourn
    Among the river sallows, borne aloft
        Or sinking as the light wind lives or dies;
And full-grown lambs loud bleat from hilly bourn;
    Hedge-crickets sing; and now with treble soft
    The red-breast whistles from a garden-croft;
        And gathering swallows twitter in the skies.

—Do you sense autumn going over into winter there?

Peter Wilson: Oh yes, especially with the swallows in the last line gathering to migrate to a warmer country. The whole stanza has a beautiful elegiac tone.

Alan Sinfield: Elegiac, yes, because he keeps on talking about dying—"the soft-dying day", "a wailful choir", "the small gnats mourn", "the light wind lives or dies". These may seem not very exceptional ways of talking about gnats and the wind, but together they give a powerful impression that everything is coming to an end. What might appear to be just a collection of things you might see around the place in autumn is in fact arranged to amount to something much more interesting and satisfying. It is this sense of movement through autumn which enables us to talk about the poem as an expression of Keats' mature acceptance of the passage of time and of change in life.

Peter Wilson: Your second element of language was syntax: the way the poet puts his sentences together. What's the contribution of syntax to poetic structure? Is there an essential difference between poetry and prose here?

Alan Sinfield: Well, the poet can certainly take extreme liberties. He is traditionally permitted to invert adjective and noun, subject and verb, verb and object—to put them the opposite way round to ordinary language. Writers sometimes do this just to get the rhyme or the metre and it goes unnoticed in many favourite poems.

But unorthodox word-order may also contribute to the heightened structuring of poetic language. It may emphasize a point by self-consciously postponing one part of the sentence so that the reader is made to wait for it. There's a good example in Donne's "The Sunne Rising". The speaker is in bed with his lover and doesn't want the sun to rise, so he abuses it; he says,

> Thy beames, so reverend, and strong,
> Why should'st thou thinke?
> I could eclipse and cloud them with a winke,
> But that I would not lose her sight so long.

If we were to put this into ordinary prose we would say, "Why should'st thou think thy beams are so reverend and strong?" By inverting the order Donne builds the sun up in the first line and sharply deflates it in the second; then he makes the lines which follow contrastingly straightforward and relaxed.

Or take this stanza from Tennyson's *In Memoriam* (section cxv)—here it's subject and verb that are inverted:

> Now fades the last long streak of snow,
> Now burgeons every maze of quick
> About the flowering squares, and thick
> By ashen roots the violets blow.

The whole emphasis is on Now and on activity, things happening, because of the way the verbs are promoted in the first two clauses.

Peter Wilson: Yes, and also there are the visual rhymes "now" and "snow" and "blow", so that the whole stanza seems to take shape around the word "Now". Some modern poets have developed a whole style based upon unconventional grammar. The two obvious examples are Gerard Manley Hopkins and Dylan Thomas.

Alan Sinfield: Hopkins' main objective is an extraordinary degree of compression. He achieves this by omitting all those grammatical particles which oil the wheels of language—indefinite articles, auxiliary verbs and so on. We seem to jump from noun to noun and verb to verb, almost as if on stepping-stones. I think this is connected with his determination to capture the unique essential quality of things in nature—quite the opposite to the aim of Augustan "poetic diction". Hopkins tries to make every word count; you feel him grappling with language, trying to seize the essence of the thing described. Take the opening of "The Windhover":

> I caught this morning morning's minion, king-
> dom of daylight's dauphin, dapple-dawn-drawn Falcon, in
> his riding

Of the rolling level underneath him steady air.

That last line, I think, is extraordinary, the way it catches the hovering of the bird: the syntax keeps you suspended, you can't come down. The voice is waiting to drop at the end of the sentence, but you can't see the end of the sentence because you can't discover any of the usual phrasal shapes in it. Nevertheless, there is plenty of scope in ordinary syntax for this kind of delay; you don't have to do such unusual things.

Peter Wilson: The famous instance from earlier poetry is the opening of *Paradise Lost*:

Of man's first disobedience, and the fruit
Of that forbidden tree, whose mortal taste
Brought death into the world, and all our woe,
With loss of Eden, till one greater Man
Restore us, and regain the blissful seat,
Sing, Heavenly Muse.

The whole movement waits upon "Sing" at the start of line six; the entire story of man is brought into the compass of the Heavenly Muse within the first sentence.

Alan Sinfield: Yes indeed. The first sonnet of Philip Sidney's *Astrophil and Stella* opens with a similar kind of effect. The main clause is postponed till the fifth line while he sets out in full how he came to be writing at all:

Loving in truth, and faine in verse my love to show,
That the deare She might take some pleasure of my paine:
Pleasure might cause her reade, reading might make her know,
Knowledge might pitie winne, and pitie grace obtaine,
I sought fit words to paint the blackest face of woe.

Peter Wilson: There are other things to notice in the syntax here, aren't there? There is a pattern like a linked chain: read, reading—know, knowledge—pity, pity.

Alan Sinfield: Yes. Patterning of various kinds is the most obvious and powerful contribution that syntax can make to the extra structuring that is typical of poetry. In the Renaissance, in Sidney's time, poets were educated very self-consciously in classical rhetoric and so they would have had the kind of structure you just remarked very much in mind. The linked chain was called *Gradatio* or *Climax* and the delaying tactic we were looking at was called *Hirmus*. As people read these poems they could pick out and recognize such patterns as they went along just as easily as we perceive a simile. Here *gradatio* confers a sense of inevitability upon the sequence: it seems as though nothing else could happen, it has to be that way—though, characteristically with Sidney, the build-up is collapsed before very long.

Peter Wilson: Pope, of course, is renowned for the formal balance of his syntax; presumably we may take that as reflecting the harmonious vision of society you were talking about earlier in relation to "poetic diction"?

Alan Sinfield: Yes, I think so. You just quoted the opening of *Paradise Lost*. It is appropriate to compare with that the opening of *An Essay on Man*, Pope's similar but very different attempt to explain why things are as they are. "Let us," Pope says,

Expatiate free o'er all this scene of Man;
A mighty maze! but not without a plan;
A Wild, where weeds and flowers promiscuous shoot;
Or Garden, tempting with forbidden fruit.
Together let us beat this ample field,
Try what the open, what the covert yield;
The latent tracts, the giddy heights, explore
Of all who blindly creep, or sightless soar;
Eye Nature's walks, shoot Folly as it flies,
And catch the Manners living as they rise. (I. 5-14)

These lines are packed with parallels and antitheses, but they are all neatly balanced and contained within the line or the couplet. There are disagreeables, Pope is saying, but they all have their place and can be analysed and explained.

The relation between the flow of the syntax and the other formal structures in a poem—line, couplet, quatrain, stanza—is such a simple thing but it's one of the most effective resources available to the poet. The technical terms here are: if the sense comes to a pause or stop at the end of a line then we say that it is "end-stopped"; if it goes on we say there is a "run-on" or an "enjambment". There's a good example in Keats' "To Autumn". He says, "And sometimes like a gleaner thou dost keep/Steady thy laden head across a brook". Where the line turns, on "Steady", the reader almost has to steady himself and balance round the end of the line. The poet orders his syntax in relation to the shapes of the lines on the page and consequently in our reading. The same is true of stanzas and internal divisions like the quatrains and couplets in a sonnet—for instance in the run-on into line five of the Sidney sonnet I quoted.

Peter Wilson: Metre is surely another area in which the poet can use methods not available in ordinary language? Even Wordsworth allowed that metre is special to poetry and not part of the language of man.

Alan Sinfield: Yes. The issue of metre, and also the sounds of words, takes us on from diction and syntax to what we called "the means of transmission": we're talking about the way we vocalize the poem. Metre is a very difficult topic and there's a lot of very advanced work being done. I think the key for most immediate purposes is to distinguish metre from rhythm. Metre is the regular pattern of stresses which the reader abstracts from the details of the poem and keeps at the back of his mind all the way through; it lurks behind the reading throughout.

Rhythm, on the other hand, is what actually happens in any given line, the way the reader feels required to speak it according to the ordinary demands of language. What we must attend to is the interaction between metre, the abstract pattern, and what actually happens, line by line, in the rhythm.

Peter Wilson: What about the technical terms for metre—spondee, dactyl, and so on? Do you think they put people off thinking seriously about rhythm?

Alan Sinfield: I expect they do, they put me off. I think there is not a lot to be gained by learning these things. They describe the different patterns, but the pattern that is used most of the time is the Iambic: *de dum de dum de dum.* The terms you need really are "iambic pentameter", which is when *de dum* occurs five times in a line; and when there are a lot of such lines that's called "blank verse". The main point is to recognise what the metre is—what the basic pattern is—and then to observe significant variations from that: moments where the rhythm, what you actually read, is at odds with the pattern behind it. Take the last stanza of Wordsworth's poem "She dwelt among the untrodden ways":

She lived unknown, and few could know
    When Lucy ceased to be;
But she is in her grave, and, oh,
    The difference to me!

In that last line we don't say, "The dífferénce to mé!" which is what the meter suggests, but, "The dífference to mé!" Up to this point the poem has jogged along fairly happily with metre and rhythm quite close to each other, but in this last line that regular pulse falters, indeed collapses, and this expresses the degree of the poet's shock.

Peter Wilson: The difference to him. What about modern poets who avoid regular metres and use "free verse"?

Alan Sinfield: "Free verse" depends only on speech rhythms, and of course on line length—where we turn the end of the line becomes particularly important then. People often talk about "free verse" as if all the writers of preceding centuries had perversely obstructed themselves by going to all that trouble of arranging *de dums* without any sensible purpose. But in art more freedom is not necessarily a gain. Metre is one of the constraints you can pit yourself against. It is only if language is set against constraints that it can be made to do anything special.

Peter Wilson: What about the sound of poetry? The vowels and consonants, assonance and alliteration?

Alan Sinfield: This troubles people too. Most text-books concentrate on a few spectacular examples like the passage in Pope's *Essay on Criticism* where he says that a long, slow line, "like a wounded snake, drags its slow length along" (II. 357), or on obvious onomatopoeia like the lines in Tennyson's "Morte d'Arthur" where the knight is walking over rocky crags in his armour—

> Dry clash'd his harness in the icy caves
> And barren chasms, and all to left and right
> The bare black cliff clang'd round him . . .

This sort of thing is very clever but it doesn't actually occur very often.

Also we need to be careful about how we identify sounds for comment. Looking at the Wordsworth line, "The difference to me!", we might think there are four *e* sounds, but in fact there's one *ee* at the end and at least two of the others are short *er* sounds. It's characteristic in English for unstressed vowels to turn into an undifferentiated grunt like the sound at the end of "china", and the critic mustn't treat them as if they are sounded fully.

Then there's the question of how far sounds really do correspond to mood. It's rather doubtful whether they have, of themselves, any specific associations at all, but in conjunction with the sense they may suggest a mood or atmosphere. If we return to

Keats' "To Autumn", the opening lines do sound warm and fruitful—"Season of mists and mellow fruitfulness,/Close bosom-friend of the maturing sun"; whereas the conclusion of the last stanza sounds considerably sharper, sparser—"The red-breast whistles from a garden-croft;/And gathering swallows twitter in the skies".

The other thing which happens is that words which sound alike tend to become associated with each other by the reader. This is specially the case with rhymes because they occur in parallel at the ends of lines. When we see words that sound the same, as it might be in rhymes, we should look for what they have in common or perhaps in contrast. Can I give an example? The poem by George Herbert called "Virtue" begins,

Sweet day, so cool, so calm, so bright,
The bridall of the earth and skie:
The dew shall weep they fall to night;
For thou must die.

The rhyme words seem to pick out the extremes within which our lives occur. The first two lines end with forms of light, the second two with forms of darkness, but the rhymes criss-cross against these distinctions and suggest that life and death are inter-woven—which is Herbert's theme.

Peter Wilson: Yes, I see. What you are doing again is relating details to the rest of the structure of the poem; it's all part of one hugely complex system. You've set out the basic categories we might use in an approach to the issue of poetic language. Where does imagery fit in?

Alan Sinfield: It's really an aspect of the lexical level, isn't it?

Peter Wilson: Well, it seems to me to raise problems, because critics speak of imagery in several different and often quite confusing ways. They talk, for instance, about Shakespeare's animal imagery, and then they talk about the Metaphysical Poets in their imagery yoking heterogeneous ideas together. Those seem to me to be quite different things.

Alan Sinfield: Yes indeed. The word image comes from the Latin, "imitari", which means just to copy or portray, so an image is simply a representation of the external world, copied or portrayed, in this case in language. It is a picture in words. When the Ghost of Hamlet's father is talking about how he was poisoned he says,

And a most instant tetter bark'd about,
Most lazar-like, with vile and loathesome crust,
All my smooth body. (I.v.71)

This is a literal picture of what actually happened, and if we were going to talk about disease imagery in *Hamlet* then we would include that.

Since the late seventeenth century, however, "imagery" has also meant figurative language—metaphor and the like—which is precisely *not* a literal picture of what happened. When Hamlet says, "the native hue of resolution/Is sicklied o'er with the pale cast of thought" (III.i.84), he means that thought, figuratively speaking, makes resolution ill, makes its face go pale and sickly. The picture of a face turning pale is not the subject; it stands in a figurative relation to it.

Peter Wilson: But if we wanted to talk about disease imagery in *Hamlet*, we might use both these examples, both the literal imagery and the figurative?

Alan Sinfield: Yes. The recurrence of images in a play or a poem of any length is often interesting. It may impart an overall tone: in *Hamlet* the disease images indicate that there's something rotten in the state of Denmark. Also we can compare successive occurrences and their differing contexts so that an awareness of previous instances contributes to the current meaning of an image. This is, in fact, a further mode of structuring in poetic language.

Peter Wilson: It's the main organizational principle in Eliot's *The Waste Land*. What are the chief types of figurative imagery, then? Before you mentioned Renaissance knowledge of technical terms for certain syntactical devices. Do we need to learn about synecdoche, metonymy, and so on?

Alan Sinfield: I don't know, I hardly ever seem to see examples of metonymy or synecdoche—that's when the part is used for the whole, isn't it? It's worthwhile remembering personification, which is when human qualities are attributed to inanimate or abstract things. The important question, though, is what a particular image is doing in its context, not whether you know the name for it. The chief categories are simile, metaphor and symbol. Simile is saying something is *like* something else: "My love is like a red, red rose". Metaphor is saying it *is* something else: "My love is a red, red rose".

Peter Wilson: The difference is clear, but does it matter very much?

Alan Sinfield: No, not usually! The point about both these figurative ways of talking is that they enable the poet to say two things at once, or possibly the same thing in two ways. In other words, they give a more highly structured way of speaking. Here's a good example. Philip Larkin's poem called "Toads" begins,

Why should I let the toad *work*
    Squat on my life?
Can't I use my wit as a pitchfork
    And drive the brute off?

Larkin can say much more about work by talking about a toad; it extends greatly the available range of resonant language.

Peter Wilson: So he says later on in the poem that he can't throw work off,

For something sufficiently toad-like
    Squats in me, too;
Its hunkers are heavy as hard luck,
    And cold as snow.

Alan Sinfield: Right, he extends this toad-language further to say something about his own personality. Metaphor, compared with simile, does assert a more complete identity between the two things, whereas simile is specially useful when the comparison is going to be extended or elaborate; where, for example, there is a figure within a figure or something like that. With simile, the basic nature of the connection is made clear at the start. That's obviously helpful with "epic simile", where an initially simple comparison is extended into a lengthy descriptive picture, or in such a case as the intricate twelve-line comparison of two lovers' souls to a pair of compasses at the end of Donne's poem, "A Valediction: forbidding mourning".

Peter Wilson: That's the most commonly quoted instance of the kind of image used by the Metaphysical Poets, the "conceit". An important part of our response is the question, "Whoever would have thought of comparing a pair of lovers to a pair of compasses?"

Alan Sinfield: Yes, I think that's what Donne was after. A conceit, I suppose, is an image where the two things compared are at first sight quite unlike each other but yet they do, when we think about it, cohere.

So initial surprise is followed by a quite special kind of satisfaction when we find that the poet has used his ingenuity to bring such incompatible elements together. There's another elaborate instance in Henry King's poem, "The Exequy". It's about the funeral of his wife, whom he compares to the sun:

Thou has benighted me, thy set
This Eve of blackness did beget,
Who was't my day, (though overcast
Before thou had'st thy Noon-tide past)
And I remember must in tears,
Thou scarce had'st seen so many years
As Day tells houres. By thy cleer Sun
My love and fortune first did run;
But thou wilt never more appear
Folded within my Hemisphear,
Since both thy light and motion
Like a fled star is fall'n and gon,
And twixt me and my soul's dear wish
The earth now interposed is,
Which such a strange eclipse doth make
As ne'er was read in Almanake.

Peter Wilson: I notice how he shifts the ground of the image several times whilst remaining with the central idea that the dead lady is the poet's sun. First she is set because it is night, and then there is an aside about how she died young and hardly reached noon, then she has disappeared like a falling star, and finally she's been eclipsed. This way of playing around with the central image but never managing to lose it is what we mean by "metaphysical wit".

Alan Sinfield: Yes, definitely. And it's a "strange eclipse" at the end of the quotation because it is the earth that has got in the way, whereas in real eclipses it's we who are on the earth and something else gets in the way of a heavenly body—what King's proposing is technically impossible. His idea is that she is in her grave and earth has been put on top of her, and he sustains the sun image wittily by calling this an eclipse. Such agile shifting of ground is one way the Metaphysicals use the conceit, as at the end of "Love's Alchemy": "Hope not for minde in women; at their best/Sweetnesse and wit, they'are but *Mummy*, possest".

Peter Wilson: How does this kind of wit compare with the imagery of Pope and his contemporaries?

Alan Sinfield: Well, we've talked about "poetic diction" and "mock heroic"; I suppose the passage I quoted from the start of Pope's *An Essay on Man* is reasonably typical. There he speaks of human life as "all this scene of Man", then he calls it "A mighty maze", then a wild or a garden, and finally he settles into an extended metaphor of an "ample field" which we are to hunt over.

Peter Wilson: This is not unlike Donne's image of the compasses, worked out in various aspects over eight or ten lines. Pope in the same way exhausts a single image, explores every possibility. But he's not, here, as bold or challenging as Donne; it all seems more controlled.

Alan Sinfield: Urbane would perhaps be a word one could use about it. Pope does employ provocatively incongruous imagery but that's usually when he is debunking his subject in satirical writings. In common with the Metaphysicals, though, there is a low premium on sense impressions: the emphasis is on the intellectual relationships he's making between the images. You could still call it witty in that sense of the word.

Peter Wilson: And the emphasis on the sensuous is what is different again about Romantic imagery?

Alan Sinfield: Broadly, yes. We could make a basic division with respect to figurative language between images of feeling and images of thought. In images of feeling the main point of introducing the metaphor or simile is to bring certain feelings or associations to bear upon the subject. In images of thought the aim of the figure is to work out a scheme of the nature of the structure of the subject. Obviously most actual images have both qualities in some degree, but we may distinguish different emphases. Nineteenth-century imagery tends to be more evocative; it often involves nature, and that's normally sure of a good response from us urbanised people.

Peter Wilson: Could you, before we move on, say something about the "pathetic fallacy", which seems to feature largely in nature poetry?

Alan Sinfield: The term, "pathetic fallacy" was coined by Ruskin to refer to the attribution of feeling to non-sentient beings—flowers, the weather, nature generally. Ruskin condemned its excessive use, but it occurs in all poetry, right back to the Greeks. It springs, I suppose, from a natural feeling that days look sunnier when you are feeling good and, conversely, that a sunny day can make you feel better. Locating feelings in the surroundings in this way is a very handy device for a poet to use.

Peter Wilson: Yes, though it does seem that since *Lyrical Ballads* poets have written with particular sensitivity to the sensuous qualities of their surroundings.

Alan Sinfield: I think also that poets and the rest of us have been driven back upon our immediate experience and the reality of its location in an immediate setting. We've discussed eighteenth-century "poetic diction" and the ordered view of the world it was based upon. Since the time of the Romantics we've had to work everything out individually, from our own experience, for ourselves. That is why reference to the immediately individual perception of our surroundings seems a proper way to represent in a poem what we personally think and mean about our own lives.

Shelley's "To a Skylark" is a typical instance of the Romantic use of natural imagery to express feeling, and of the poet striving to discover a way of defining the individuality of his experience. Shelley is struck by the way the skylark hovers out of sight singing; he says, "What thou art we know not;/What is most like thee?", and six stanzas of images follow. Here are a couple:

Like a glow-worm golden
    In a dell of dew,
Scattering unbeholden
    Its aëreal hue
Among the flowers and grass, which screen it from the view!

Like a rose embowered
    In its own green leaves,
By warm winds deflowered,
    Till the scent it gives
Makes faint with too much sweet those heavy-wingèd thieves.

Through the sensuous picture he attempts to evoke feelings similar to those inspired in him by the song of the skylark. He can't explain what it means to him any other way.

Peter Wilson: It is sometimes suggested that this is a rather sloppy way to write poetically—that everyone has good feelings about glow-worms and roses and the poet doesn't have to work very hard to produce the right sort of approximate response in his readers.

Alan Sinfield: I feel this myself sometimes, but when it does come off it's marvellous. I've talked about images of thought and images of feeling: for an image to work well one has to control the other. I think what Shelley is doing there is quite precise. The glow-worm and the rose in its leaves are both examples of a mysterious source, one of light, the other scent; he gives us two kinds of teasingly paradoxical situations, both of them like the skylark but neither quite the same. The successive approximations act out the Romantic belief that one may approach the essential quality of individual experience through poetic images but, at the same time, they *are* only approximations, and that reminds us that each experience is unique and that no real equivalent can exist.

Peter Wilson: We have talked about simile then, and metaphor. What about symbol?

Alan Sinfield: Symbol is one of the stickiest literary terms there is. The general meaning of symbol is "something which stands for something else". This, of course, is extremely broad. Most words stand for something else; they stand for objects, concepts, or people. For our purposes symbol is something much more confined: it's an image which we understand represents something beyond itself, although there's no straightforward cue. It's a metaphor without the literal element. Instead of, "My love is a red, red rose", or "My love is like a red, red rose", the poet says, as it were, "O rose", and leaves us to interpret what else he has in mind.

Peter Wilson: It sounds as though you're thinking of Blake's "Sick Rose":

O Rose! thou art sick!
The invisible worm,
That flies in the night,
In the howling storm,

Has found out thy bed
Of crimson joy;
And his dark secret love
Does thy life destroy.

Alan Sinfield: Yes. The poem *appears* to be about a rose but in fact we are pretty sure it is more than that. In fact most people think it is about a lady and some aspect of sexual relations. It's a matter of emphasis; we feel the poem *must* be about something more than roses!

Peter Wilson: But we are not quite certain what.

Alan Sinfield: Right. I think a principal point about the quality of literary symbolism is that it shouldn't be too simply explicable. If it is, it strikes us as too flat and easy. Breadth of meaning is part of the strength of symbol; perhaps there should be a precise core of meaning but a vaguer penumbra. It is like the difference between a cross on a road sign, meaning simply a road junction, and a cross in a church, which is involved with two thousand years of religious tradition.

We could take another illustration from Yeats' poem, "Among School Children". Seeing children in a classroom makes Yeats think about the woman he has loved at various stages of her life and then about life in general. In the last stanza he ends the poem with symbols of a tree and a dancer:

> Labour is blossoming or dancing where
> The body is not bruised to pleasure soul,
> Nor beauty born out of its own despair,
> Nor blear-eyed wisdom out of midnight oil.
> O chestnut-tree, great-rooted blossomer,
> Are you the leaf, the blossom or the bole?
> O body swayed to music, O brightening glance,
> How can we know the dancer from the dance?

The first line quoted sets up the symbols of the last two lines, but they nevertheless stand by themselves as images whose relation to the rest of the poem we are obliged to work out for ourselves. It seems to be a matter of the wholeness of experience and of an overall shape emerging in a life through a succession of changing moments.

Peter Wilson: I'm glad you brought up Yeats because, after all, symbol had a special place in his theory of poetry. He developed a whole system of symbols which he believed were of permanent significance in the minds of men, and he used these symbols in poem after poem.

Alan Sinfield: I think Yeats illustrates how there are two main ways of developing imagery with symbolic resonances: one is to use images which have a long tradition of significance in our culture—that's what happens with Blake's rose. The other is to build up images into symbols by repeating them. Yeats does both of these things.

Peter Wilson: A system of symbols isn't allegory, though, is it?

Alan Sinfield: No, I wouldn't say so. Allegory is reached when the details and the whole shape of the story have a correspondent set of meanings, item by item, within another whole system. We've been talking about intermittent heightening by use of symbols.

The other special feature of imagery in modern poetry we might pick out is the sharp juxtaposition of images—not in comparisons so much, like the Metaphysical Poets, but just left to stand one after another. In the poems of Dylan Thomas this cascade of images represents a sense of one life running through everything; with other poets the theme is more the fragmentation of modern life. Recently the technique has figured largely in pop music and in poetry connected with it, incorporating to an unprecedented degree the language and attitudes of other than the higher income groups.

Love is feeling cold in the back of vans
Love is a fanclub with only two fans
Love is walking holding paintstained hands
Love is

Love is fish and chips on winter nights
Love is blankets full of strange delights
Love is when you don't put out the light
Love is

That's from "Love Is" by Adrian Henri; notice how the method of successive approximations is ultimately the same as Shelley's with his skylark. It's rather self-conscious and whimsical, but there is potential for growth here.

Peter Wilson: You have described three constituents of the language of poetry, we have spoken of images and symbols and we have been on a brief historical ramble. Where do you think we have arrived?

Alan Sinfield: The first question we asked ourselves was whether there is an essential difference between poetic language and other language. The basic answer we've arrived at is that poetic language is more highly structured than other language. In part poetry does this by a more intense and systematic deployment of the elements that we use all the time in ordinary speech and writing. There are also, however, a number of conventions that the poet is traditionally allowed to employ to rearrange ordinary language even more radically. That's what's meant by "poetic licence". The way to read, therefore, is to notice all the kinds of things that occur, but also to try to get a very clear idea of the overall shape of the poem, of what it is doing altogether. Observations about a metaphor here or alliteration there are only interesting when they are related to the overall structure.

I think for myself that this is the attraction, the excitement, of works of art of all kinds. Experience in life is inevitably ragged and bitty. Even when someone dies you still remember them and think about them so they aren't ended. There isn't a stop; you can never say all the ends are tied up. Even in an hour when you decide, "I am going to concentrate on this," in fact you think about any number of things. In a poem everything that needs to be said is there and there should be nothing that doesn't need to be said, that doesn't contribute. The experience is complete.

Further Reading

F.W. Bateson, *English Poetry and the English Language* (Oxford, 1973)
Cleanth Brooks, *The Well-Wrought Urn* (Harcourt, Brace, 1947)
C.B. Cox and A.E. Dyson, *The Practical Criticism of Poetry* (Arnold, 1965)
Elizabeth Drew, *Poetry* (Dell, 1959)
William Empson, *Seven Types of Ambiguity* (Penguin, 1961)
Paul Fussell, Jr., *Poetic Meter and Poetic Form* (Random House, 1965)
F.R. Leavis, *Revaluation* (Chatto, 1936)
Laurence Lerner, *An Introduction to English Poetry* (Arnold, 1975)
C. Day Lewis, *The Poetic Image* (Cape, 1947)
Winifred Nowottny, *The Language Poets Use* (Athlone, 1962
Christopher Ricks, *Milton's Grand Style* (Oxford, 1963)
Alan Sinfield, *The Language of Tennyson's "In Memoriam"* (Blackwells, 1971)
Barbara H. Smith, *Poetic Closure* (Chicago University, 1968)
Geoffrey Tillotson, *Augustan Poetic Diction* (Athlone, 1964)
Brian Vickers, *Classical Rhetoric in English Poetry* (Macmillan, 1970)
William K. Wimsatt, *The Verbal Icon* (Kentucky University, 1954)

II

CHAUCER'S REALISM

Elizabeth Salter, Professor of English at York University
Derek Pearsall, Reader in English at York University

Introduction

Some people think that there are two distinct kinds of literary appreciation, the scholar's and the critic's. That the two are in fact interdependent is evident time and again in the present volume, but it is most obvious in the case of the medieval writer. We need guidance not just about what the words mean, and not even just about the historical and cultural background; often the delight of reading Chaucer resides in the slightest nuance of phraseology, which may provoke an ironical smile or even a sharp hint of a frown. Elizabeth Salter, in an extract from a talk on the difficulty of medieval poetry, draws attention to some interesting and salutary examples of this kind of effect.

Elizabeth Salter: Many of Chaucer's sly felicities need no interpretation at all; his comment, for instance on the Sergeant of Lawe: "And yet he semed bisier than he was" ("General Prologue", l.322). At other times interpretation can widen but not totally change our first untutored glance at the meaning. Take the old man January's comment on marriage in "The Merchant's Tale": "'Noon oother lyf,' seyde he, 'is worth a bene;/For wedlock is so esy and so clene'" (1.19). You recognise immediately, I think, in those two crisp adjectives "easy" and "clean" the point that Chaucer or the Merchant is making about the appalling jauntiness of this old sinner who is giving up promiscuity only because of the greater convenience of marriage in accommodating his lust. The line might be best rendered as, "For marriage is such a comfortable and sanctified way of life", but our initial response to the ludicrous and dangerous simplicity of, "For wedlock is so easy and so clean", wouldn't be at all mistaken in the light of the sorry and sordid tale that follows.

The whole question of how to manage a reading of Chaucer's verse without becoming either careless or depressed is very complex. We could recommend two entirely different approaches, depending upon the needs of the moment. First, if we are taking part (not always of our own free will!) in the intellectual game of accurate translation, we could say that it is best to regard this poetry, which is written in a language distanced from us by nearly six hundred years, as an alien art form, and never to assume that words which seem familiar will turn out familiar on closer study. Then we will not only refuse to be misled by modern associations when we read that the Cook was specially skilled at making "blankmanger" ("General Prologue", 1.387); we will go to medieval cookery books to find out that this was in fact minced chicken with rice.

If, on the other hand, we are not so much concerned with the business of translation as with a more general and comprehensive acquaintance, we might change our tactics and advertise medieval poetry to ourselves and to others as part of a total harmonious tradition of English literature, as accessible to us as, say, Donne's love poems, Keats' Odes, or Eliot's *Four Quartets*. If this is the case perhaps we would not want to linger over every word, but to look for broader similarities and affinities, thinking not so much of historical as of universal contexts.

Of course in practice neither approach can be kept quite distinct and separate. Indeed, it may be that we can only get the best out of this earlier verse of ours by a judicious and sympathetic arbitration between the scholar's passionate concern for truth and the common reader's hunger for imaginative experience. The wider implications of accuracy are never hard to prove. Chaucer's heroine, Criseyde—in the finest treatment of human love the Middle Ages would ever produce—is here weighing up the advantages and dangers of taking a lover: "Shal I nat love, in cas if that me leste?/What, par dieux! I am naught religious" (II, 759). Now if we were tempted to take that to mean, "Can't I love if I want to? I'm not of a religious disposition", when it really means, "Heavens above, I'm not a nun", we would damage the lively irony of the passage. Here Criseyde decisively puts behind her all earlier resolutions to live out her widowhood as chastely and sadly as a recluse in a cave.

Accuracy matters also when we are thinking of the exact significance that certain descriptive details may have had for Chaucer. Work now being done on the Reeve, for instance, suggests that here is a rather more complex portrait than we may have imagined. He is written off in "The Miller's Prologue" as "a cherl" (I. 74), yet in the "General Prologue" (II. 587-622) he is a highly respected craftsman, an excellent businessman, and a man with pretensions to courtly appearance. If his sword is rusty, his hair is cropped in a style which was becoming more fashionable as the fourteenth century went on. His "long surcote of pers" is expensive and he rides a very respectable kind of horse. Now the apparent lack of consistency in these details does not necessarily mean that Chaucer was being careless, but that we've lost the point he was trying to make about this particular man. Just that small reference to his close-cropped hair, which earlier editors took to be a reference to his servile station, may in fact set him for Chaucer's readers as a mobile member of society, a man of hard-headed ability—not particularly likable, but very much a man of the future, with his young lord in the palm of his hand and a secret contempt for the old fashioned aristocracy off whom he lives. Compare the young squire's elaborate curly hair: "lokkes crulle as they were leyd in presse" (I. 81). This is a courtly style certainly, but the Squire's hair style is probably slightly more traditional than the forward-looking style favoured by the Reeve.

Then there is the Squire himself. If we were persuaded to think on a quick reading of the portrait in the "General Prologue" that

Chaucer is presenting us with a typical young man of the fourteenth century, we would be very much misled. He is about as typical as a present-day debutante. He is engaged in all the traditional storybook rituals of medieval youth—the references are to romances of chivalry and love lyrics, and to associated symbols and patterns of emotion: the nightingale, sleeplessness, desperate longing and aspiration.

He koude songes make and wel endite,
Juste and eek daunce, and weel purtreye and write.
So hoote he lovede that by nyghtertale [night-time]
He sleep namoore than dooth a nyghtyngale. (I. 95)

For me the key to the portrait of the Squire is in the line, "He was as fressh as is the month of May" (I. 92); this gives the proper context for the description. Medieval readers would at once think of the pictures of the months which were painted in manuscripts or on the walls of great palaces, or sculpted over doorways to cathedrals. In these calendars May is nearly always represented as a young knight riding out into early summer fields; and those fields are often studded with the same "fresshe floures, whyte and reede" that the Squire has embroidered on his clothes (l.90). Like his father, the Knight, the Squire has much more to say to us of the ideals of the Middle Ages than of its raw and uncomfortable substance. The minutiae of the portrait make this quite clear, preparing us for the impossible sort of tale that the Squire begins to tell so eagerly but fails to finish.

With some provisos, then, we may feel justified in exchanging the word "difficulty" for "difference", as a way of indicating how we can get most out of Chaucer's poetry. A sympathetic awareness of difference can enlarge our response. For instance, the opening to *The Canterbury Tales* can be simply appreciated as a breath of uncontaminated springtime, and such a direct reaction to the seasonal dance—all bird-song, gentle rain, buds, sun and breezes—isn't to be lightly dismissed. But we could supplement and sharpen our response to take in more of what Chaucer really intended. That opening to the "General Prologue" invites the reader to think not just of a walk into a spring landscape but of the delicate processes of growth in plants, beasts and men, and of the divine control of seasonal rebirth witnessed in the regular movement of the sun in the heavens. There's a lot of mind in that passage as well as a lot of sensation, and it is much more like T.S. Eliot on spring than it is like Dylan Thomas.

The truth of the matter is that we can never be totally at home in the fourteenth century, just as we can't be totally at home in a castle or a Gothic cathedral. But isn't it rather dull, this longing to be always in the same place, to keep recognizing the familiar rather than discovering the new?

Editor: An even more elusive problem for the modern reader is the kind of relationship Chaucer assumes between the world of his fiction and the world we actually live in. In the majority of modern novels and plays the characters are supposed to be saying and doing things that we might see going on around us, but Chaucer's stories often seem to have more in common with a fairy tale or a pantomime. The action may be fantastic and obviously designed to point a moral, the characters one-sided and symmetrically balanced against each other, and the language highly stylized and artificial. Yet, at the same time, we often feel the immediate pressure of life as it is actually lived and the direct appeal of personal joy and sadness.

In the dialogue which follows Elizabeth Salter and Derek Pearsall discuss the nature and extent of Chaucer's realism. They consider the balance between apparently incidental detail, grotesque exaggeration, traditional moralising and formal structuring in several poems: the "General Prologue", the linking passages and the tales of the Clerk, the Knight, the Franklin and the Merchant in The Canterbury Tales, and Troilus and Criseyde. They distinguish different kinds of realism, and find that often the balance shifts within a work as Chaucer develops his treatment of a theme; sometimes his sympathy for his characters intrudes upon the ostensible purpose of the tale. The fullness of imaginative energy we experience when we read Chaucer perhaps arises in large part from the interaction of various levels of realism.

Derek Pearsall: I'd like to begin our discussion about realism in Chaucer with the "General Prologue", because one of the strongest impressions it makes on a reader is of realism and immediacy and vividness. When you think of some of the most famous portraits in the "General Prologue" it is the accumulation of detail to produce an impression of realism that you most remember. For instance, when Chaucer tells us that the Reeve came from "a toun men clepen Baldeswell" (1.620) it seems that he can have had no other reason for telling us that the Reeve came from there except that that was where he came from. And when he tells us that he doesn't know the name of the Merchant, again the only reason that he doesn't tell us seems to be that he actually doesn't know. These features of the "General Prologue" seem to suggest to us that

Chaucer is in fact describing real people.

Elizabeth Salter: But in fact that isn't quite the impression one gets from a more complex, or more subtle look perhaps, at the "General Prologue". So many of the characters on second consideration really have very little to do with realism at all—one can list the Knight and the Squire even, and the Parson and the Plowman who are modelled on ideals of the Middle Ages rather than on a realistic observation of what parsons and plowmen and knights were really like.

Derek Pearsall: But those are characters that you've had to select very carefully, because there are only a few like them. In fact it is quite obvious in the "General Prologue" that some of the pilgrims —well, one at least—is actually taken from life: Harry Bailey, whom Chaucer portrays as the host, really existed. In other cases he gives us detail, for instance of the Cook and to some extent of the Shipman, which has been documented and shown to have applied to real people. So here we have to reckon with a kind of realism which has reference to the actualities of Chaucer's own time as well as the more idealistic kind that you are talking about.

Elizabeth Salter: Nevertheless, I feel that to be looking for real people in all these portraits is a temptation to be resisted; one tends to impoverish Chaucer's characters by wanting to tie them down. There are degrees of realism even in the characters one accepts as being "real": there is for example the grotesque exaggeration of the Summoner and Pardoner, where you feel that the portraits are not just like life, but larger than life. There is a whole gradation of qualities of realism in the "General Prologue", shading from accurate observation linked to contemporary records right through to the idealised portraits such as the Knight or the Parson, or the Clerk of Oxenford.

Derek Pearsall: Yes, it would be interesting to take some detail which has the arbitrariness of complete realism, and find out whether Chaucer conveys some underlying meaning by it. For instance, the "mormal" or ulcer that the Cook bore upon his skin (l.386) may seem to us something which Chaucer just happened to observe, but underneath, presumably, it must have some important significance.

Elizabeth Salter: You mean the connection between the corruption of the body and the fact that this man was very much concerned with the preparation of food? Or an indication of the inner character of the cook? Is it an interesting and rather horrifying point about hygiene, or is it something more indicative of the degraded moral nature of this man?

Derek Pearsall: Well, whichever it is, it means something more than its surface reference. In other words it has to do with what we usually call irony, the level of meaning which lies below the surface reference. This is the sort of structure that we are constantly finding in the "General Prologue" for all its appearance of immediacy and accuracy. It usually has reference also to some structure of judgement and discrimination.

Elizabeth Salter: Yes, and some of these references are not totally clear to us even nowadays. We can usually gauge generally what Chaucer meant, for instance, by the different kinds of clothes that the pilgrims wear, but we are not totally certain what all these details mean. We might understand what the red stockings of the Wife of Bath signify (l.456), but it's not so clear what Chaucer meant by, say, the Reeve's rusty sword (l.618). That's a detail that looks too haphazard to be anything but real, but what could its significance in fact be?

Derek Pearsall: Yes, I think that is also true of the ordering of the portraits in the "Prologue". We often find it said that this has the haphazardness of life, but it is in fact intended to enhance our sense of the judgements that are being made under the surface. For instance, the Clerk is sandwiched between the Man of Law and the Merchant so that you get a stronger sense of the stringency and austerity of the Clerk's character by having him set between those two windbags. Other juxtapositions and arrangements confirm one's sense that there is constantly at the back of the realism a judging and discriminating mind enforcing a pattern on the "General Prologue".

Elizabeth Salter: You've been talking about characteristics of the "Prologue", where this kind of structuring is apparent, but do you think these kinds of realism are characteristic of the *Tales* in general?

Derek Pearsall: Well, I think of the kind that we've been talking about as being real realism—the kind that one can recognize in the accumulation of detail, the constant references to life and the surfaces of life. That kind is present to some extent in the *Tales*, and particularly in the linking passages, which often get neglected.

Elizabeth Salter: Wouldn't it be important here to consider the two statements that Chaucer makes about what he intends to do with the Pilgrims? Towards the end of the "General Prologue" he talks about how he's going to have to reproduce the language just as it was spoken by some of the lower orders of the pilgrims:

Whoso shal telle a tale after a man,
He moot reherce as ny as evere he kan
Everich a word, if it be in his charge,
Al speke he never so rudeliche and large,
Or ellis he moot telle his tale untrewe,
Or feyne thyng, or fynde wordes newe. (I. 731)

Again immediately before "The Miller's Tale" he apologises for the slightly vulgar language that's going to be used by the Miller and Reeve and the like. This is a plea for realism of portrayal: the language that's used is going to be the language really used by men. This is perhaps important if we are trying to judge his intent in the whole of *The Canterbury Tales.* Part of the time he wants to persuade us that he's going to be extraordinarily concerned with realism, doesn't he?

Derek Pearsall: Well, I think those passages are important, but not quite in that sense. I'm sure that when Chaucer says that we are to accept what he says because it is the very words of the people that he is describing he means us to take this with a pinch of salt; he's got his tongue in his cheek. We know perfectly well that this plea for realism is a trumped-up one and that he is in fact inventing everything.

Elizabeth Salter: But nevertheless he provides his audience there with a kind of guide-line which they are not properly allowed to forget. As far as the links to the *Tales* are concerned I think a statement like that really does mean something, because there, surely, he is portraying the pilgrims in themselves, and as they were.

Derek Pearsall: Yes, but the reference that's made in the "General Prologue" is not so much to the links, but to the actual tales told by the pilgrims, isn't it? And in that sense it is a complete delusion.

Elizabeth Salter: Well, I wonder whether it is. After all, it's a rather unusual thing for a medieval author to say he's going to do.

Derek Pearsall: Well, the reasons for it are obvious, aren't they? Chaucer, who had just written *Troilus and Criseyde*, a poem of high nobility and romance, was now writing *fabliaux*, and to some extent these needed a different kind of approach. So here he is defining his position in relation to his audience.

Elizabeth Salter: Yes, I think that's true, but it also seems to me, especially in "The Miller's Prologue", that he was pleading for writing of a dramatic and realistic sort in a way that hadn't been done before—

I moot reherce
Hir tales alle, be they bettre or werse,
Or elles falsen som of my mateere. (I. 65)

I wonder whether this isn't rather more than a simple excuse for the rough language the lower characters are going to use? Mightn't it have a more general significance?

Derek Pearsall: I agree that whatever interpretation we put on those individual passages, there's no doubt that Chaucer does go a long way towards realism in these links, and in the portrayal of two of the most fully developed characters, the Wife of Bath and the Pardoner. It is really noticeable that these are the two characters who are given long autobiographical monologues in which they talk about themselves in a way which bears a close relationship to what we think of as being alive. The Wife of Bath is not merely (as one critic has suggested) an iconographic figure portraying various heretical attitudes towards women. She is a fully realised woman, and the way in which her monologue develops—the apparent inconsequentialities, the sense we have that she is not fully in control of what she is saying, the way she loses the thread of her argument—these give us the strongest feeling that we are actually listening to a dramatic revelation. To a lesser extent this is true of the Pardoner too.

Elizabeth Salter: Yes, I was going to mention the Pardoner here because this sense of a personal revelation is less strong in "The Pardoner's Prologue". There we are on slightly different ground, aren't we? At times a different mode of writing shows through. In "The Pardoner's Prologue", it is less a man talking about himself than a sinner justifying himself to Christians in order that they may reject the sin. There is a glut of what I would call "straight writing" here, whereas there is very little of a straight, moral kind of writing in "The Wife of Bath's Prologue". I would distinguish between two kinds of realism here.

Derek Pearsall: Yes, I think Chaucer is closer to his traditional sources with the Pardoner than he is with the Wife of Bath. Both characters are based on suggestions in *The Romaunt of the Rose*, but in the Pardoner he has kept more strictly to the figure of False-Semblant, who represents hypocrisy.

Elizabeth Salter: Is it perhaps that the Pardoner is more of an evil character? With the Pardoner Chaucer can't really allow his artistic licence fullest play, whereas he can allow it with the Wife of Bath because at least there is some redeemable element in her character.

Derek Pearsall: I think it is a very moot point whether the Wife of Bath is less evil than the Pardoner . . .

So far we've been talking about some of the tales and characters where realism of this kind is most evident. What about the tales and characters that lie at the other extreme, "The Knight's Tale", for example, and "The Clerk's Tale"?

Elizabeth Salter: Well, these tales do again, on first acquaintance, seem to be rather formally structured, with very little to do with realism. But I think the interest of these tales lies in the way Chaucer uses a conventional structure but allows realism to creep through. "The Clerk's Tale", for example, is based on a very well articulated medieval form. It is in fact a sort of parable, but even so Chaucer can't resist the lure of realism. So the tale ends up very perilously poised between a moral structure and a realistic structure which might in the end destroy the moral.

Derek Pearsall: By "the lure of realism" in "The Clerk's Tale" you mean things like the suggestions of pathos attaching to Grisilde, and the way in which motives are offered for Walter's behaviour—quite improperly if we are supposed to regard him, allegorically, as God?

Elizabeth Salter: Yes, and the intrusion of the narrator's objection to Walter's testing of Grisilde—

But as for me, I seye that yvele it sit
To assaye a wyf whan that it is no nede,

And putten hire in angwyssh and in drede. (I. 404)

This is a natural response, but it's quite inappropriate to a parable of human obedience to God, which is what the story was originally intended to be. Chaucer is stirred imaginatively by the plight of Grisilde, though he really shouldn't have been if he was going to make his moral point adequately. But part of the fascination of the tale for the modern reader is the fact that he can't prevent the human element making itself felt.

Derek Pearsall: I agree. But I don't think the rest of "The Clerk's Tale" should be thrown overboard. The moral and allegorical and homiletic parts of the story have an extraordinarily fine austerity of style which is not often found in Chaucer. This is something that is worth valuing for its own sake.

Elizabeth Salter: Yes. The realism in "The Clerk's Tale" is only a gleam of a different kind of light peeping through chinks, but it is an interesting shaft of light when it comes. Perhaps more important is the adjustment of realism and formalism in "The Knight's Tale", which seems at first to be almost totally concerned with a structured set of values and has a very composed philosophic ending. When you read it again, though, the tale seems so much concerned with perplexity and human suffering and the adverse side of all those medieval institutions which at first look admirable—like chivalry.

Derek Pearsall: I think that when we first assess "The Knight's Tale" and compare it with the source in Boccaccio we assume that what Chaucer has done is to turn it into a philosophical romance: he's added great philosophical speeches and has attempted to subdue what we would think of as the human interest of the story by making Arcite and Palamon almost indistinguishable, and Emelye into a cipher. Although he is trying to make it into a philosophical rather than a personal or tragic story in the end, to some degree, he is defeated by the nature of his own imaginative energies, isn't he? After all, the portrayal that he gives, for instance, of the death of Arcite is tragic to such an extent that it disturbs the philosophical balance of the story as a whole.

Elizabeth Salter: Yes, and I think that disturbance is present from the very beginning of the poem, in some of Palamon's speeches against the gods, which are very moving imaginatively; likewise the additions that he makes to the portraits on the walls of the Temple of Mars—the cruelty of human aggression and the misery of violence is there. The poem is very much concerned with human suffering, as well as with human beings in institutionalised, formalised attitudes of triumph. I think this theme of human suffering runs right through to Arcite's dying speech and his pathetic last questions: "What is this world? what asketh men to have?" (I. 1919).

Derek Pearsall: Yes, you're talking about a theme of confusion, but I think we should accept a degree of confusion on Chaucer's part too, both in "The Clerk's Tale" and "The Knight's Tale". He isn't quite sure in which direction his imagination and his energies are leading him.

Elizabeth Salter: You've been giving examples in these two tales of Chaucer faced by a dilemma, telling a tale which cannot really be told realistically and yet all the time hankering after realism. Are there any tales in which he manages to reconcile these opposing tendencies?

Derek Pearsall: I think there is probably one, though opinions might differ about this, and that might well be "The Franklin's Tale". This story is at first developed on a human, realistic and even tragic level. The dilemma in which Dorigen is placed and the promise that she makes as a result of the conflict within her—all this seems to be writing of a very dramatic and realistic kind, and yet Chaucer is still dealing with a story which is essentially ridiculous. Our interest in "The Franklin's Tale" must be how Chaucer manages to modulate from the well-expressed and well-presented realism of the early part of the tale to the romantic congratulatory quality of the last part, where the only question to be asked is, Who was the most generous of the three characters? That modulation in the central part of "The Franklin's Tale" is one of the triumphs of Chaucer's efforts to reconcile this opposition between realism and convention.

Elizabeth Salter: Do you mean that moment in the tale when Dorigen realises what has happened and makes that long lament about the plight of ladies in the past who have suffered (ll.636-728)? This seems to me a rather curious moment, when realism, in a sense, finishes and formalism takes over. It is a very unrealistic thing for Dorigen to do at that particular point. The natural impulse of anybody in such a situation would be to run for some kind of remedy, but she sits down and meditates over unhappy stories of the past before she moves on. Is it a warning to the reader that he must now stop expecting realism and look for solutions of a more formal kind?

Derek Pearsall: Well, it's a good example of the difficulties of reading Chaucer according to modern realistic canons, because our tendency is to feel that Dorigen is not behaving like a real person and to lose interest in the telling of the story on that level. But what in fact is happening, as you say, is that Chaucer is changing the mode of the story and is now making us think of Dorigen not so much as a real person but as a participant in a story, in an action. So after that lament we think of her in a rather more external way than we have thought of her before.

Elizabeth Salter: Yes, I think that's very evident in the last part of the poem where everything has changed, even the garden that Dorigen goes to. Chaucer seems to forget, or to neglect the fact that although it is now December, Dorigen goes into the garden to meet Aurelius (l.776). It is a point which could be objected to on realistic grounds, but it doesn't matter. The May garden in which he first was tempted has changed into a December garden, but we are not encouraged to think in realistic terms at all; it is simply a place of meeting.

Derek Pearsall: And I think there is an even better example from the point of view of the novel reader, when Chaucer actually enters into the narrative and warns his readers not to be too worried about the plight of Dorigen because it will all turn out well in the end:

> Herkneth the tale er ye upon hire crie.
> She may have bettre fortune than yow semeth;
> And whan that ye han herd the tale, demeth. (l. 768)

This is the very sort of thing that is deplored by Henry James when he says that in the telling of the novel you must maintain an illusion of realism. Here Chaucer chooses not to do so because he is not committed to that conception of realism.

Elizabeth Salter: And doesn't Arveragus also seem to have some inkling that everything is going to be well? When he talks to Dorigen about it, although he weeps, he seems to have something up his sleeve when he sends her off to meet with Aurelius—"It may be wel, paraventure, yet to day" (l.745). There's a sense that we are not to worry too much about suffering because suffering is liable to be resolved.

Derek Pearsall: Yes, romance has taken over. But the tale which, amongst all *The Canterbury Tales*, causes us most trouble is probably "The Merchant's Tale". I'm not sure how this would fit into our various concepts of realism. Perhaps we would have to use the idea of the Merchant narrator of the tale to explain the extraordinary tone of cynicism and disgust which pervades it.

Elizabeth Salter: Isn't this in a mode somewhat similar to that of the Summoner and Pardoner in "The General Prologue"? It is almost a tone of grotesque realism that is being used in "The Merchant's Tale". We have that very famous picture of January when he takes his young wife to bed:

And Januarie hath faste in armes take
His fresshe May, his paradys, his make.
He lulleth hire, he kisseth hire ful ofte;
With thikke brustles of his berd unsofte,
Lyk to the skyn of houndfyssh, sharp as brere—
For he was shave al newe in his manere . . . (I. 577)

This is the same kind of style of writing as the description of the Summoner and Pardoner. It is almost warning us that realism is going to be extreme in this story, even running into the realm of grotesquerie.

Derek Pearsall: Yes. You think that when we read "The Merchant's Tale" we should relate it to concepts of the grotesque?—because Chaucer doesn't actually give us that hint to start with. He pretends that this is the tale told by the Merchant, and invites us to place it in the context of the Merchant's character as the sort of tale that a man might tell who had made a mistake in marriage.

Elizabeth Salter: But I don't think we can possibly maintain the Merchant for long as the actual teller of this tale; even the reactions of the pilgrims after the tale is over seem to prove that a stronger voice has taken over than could possibly belong to that particular Merchant. His personal circumstances being what they are, we still wouldn't expect quite such a bitter tone of telling, nor such an eye for grotesque chance.

Derek Pearsall: So the context for realism in "The Merchant's Tale" would be provided by what we take to be the tone of voice of the narrator rather than the Merchant, and this would be Chaucer's device, perhaps thought of at a later date, for fitting it into the framework of *The Canterbury Tales*?

Elizabeth Salter: I think so.

Shall we move on to *Troilus and Criseyde*? There we seem to have a kind of network of realism and convention about which it would be difficult to generalise, because it varies so much from book to book. This is one of the most interesting of Chaucer's poems because here we see him changing his mind about what he is doing as the poem progresses. Characters who are totally conventional at the beginning of the poem are totally real by the end of it. A character who may be developing in one direction in Book I may take a slightly sideways swing in Book II and turn out to be slightly different.

Derek Pearsall: Perhaps I might take up that point. One might well say that the characters appear different at the end of Book III, but by the end of Book V, and to some extent IV, former categories of judgement have reasserted themselves. We could say that in Books II and III Chaucer allows characters, particularly Criseyde and Pandarus, to develop in ways that we recognise as being inherently lifelike and, indeed, life-enhancing. This would not be true to such an extent of Troilus, and it is of course Troilus who survives Book III and who is the subject, on the whole, of Book V.

Elizabeth Salter: Yes, it is really Troilus that I had in mind, because he is very much a man of attitude and gesture, though we sympathise with him, in the earlier books of the poem. He comes to life in Book III, but it is only in Book V that one properly feels for his suffering—at that moment on the walls of Troy where he is still hoping against hope that Criseyde is really coming back and Pandarus is watching him and feeling helpless. I think there is a very strong development of Troilus over the whole of the poem.

Derek Pearsall: Yes, but perhaps we should take it a little further when we are talking about the reassertion of former categories of judgement in contrast to the development of realism during the course of the poem. We should ask precisely what Chaucer was doing in the Epilogue.

Elizabeth Salter: Well, in the Epilogue Chaucer has to put right what has gone wrong. The artistic licence he has allowed himself has not got to be reconciled both with the actual narrative which has now got to be reconciled both with the actual narrative which he inherited from Boccaccio and with a moral framework. Con- the Epilogue.

Further Reading

Muriel Bowden, *A Commentary on the General Prologue* (Macmillan, 1967)
Derek Brewer (ed.), *Geoffrey Chaucer* (Bell, 1974)
John Burrow (ed.), *Geoffrey Chaucer* (Penguin Critical Anthologies, 1969)
T.W. Craik, *The Comic Tales of Chaucer* (Methuen, 1964)
Maurice Hussey, *Chaucer's World, a Pictorial Companion* (Cambridge, 1967)
P.M. Kean, *Chaucer and the Making of English Poetry* (Routledge, 1972)
John Lawlor, *Chaucer* (Hutchinson, 1968)
Edith Rickert (ed.), *Chaucer's World* (Columbia, 1948)
Beryl Rowland (ed.), *Companion to Chaucer Studies* (Oxford, 1968)
Edward Wagenknecht (ed.), *Chaucer, Modern Essays in Criticism* (Galaxy, 1959)

III

THE METAPHYSICAL POETS

Frank Kermode, Professor of English at the University of Cambridge
A.J. Smith, Professor of English at Keele University

Introduction

John Donne and the poets who followed him in the seventeenth century have been both popular and controversial ever since H.J.C. Grierson's edition of their poems in 1921 and the highly laudatory essays of T.S. Eliot and F.R. Leavis which were published soon afterwards. Since then critics have sought to explain the strange human appeal of poetry which often appears to be self-consciously intellectual in theme and tortured in expression. The notorious "conceits"—comparisons which at first sight seem merely far-fetched and clever—have been analysed and debated, and the complex and sometimes enigmatic personalities of these writers have been explored at length.

The Metaphysical Poets sometimes wrote in dialogue form, and the exchange which follows is nearly as sharp as their work, though not quite so complicated. Frank Kermode and A.J. Smith agree that Donne introduced a new kind of poetry which affected other writers, but they don't succeed in their initial attempt to define Metaphysical Poetry, largely because although Smith is prepared to discover a common mode of apprehension Kermode is more impressed by the differences between Donne, Herbert, Vaughan and Marvell. To establish their positions they discuss a wide range of poems, and they work closely upon Donne's "Good Friday, Riding Westward" and "A Valediction: of Weeping", Herbert's "Prayer (I)" and Marvell's "The Garden". The shared and distinctive features of these poets are identified with unusual precision.

THE METAPHYSICAL POETS

A.J. Smith: I think we should start off by trying to define what we mean by Metaphysical Poets and Metaphysical Poetry. It seems to me that the poets coming into this category range from Donne to, shall we say, Cowley. Do you agree that it is possible to group these poets together, not perhaps in a definite school, but with certain preoccupations, interests, modes of apprehension, or simply ways of writing in common, which were not shared with people who wrote before or immediately after?

Frank Kermode: Yes, I suppose in a sense the Metaphysical Poets are whoever we say they are; these are really just labels applied by literary historians. In fact, the expression "Metaphysical Poetry" was meant as a sort of nickname, or even insult, to begin with. We sort of scooped them together by a later process, trying to find out things about them that justified them being put in the same bag. However I do agree with you that the old problem of whether Donne introduced a new poetry or not is now solved; we can accept that he did.

A.J. Smith: Yes.

Frank Kermode: And that this new way of writing affects the sensibility, to use another old-fashioned word, of a lot of poetry in the succeeding half century. I don't think we can actually speak of a school of Donne, as you pointed out, but we can find, if we look for them, and if we're clever enough about it, traits of sensibility and expressiveness which are common to all these poets, and which die out after them.

A.J. Smith: Exactly. If we look at Donne, or Herbert, or Vaughan, or Marvell, and then move backwards to poets who are writing before them, we can see that they have something in common which earlier poets didn't have. We can see this even more markedly, I think, if we move on from them to Dryden, Sedley, Buckhurst, and the other poets of the Restoration, who plainly haven't got this kind of shared sensibility, apprehension, or way of writing.

Frank Kermode: In fact this shared sensibility begins to break up even before the Restoration poets. For example, if you take Dryden's "Upon the death of the Lord Hastings", which he wrote in 1649, there he was trying to write this earlier kind of poetry, which we call metaphysical, and doing it very badly. Again, at the end of that tradition, we have a poet like Cleveland, or even to a lesser extent Cowley, trying to write like Donne and failing. Something has happened to turn Metaphysical Poetry into jokes, and a great poet like Dryden finds it is not his true mode. The Dryden we're all familiar with, after the Restoration of course, does not write like that at all; though he's still a witty poet, he's wittv in a different sort of way.

A.J. Smith: Yes, and I think this helps us towards a definition. You said that something had happened which turned poetry into jokes, and it seems to me that really focuses our attention on one aspect of Metaphysical Poetry which has sometimes been taken for a definition of it. In Johnson's essay on the Metaphysical Poets, for example, he describes them as yoking heterogeneous ideas by violence together (*Life of Cowley*). This obviously emphasises their extreme figurative ingenuity, and is one aspect which I take it Cleveland and Cowley share with Donne, Herbert and others of the school. But it is not to my mind a defining characteristic, and I would in fact want to repudiate that definition for the major poets, because it seems to me destructive.

Frank Kermode: Well, it clearly can't be the major defining characteristic, simply because Cleveland and Donne, two very different kinds of poet, do have it in common.

A.J. Smith: Exactly, exactly; and I think that moves us on to suggest perhaps a peculiar metaphysical mode of sensibility. I'm thinking here of T.S. Eliot's account of poets like Donne as "feeling their thoughts" in some special or peculiar way. This is another standard definition of Metaphysical Poetry, but has the advantage that it evidently wouldn't apply to Cleveland and Cowley.

Frank Kermode: I think it's a very dangerous way of talking about it, though, because it leads to large historical generalisations about the dissociation of sensibility, how the Civil War ruined England and so on, which I don't think are really relevant to what we're talking about at all.

A.J. Smith: No, I agree.

Frank Kermode: In many ways what is most relevant is also the hardest to understand—the fact that there were some very good poets at the beginning of this tradition and some rather poor ones at the end of it. I don't know whether we can generalise about it. If you think of Donne for example, then almost the first thing to say about him is that he's a poet of argument; that all his poems contain argument or false argument, syllogisms and so on. Donne characteristically starts off a poem with some extreme intellectual proposition, and then refutes it in the second stanza or develops it in some slightly absurd way. If you can't find the argument of a Donne poem, in fact, you can't read the poem; he is one of the few exceptions to the rule that Eliot laid down that good poetry can please before it's understood.

But the later Metaphysicals, as we've agreed to call them, are not in anything like the same way dependent on argument. Vaughan, for example, is a very poor arguer; he runs out of steam very quickly when he tries to maintain an argument.

A.J. Smith: Vaughan is a special case, I think.

Frank Kermode: Yes, but even Herbert's poetry is not in that sense a kind of charge on the argument, if you see what I mean.

A.J. Smith: Yes.

Frank Kermode: So it's possible to say that the prime Metaphysical Poet, Donne, has one characteristic which the others lack.

A.J. Smith: Yes, though a good deal of what is very distinctive about Donne is not metaphysical at all, except in a very arbitrary and artificial sense. A poem like "Woman's Constancy", for example, has no metaphysical elements or none that I can attribute to it, anyway; or perhaps I should say that in this poem or in, for instance, "Fond woman, which would'st have thy husband die" ("Elegie I"), some of Donne's most striking and characteristic effects of voice, attack or tone are only metaphysical, as you suggested, in their implied dialectic—the implied affront to normal ways of looking at things, the very notion that he should argue out the very novel and almost shocking proposition that he puts forward.

Frank Kermode: Yes, I think that's very characteristic. The proposition may not be metaphysical in itself at all; it could be just a dramatic declaration which the poem continues.

On the other hand, Donne can write poems which are metaphysical in whichever sense you want to take them, like "The Extasie", which is metaphysical in Dryden's sense: it "perplexes the mind" by its combination of thoughts of the fair sex and nice philosophical speculations. It's metaphysical in the sense that it talks about love, about the relationship between personalities, in terms of the way they apprehend each other and so on.

"The Extasie" is not to my mind a very good poem, incidentally, largely because it seems to plod through its argument much more than Donne usually does. Because it is a highly metaphysical poem in every sense, and a poem about which there is a greal deal of argument, people who want a central Donne poem always choose "The Extasie" and take it very seriously. Whereas those who think of Donne as a very much more diverse personality, as I do and I think you do, are inclined to think that the tone of "The Extasie" is very hard to seize on, and that it is in fact playful, despite its great freight of serious allusions.

A.J. Smith: Actually I'd want to make larger claims than that for "The Extasie". I see it as at least an attempt to make sense, perhaps a final sense, of a particular relationship between two people. It's a very human poem in that way, though its mode of proceeding may appear very scholastic, and even dry.

Frank Kermode: But so huge is the load of metaphysical allusion in it that though we may *feel* that we know exactly what it is driving at we can't be sure. In fact there is great difference of opinion about what it means, and which way it goes. That seems to me to make it a different sort of poem from some others, like "The Apparation", which is relatively very direct, or that very beautiful poem which almost belies what I was saying earlier about Donne's poetry pleasing by its sound, "Aire and Angels". That is another puzzle poem, because of the difficulty of the direction of the argument, but it nevertheless strikes one instantly as having direct sensuous force of the kind that you were talking about.

A.J. Smith: Yes, yes. But in a poem with this kind of attack or dialectical approach, the attack itself need not necessarily involve a dialectic. It may in fact involve, though not often in Donne, I think, a direct kind of metaphysical apprehension. For example, Vaughan's "They are all gone into a world of light" is a very challenging statement in a way, but immediately plunges one into a very special kind of apprehension, involving a perception of this world in the final context of eternity.

Frank Kermode: Yes, but that line from Vaughan raises the question of the ways in which these poets differ from one another. Of all of them Vaughan, and perhaps Herbert, is the one who most requires a reader to feel his way into the whole sense of the poem. It doesn't matter whether you know that Vaughan was hooked on hermetic philosophy or not, though it's useful to know; there are all kinds of allusions in Vaughan's poetry, references to light, to stars and so on, which in the end form a sort of star-map of his own mind, and which you don't need a lot of critical help to understand if you're willing to submit yourself to the poem itself. You can understand Vaughan without knowing anything about hermetic philosophy, whereas you can't understand Donne without knowing something about scholastic philosophy. I would have thought that was the difference.

A.J. Smith: Yes, that is quite true. But it does seem to me that it is nonetheless characteristic of these poets, and I'm including Vaughan here, that they do have, to put it in a very minimal way, a distinctive figurative life. There's a constant play of the mind, a kind of inter-involvement of the mind with the experience that is going forward.

Frank Kermode: Yes, that is true, but it's not inconsistent with the view that, unlike some earlier poets, they're each asking us to apprehend a different set of meanings, so that we distinguish Herbert from Vaughan very easily, despite the fact that their relationship is said to be closer than any two other English poets.

A.J. Smith: It isn't at all, though; I think they're very different poets.

Frank Kermode: Well, we distinguish them very easily because Herbert's whole range of reference is entirely different from Vaughan's. The same applies to Donne. These poets have, as it were, three separate referential worlds, in a way that, say, Sidney, Daniel and Greville do not. There is a kind of diversification of reference. Their particular form of allegiance to these other worlds of reference may be what you mean when you say that they share something in the way in which they apprehend the world outside.

A.J. Smith: Well, let's take a precise example. I was thinking of such an image as the one in Donne's "Good Friday, Riding Westward":

Could I behold those hands which span the Poles,
And turne all spheares at once, peirc'd with those holes?

The crucified Christ is superimposed upon God, the all-powerful Being who has the whole of creation in his grasp. The outspread hands are the same in both cases: an image of absolute degradation and abasement is superimposed upon an image of absolute power.

Now that superimposition of the two images, seeing that in some senses they are the same thing, seems to me a characteristic mode of apprehension that one would find also in Herbert. In "Church Monuments", again, Herbert goes through the Church and looks at the monuments about him, the effigies of the great and the dust with which they're covered, and sees that in some way they represent his own life and his own inner state. He's not only concerned with an exemplification of worldly fame and what it amounts to, but with the fact that the worldly fame itself means nothing. In the dialectic of the poem he sees his own life and his own pattern of inner experience as identical with the monuments.

Frank Kermode: Well, the basis of "Good Friday, Riding Westward" is precisely the paradox that on the day when you ought to be facing East, Donne is being compelled to ride West. This seems to me a very characteristic Donne situation, with its curious, built-in paradox. Out of this same notion he made another poem, "The Annuntiation and Passion". This kind of juxtaposition in a sense amused him, though I don't mean to say that he treated it trivially.

Now, the Herbert poem is in principle about a much simpler subject, as you can tell from the tone of it; a line such as "To sever the good fellowship of dust" has a sort of marvellous rotundity, which you would never find in Donne. The whole feeling is very much more generalised; there's not the desperate attempt to be unique and specific that you find in Donne. That would seem to me an important difference between them.

A.J. Smith: Yes, I would certainly agree with that difference, but it still seems to me that they do have in some sense a common way of looking at things, which is bound up with this direct interinvolvement of the mind with an immediate experience going forward. Donne finds himself riding westwards on Good Friday. His mind plays about this, and the point is surely, as with the Annunciation and the Passion falling on the same day, that he finds it in some way meaningful.

Frank Kermode: Yes, but what I mean is that the great charge of feeling in Donne very often arises from some unexpected collocation of events of that sort and he writes good poems about it. You may not agree with this, but I should have thought Herbert tends to be a less good poet when he is meditating on some quite trivial occasion—for example in the poem called "Jesu", where he imagines the word split up into the words "I ease you".

A.J. Smith: Yes, I certainly do agree with that.

Frank Kermode: Herbert is really at his least interesting in poems like this, whereas Donne happens to be at his most interesting in roughly parallel situations.

A.J. Smith: Yes, I think that is a real difference between them. But what strikes me is that in a sense they're both doing, or trying to do, the same thing, because they both see significance in the same kind of events. Take for example the play on Donne's own name and on 'son' and 'sun' in "A Hymne to God the Father". There the poet not only sees significance in the fact that the two words have an identical sound but different meanings, but he seems to expect that significance.

Frank Kermode: Well, let's consider for a moment the way in which Donne and Herbert use emblems, because this is clearly relevant to what you are saying. Herbert is well-known for his interest in emblem poetry and emblem books. In an emblem book you actually get an enigmatic picture and a poem that comments on it, but of course you don't get the picture in Herbert. What you get instead is a poem, like "Hope", for example, which contains a number of apparently unexplained references to an anchor, a watch and so on, and has to be explained as you'd explain a stained glass window in a church. This is Rosemond Tuve's argument in *A Reading of George Herbert*, of course. Now that kind of appeal to a traditional enigmatic wisdom is something which Donne does not have, and I think it's a very important difference.

A.J. Smith: Yes, but could we move over towards Vaughan, because I think what you've just said brings up the sense in which all these poets are related. I would see Vaughan's poems almost as a series of attempts to read the book of creation in a series of divine hieroglyphs, or emblems if you like. But the difference between an emblem that one might encounter in an emblem book and a divine hieroglyph such as one encounters in Vaughan or Herbert's poetry seems to me to be immense. The one has no metaphysical reference whatsoever, while the other assumes that temporal instances, for example natural phenomena, will have extra-temporal meanings; in other words that they are hieroglyphs of another order of being.

Frank Kermode: Of course Vaughan happened to subscribe to a philosophy which developed in a very extreme way this idea that everything below reflects something above.

A.J. Smith: Yes, but that was a fairly common assumption in his time; it goes back in fact to the sixteenth century. The only difference between Vaughan and the people who wrote up the programmes for the Italian academies is that Vaughan's version of the direct relationship between natural phenomena is more extreme.

Frank Kermode: Largely because of the influence of his brother, who was a metaphysical philosopher. The notion that there is a direct communication between stars and planets, for example, was very important to Vaughan. If Donne had ever bothered to mention such a notion, which I don't think he does, it would have been by way of an illustration just in passing, whereas it's got into the very fabric of Vaughan's work.

What these poets have in common, although they're all so very different and there isn't any kind of common voice as there is in the poetry of some periods, is their quality of colloquial directness, and their immense dispatch of poetic business. But the business that they're dispatching tends to be different, and to reflect very different ways of looking at the world. It is after all what you'd expect in this period, with the whole religious establishment in collapse and the new science building up.

A.J. Smith: Yes, all right, certainly their voices are very different, and the kinds of concern that they have are also often very different, but it still seems to me that there is a degree of common apprehension which was not shared, for instance, with the people who were writing in the full tide of the scientific movement you mentioned. I'm thinking now of Donne's "Hymne to God, my God, in my Sicknesse":

We thinke that *Paradise* and *Calvarie*,

Christ's Crosse, and *Adam's* tree, stood in one place;
Looke Lord, and finde both *Adams* met in me;
As the first *Adam's* sweat surrounds my face,
May the last *Adam's* blood my soule embrace.

So, in his purple wrapp'd receive mee Lord . . .

I think you have here an attempt to see in the physical details of sickness—the sweat, the fever, the flush—a kind of final, metaphysical sense. The details of Donne's sickness are, as it were, superimposed upon the details of the Crucifixion. That kind of apprehension is, I think, peculiar to someone who sees temporal events as having a metaphysical force, and layers of metaphysical force within the one event.

There's one other thing that I would like to say about this. I have a quotation here from a poem by Herbert called "Man" that seems to me to sum up the kind of shared apprehension that I've been trying to define—though of course I'd entirely agree with you about the differences, and how important it is to be sharply aware of them.

More servants wait on Man,
Then he'l take notice of: in ev'ry path
He treads down that which doth befriend him,
When sicknesse makes him pale and wan.
Oh mightie love! Man is one world, and hath
Another to attend him.

That sense of inter-involvement of another world with this one, and of another order of being which resonates with our own, seems to me to be common to Herbert, Cowley, Vaughan, and also at times to Donne.

Let's now move on to discuss one of Donne's poems in more detail. I think "A Valediction: of Weeping" introduces a number of the characteristics that we've been talking about. First of all it's a poem of situation, the situation of parting. This was a familiar topic, of course, in Renaissance poetry. There are hundreds, literally hundreds of poems of parting, and Donne himself wrote a number of valedictory poems. But if one thinks firstly of this poem as in some way written up out of a situation, then it seems a very curiously detached, if not bizarre, rendering:

Let me powre forth
My teares before thy face, whil'st I stay here,
For thy face coines them, and thy stampe they beare.

He then continues with a very intricate, elaborate, complex play upon the notion of someone crying because he has to part from someone else. If we thought of this as an immediate rendering of the situation it would look very bizarre indeed, and the more bizarre because of the poet's immediate dramatic involvement.

Frank Kermode: It's very characteristic, though, of Donne's style, that he is able to prevent you from noticing the bizarre quality at first. Obviously some people always have noticed it first; Dr Johnson was clearly one of them. There are also one or two poems like "The Flea" where we're meant to admire it. But there are several factors in the poem which prevent one from simply thinking, "How bizarre", and one of them is the way it sounds. Everybody ought to read these poems aloud, because they often tell you how to read them. For example, if you take the line, "When a teare falls, that thou falst which it bore", most people read it wrongly first time because they don't realize that "thou" is an object, the image of the lady in the teardrop.

The other thing about the poem that distracts one's attention from the weirdness of the development of the tears imagery is the form in which it's written, which is presumably unique, certainly arbitrary, and yet very carefully repeated through three very complicated stanzas. Not only is it very difficult in itself, but it has to bear a very difficult argument. So one's involved very much in an awareness of the intense thinking and hard poetic work that's going on in the poem, as well as the *recherché* quality of the imagery.

A.J. Smith: Yes, that's entirely true; I was going to say that one doesn't in fact notice the bizarre element at first, because the poem moves so convincingly. Its rhetoric and its dramatic force take one with it. Nonetheless, I think one has to be conscious that this is not, as it were, a spontaneous overflow of powerful emotion; it's a mind working upon a particular situation, but ultimately directed to presenting a certain account of that situation. In other words, the mind is playing about it purposefully, to an end which discloses itself.

Frank Kermode: But it's worth adding that the poem earns itself the right to be not only very intelligent, as it obviously is, but also very emotional in the final stanza. Once you've worked through the first two stanzas, and held on to the sense of the poem, then somehow you're ready for the great outcry in the last stanza:

O more then Moone,
Draw not up seas to drowne me in thy spheare,
Weepe me not dead, in thine armes, but forbeare

To teach the sea, what it may doe too soone.

The kind of passion which you might find in a much simpler kind of poem is here much stronger, because it's enforced by the intellectual pressure of the argument.

A.J. Smith: Exactly. So one can now turn the argument around, as it were, and see the real occasion of the poem as highly passionate and highly moving, where it could very easily have become sentimental and melodramatic. One can now see the ingenuity of the poem partly as a way of distancing the extreme of passion which the situation naturally begets, and also as a way of exploring the sense of parting or valediction, of finding out what this involves for either of them, or both of them together. Thus there are two ingredients here—the very strong passion and the mind reflecting on that passion—but they are in a sense one and the same, for they are both reactions that would affect any man placed in that situation.

Frank Kermode: Yes. This poem explores what may have seemed the sterile possibilities of the poetry of tears. After all, it has a long history, hasn't it?; we think of this as a Petrarchan theme.

Here the lovers' tears are compared first to coins—his tears are valuable because her image is reflected in them, so they're like coins with the King's head. They're then compared to the whole world, since you can make a world by taking an empty globe and placing the countries of the world on it. They're then compared to a flood which can drown the whole world. Finally at the end of the poem the wind is compared to the lovers' sighs, reminding us that this is an old conceit. But here the mind is putting emotional content into the banal notion.

A.J. Smith: Yes, in fact one of the poem's striking qualities, for a love poem, is the range of its reference. A number of very humdrum and practical elements enter the world of the poem:

On a round ball
A workeman that hath copies by, can lay
An Europe, Afrique, and an Asia,
And quickly make that, which was nothing, *All.*

That would seem, and has been taken to be, a very curious and in some ways grotesque analogy in this situation. What Donne is moving towards is the sense of the lovers' inter-involvement which their parting directly raises. Is their parting a kind of finality, or are they in some way so intricately inter-involved that there is no final parting? This seems to me entirely to remove one's first feeling that this is in some way a grotesque or a fantastic image. It isn't so at all; it's a way of expressing the complexity of their relationship.

Frank Kermode: Nor is the image frigid, as it very well might be in another poet. This is exactly the same basic figure that we associate with a kind of Petrarchan frigidity, but here it's driven out, not by a naked candour of emotion but, as you say, by hard thinking and an elaborate working of the idea.

This hard thinking is very typical of Donne. We see it in the "Nocturnall Upon St Lucie's Day", which illustrates the well-worn figure "My mistress is dead, so I am as good as dead", but is worked out with an extraordinary cold, passionate intensity. That poem develops a set of images from alchemy which seem to have nothing to do with the subject at all, but which totally engage the "mind" of the poem. That's why "The Valediction: of Weeping" is a good example of a certain kind of Donne poem.

Herbert has a comparable resourcefulness and ingenuity in stanza form, and a comparable colloquial directness. His are always religious poems—about the validity and pride of prayer. It's impossible to choose any one poem to represent the whole range of Herbert, but I think we should talk about the sonnet "Prayer (I)":

Prayer the Church's banquet, Angels' age,
    God's breath in man returning to his birth,
    The soul in paraphrase, heart in pilgrimage,
The Christian plummet sounding heav'n and earth;
Engine against th'Almightie, sinners' towre,
    Reversed thunder, Christ-side-piercing spear,
    The six-daies world transposing in an houre,
A kinde of tune, which all things heare and fear;
Softnesse, and peace, and joy, and love, and blisse,
    Exalted Manna, gladnesse of the best,
    Heaven in ordinarie, man well drest,
The milkie way, the bird of Paradise,
    Church-bels beyond the starres heard, the soul's blood,
    The land of spices; something understood.

This is a curious poem because it contains no main verbs. It's a series of glosses on the word or the idea of prayer. What is striking about these glosses is that although they are very various and apparently random they all have the same external reference. Many of them are witty, some of them are obscure, like little riddles which you have to interpret; but in the end you're not told anything about prayer that you didn't know, it's simply that the general emotion aroused by the idea of prayer is refined and expanded.

Take for example the opening phrase. It takes a little cracking; what it means is that between the feasts of the Church, between Eucharists, as it were, you have a sort of snack, a little meal, which is the seventeenth century sense of the word "banquet". So the phrase compresses something which if you wanted to spell it out would take you a couple of sentences. Similarly we have "The soul in paraphrase" as another way of describing prayer. A paraphrase is not necessarily as we would understand it, something shorter than the original; at that time a paraphrase was normally longer than the original. So this is a way of expanding the soul to make it more intelligible; prayer therefore becomes "The soul in paraphrase". Then it's called an "engine" or "weapon" against God, and "Reversed thunder", thunder that goes up instead of coming down.

The sestet of the sonnet begins with the very simple line, "Softnesse, and peace, and joy, and love, and blisse", as if to say, "We can now give up all these fancy definitions and paraphrases and come down to simple terms". But immediately after that we are directed into a lot more witty, conceited descriptions of prayer: "Exalted Manna", manna which gets to heaven instead of coming from it, "The milkie way", "the bird of Paradise" which never lands on the earth, and so on. One could write a little commentary on each one of these witty equivalences for prayer, but at the end it's described as "The land of spices", which is a lapse into a kind of pure simplicity, as if to say, "We don't need all these fancy definitions anyway, because their whole idea is common to all of us". This is very characteristic of Herbert in concentrated form.

A.J. Smith: Yes, it's the movement forward of the poem as a sonnet which is so interesting. It's very unlike the traditional movement of a sonnet as it developed in Europe from Dante through Petrarch. This one moves forward in what seems at first a very bitty way. At first glance there seems to be no overall coherence—dramatic coherence or coherence of argument; it proceeds through a series of little, witty strokes, as you were saying, each one contained in itself. You have to stop and think, "What does this mean?" What one really wants to ask is how this holds together overall as a poem and how it moves to its final resolution; how the resolution is related to the various apparently separate, disparate definitions that precede it.

Frank Kermode: Well, in a way the resolution expresses the inutility of the definitions, but on the other hand, by saying so many simply interesting things about prayer, they do make the idea of prayer more attractive. The poem illustrates what you called earlier the hieroglyphic approach to reality, because here Herbert is composing a series of perhaps a dozen or more little hieroglyphs for the idea of prayer, each of which, in the nature of a hieroglyph, contains both the idea of prayer and something else beyond it. Throughout the poem he is expanding the idea of prayer, and then at the end he comes back to the root of the matter, which is that it is something implicitly understood, however much we may range about in order to attempt to explain it.

Donne's "Anniversaries", too, are kept firing by a series of conceits or squibs that keeps them rattling along like a firework. And a lot of the funeral elegies of the time are like that, of course. But what's unusual here is that the idea should be applied to prayer, rather than to love; or death, as in the funeral elegy. Here it's prayer that's the recipient of human wit. The poet is trying to make as many ingenious comparisons of prayer to other things as he possibly can; and again one comes down to the idea that all this is unnecessary.

A.J. Smith: Yes. This is one form of Herbert, isn't it? and one form of metaphysical poem. I suppose you could find similar poems by Crashaw where the wit takes the form of a series of witty voluntaries, one after another. Vaughan also has poems of this kind.

Of course there are other poems by Herbert which move in a very different way. We have mentioned some already, but some of the affliction poems, "Affliction (I)" or "The Flower", seem to move forward through the whole process of a man's life, with a complex, tense, up-and-down dialectic. There are also poems like "Redemption", which passes through a kind of anecdote to a degree of simplicity at the end, or "The Collar" which starts from a dramatic rebellion, with a very different kind of movement.

Frank Kermode: Now, Marvell's is another kind of wit, although we've already agreed that it's not unrelated. If you take a poem such as "The Garden", which is I suppose the best known of his poems, you find that it too is about meditation and contemplation, and proceeds by a long series of witty remarks, conceits of one sort or another. But they don't attract our attention by their pure ingenuity in quite the way that Donne's do.

The argument of "The Garden" is basically that, of all the kinds of gardens that people celebrate—those lovers like as a setting for licensed or unlicensed sensuality, or those busy people like to escape to when they're tired—the kind that the poet likes, although he values the garden's sensual pleasures, provides a setting for the mind to withdraw from created things into a quite different world of meditation where the soul is, as it were, on the point of leaving the body. Then the poem ends with a kind of joke again, saying that Adam must have been rather like that before he had to take on Eve, and that's what it would have been like to live in Paradise alone. So there's fluctuation in this poem between serious meditation and a joke about women, if you like.

This tone is very characteristic of Marvell, who is in many ways the most difficult poet of the period to characterise, because he's so eclectic and refers to so many traditions. So many of his poems, like the "Horatian Ode" or "To His Coy Mistress", or "The Garden", which in their own right are the best poems of their kind in the language, are in some way derivative. They're also all very different from each other. He's a poet who belongs at the end of a tradition, and draws heavily upon its different aspects.

A.J. Smith: Could I raise a general point about this? There's something we haven't said so far which I think we ought to consider when talking about Metaphysical Poetry. My point is that a garden meant something special for the mid-seventeenth century. Take Vaughan, for example, who deliberately retired for the greater part of his life to rural Breckonshire, to practise as a kind of hermetic doctor. This retirement into rural places, particularly into innocent nature, was very important for these people. It seems to me that they had the notion that their own time was placed in the context of all time since the Fall, and that for them walking through a garden was related in the larger context to the notion of a Paradise which we have lost.

Frank Kermode: Yes, but I do think it important to remember how many-sided the emblem of the garden was at the time, and how very conscious Marvell was of this. In his poem "The Mower against Gardens", for example, he is actually replying to a poem by Thomas Randolph, which portrays the garden as a place of libertine pleasure. The garden was very firmly associated with sexual misbehaviour; there is another poem of the period which says that you can hardly mention gardens now because "maids and matrons blushing turn away" if you do so. In this sense the whole idea of the garden, which could mean an interference with nature as well as the exact opposite, the liberation of man into nature, was very much in Marvell's mind. That is very much the kind of poet he was: extremely allusive, very powerfully minded, very witty, very sophisticated. This poem is an attempt to sum up, partly by refuting, partly by accepting, and partly by joking, the figure of the garden, which was a very complicated one in the minds of contemporaries.

A.J. Smith: Yes, I'd agree entirely. Mark you, a lot of these themes, like the involvement of sexual frailty in the Fall, run right through the poetry of the period, and culminate in a poem like Rochester's "The Fall", where it's put entirely in terms of inadequate sexual performance:

How blest was the Created State
    Of Man and Woman, e're they fell,

. . . .

But we, poor Slaves to Hope and Fear,
    Are never of our Joys secure:
They lessen still as they draw near,
    And none but dull Delights endure.

This element is present in Marvell, but it seems to me that it is largely the sense of innocence and guilt that he's playing with here, associating guilt perhaps with worldly success:

How vainly men themselves amaze
To win the Palm, the Oke, or Bayes;
And their uncessant Labours see
Crown'd from some single Herb or Tree . . .

That is perhaps inherited from Donne—the awareness that the world and all the ways of winning praise and glory in it are just a waste of time. But the blandness of tone is characteristic of Marvell alone; no one else shares that really.

Frank Kermode: What is very worrying about Marvell, and what makes him in some ways the most mysterious of all these poets, is that he has their intellectual strictness, so that when he wants to be very specific he is, and yet there's a great "penumbra of emotion", in Eliot's phrase, which is very difficult to penetrate. Take "The Nymph Complaining for the Death of her Faun", for example: nobody really knows, in a crude way, what the poem is about, and yet it's obviously written by a poet of extreme self-control, so that it's a puzzling and difficult situation.

A.J. Smith: I would have thought, though, that the poem is basically concerned with the loss of innocence, and the wanton destruction of what is innocent. Wouldn't you?

Frank Kermode: Oh, these themes are in it, but then there are many other hints as well—references apparently to the Cricifixion, to the Church of England and so on, which nobody knows quite how to fit in.

A.J. Smith: No, quite, except that one has again a somewhat general sense that they all refer to the way that innocence, purity and truth are trampled and destroyed by the processes of the world.

Frank Kermode: Yes, I agree, but I think I can explain the difference of tone that I'm trying to get at by comparing Marvell with Donne. We've agreed that Donne made a new poetry, although lots of his themes were old ones. Marvell in a sense does not make a new poetry; his themes are very often ancient, in fact. Poems about girls complaining about the deaths of pets are part of a long tradition all through the sixteenth century, and probably earlier too. Poems or orations complaining about gardens certainly go back to the Roman schools of rhetoric. In this sense Marvell stands at the end of a line. Eliot described him as a poet of civilisation, a poet who is conscious, as in the "Horatian Ode", of a great historical crisis, and who, standing at that point of crisis, looks back at the whole past and values it in a very modern way: he makes a selection from this past and uses it as the basis for his poetry.

Further Reading

A. Alvarez, *The School of Donne* (Chatto, 1961)
Joan Bennett, *Five Metaphysical Poets* (Cambridge, 1964)
Ann E. Berthoff, *The Resolved Soul, Marvell's Major Poems* (Princeton, 1970)
Malcolm Bradbury and David Palmer (eds.), *Metaphysical Poetry* (Arnold Stratford Studies 11, 1970)
John Carey (ed.), *Andrew Marvell* (Penguin Critical Anthologies, 1969)
T.S. Eliot, *Selected Essays* (Faber, 1932)
Helen Gardner (ed.), *John Donne* (Prentice Hall Twentieth Century Views, 1962)
H.J.C. Grierson (ed.), *Metaphysical Lyrics and Poems* (Oxford, 1921)

Hugh Kenner (ed.), *Seventeenth Century Poetry: Donne and Jonson* (Rinehart, 1964)
Frank Kermode (ed.), *Discussions of John Donne* (Heath, 1962)
F.R. Leavis, *Revaluation* (Chatto, 1936)
J.B. Leishman, *The Monarch of Wit* (Hutchinson, 1951)
The Art of Marvell's Poetry (Hutchinson, 1966)
George de F. Lord (ed.), *Andrew Marvell* (Prentice Hall Twentieth Century Views, 1968)
Julian Lovelock (ed.), *Donne, Songs and Sonets* (Macmillan Casebooks, 1973)
M.M. Mahood, *Poetry and Humanism* (Cape, 1950)
Earl Miner, *The Metaphysical Mode from Donne to Cowley* (Princeton, 1969)
A.J. Smith, *John Donne: the Songs and Sonets* (Arnold, 1964)
Joseph H. Summers, *George Herbert, his Religion and Art* (Chatto, 1954)
Rosemond Tuve, *A Reading of George Herbert* (Chicago, 1952)
Michael Wilding (ed.), *Marvell* (Macmillan Modern Judgements, 1969)
George Williamson, *The Proper Wit of Poetry* (Faber, 1961)

IV

PARADISE LOST, *COMUS* AND *SAMSON AGONISTES*

John Broadbent, Professor of English at East Anglia University
Lorna Sage, Tutor at East Anglia University

Introduction

In the introduction to the previous chapter I mentioned the twentieth-century re-evaluation of the Metaphysical Poets; this has been accompanied by a hard-fought dispute about the merits of the poetry of Milton, whose greatness had scarcely been challenged for two hundred years.

Of the two speakers here, Lorna Sage is disposed to maintain the integrity of the intellectual and emotional structure of the poems. She locates the focus and source of the tremendous power and energy of Paradise Lost *in the negatively defined God of Book Three and regards the attractions of Hell as placed in order that we should embrace them and then reject them; in* Comus *she defends the emphasis on chastity as part of a more comprehensive wholeness of body and soul which slights neither; and in* Samson Agonistes *she sees the hero's death as a positive act of self-sacrifice which makes retrospective sense of his life.*

John Broadbent is more inclined to question Milton's attitudes. In Paradise Lost *he is uneasy at the repressive use of sheer force of language and action, even when directed against evil and tyranny, and disturbed by the condemnation of art and human activity which are not dedicated to religious ends; he is repelled by the stony chastity of the Lady in* Comus; *and he suspects the suicide of Samson as self-dramatising. The discussion ends peaceably with "calm of mind, all passion spent", but neither speaker really converts the other. Ample scope remains for the reader to pursue the argument further.*

John Broadbent: *Paradise Lost* often makes readers rather cross, because it oppresses them; they feel that it's a poem which is not only about virtually everything that exists, but also that Milton deals with everything in a thoroughly oppressive way, as if he is being totalitarian about the totality. From the very beginning—"Of Man's first disobedience, and the fruit/Of that forbidden tree"—one is hammered with prescriptive words, "not" words, "disobedience", "forbidden". One is also hammered with the constant repetition of an "au" sound—which runs through the whole poem—"whose mortal taste/Brought death into the world, and all our woe". This "au" noise goes on and on and yet, although I feel this critical anxiety myself and often have to resist reacting with impatience, I feel that Milton is actually using his admittedly oppressive language in order to attack what he felt to be genuinely oppressive and tyrannical.

There is an example in Book One in that long catalogue of fallen angels:

> Belial came last, than whom a Spirit more lewd
> Fell not from heaven, or more gross to love
> Vice for itself. To him no temple stood
> Or altar smoked; yet who more oft than he
> In temples and at altars, when the priest
> Turns atheist, as did Eli's sons, who filled
> With lust and violence the house of God?
> In courts and palaces he also reigns
> And in luxurious cities . . . (I, 490)

It seems to me that the reader is very conscious of Milton's violent dislike of Belial and tends to lose sympathy with such extreme passion. Because of this we may forget, or not notice, that Milton is often attacking something that we would even now regard as a vice deserving of such hostility. Notice, for example, the confusion pointed by the strange anti-rhyme between "lewd" and "love" at the end of the first two lines quoted, a confusion between what is lewd and loving which Belial's followers build into a religion.

Lorna Sage: You are saying then—and it's somewhat complicated, isn't it?—that Milton "batters" us with his distaste and disapproval, batters us in terms of attitudes as well as language, but that although, in a sense, he too is glorying a little in a use of power, from which we may instinctively recoil, Milton is nonetheless using that power to get at abuses of power. He is using power against power. This is what causes the reader to feel anxious about the poem or puzzled by it.

In a way I too wanted to talk about this. I think one has to look for the centre of power in *Paradise Lost*. We don't reach this centre in the first two books; in fact not until we arrive in Heaven in Book Three and are confronted with Milton's God. This God is very much the still centre of all that goes on in the poem: from Him all the energy comes and to Him it eventually returns.

John Broadbent: When you say that are you talking about the poem, or about a belief that you personally have about the cosmos?

Lorna Sage: No. I'm talking about the poem and the structure of the poem. As you read through the first two books it is very obvious that Milton, as well as battering you with disapproval, is inviting you into various sorts of complicity with the Devils. It is only in Book Three that you arrive at a clue to where Milton stands and at the source of his ironies against the Devils.

John Broadbent: You use the phrase "the source of power in the poem". This interests me because people talking about power colloquially often refer to such things as "the power structure" or "the power struggle" as though power was, as it were, free-floating. Now you're saying that it *isn't* free-floating in *Paradise Lost*.

Lorna Sage: No, I don't think it's just a general energy. It comes from a very fixed point. That point is Milton's God, someone very still, inaccessible, that the angels circle round; all the motion is outside God, but God is the source. I think this is a comment on the structure of the poem and not on my own belief!

John Broadbent: Don't you think that it is difficult, though, to take seriously a power which is fixed, still and inaccessible, when it's surrounded by all sorts of other kinds of power which are much more solid?

Lorna Sage: I think that if we only respond to certain kinds of rhetoric in the poem, if we only respond to the rhetoric of Hell or to the descriptions of Paradise, then that is probably true. However, there are many kinds of rhetoric and one of them Milton uses very consistently to enable us to approach or to feel in a certain way about his God. I think he's perfectly right not to try to describe his God. What he does instead is to take us through passages like this about the praise of the Angels:

Thee, Father, first they sung omnipotent,
Immutable, immortal, infinite,
Eternal King; thee Author of all being,
Fountain of light, thyself invisible
Amidst the glorious brightness where thou sitt'st
Throned inaccessible . . . (III, 372)

This tells us very thoroughly that we can't describe God directly; what we can do instead is to move round him. We can say that He's not mutable, He's not mortal, He's not finite, He's not the things we know about. This is a kind of reverse rhetoric, but I think it works.

John Broadbent: How does this power of God compare with the other orders, what I suppose you would have to call the "pseudo-powers" in the poem?

Lorna Sage: Well, I think this is very abstract, though I think we're given instructions as to how to take it. When Raphael is telling Adam about the creation he says:

Immediate are the acts of God, more swift
Than time or motion, but to human ears
Cannot without process of speech be told,
So told as earthly notion can receive. (VII, 176)

There I think Milton is giving his instructions about how we should react to God in the poem. For God, who beholds things "from his prospect high,/Wherein past, present, future he beholds" (III, 78), the whole action is a pattern; it's instantaneous; it's not got the mess of development and mortality. Putting it in formal terms, it has no narrative or drama, just pattern. And it's pattern that Milton is trying to express in the way he describes God.

John Broadbent: That's interesting about "the mess", but could I halt you just for one moment. You are reading the poem as a set of instructions, and this seems to me something that you'd refuse to do if you were reading a novel; you'd be very cross if a novelist gave you instructions!

Lorna Sage: I'm not sure . . . I don't think so. Don't novelists also use characters to tell the reader what to think, or rather *how* to think? That's a distinction I'd want to make. These instructions about how to read, not what to think.

John Broadbent: It's a useful distinction. But can we take up what you have called "the mess", that is to say all the other kinds of power and exercises of power in the poem? I'm very conscious in Book One particularly, of the way in which human power, either heroic, military, or aesthetic, is undercut; it's constantly built up and then undercut. The most obvious example is the construction of Pandemonium in Book One: it is

Built like a temple, where pilasters round
Were set, and Doric pillars overlaid
With golden architrave; not did there want
Cornice or frieze, with bossy sculptures grav'n;
The roof was fretted gold. Not Babylon,
Nor great Alcairo such magnificence
Equaled in all their glories, to enshrine
Belus or Serapis their gods, or seat
Their kings, when Egypt with Assyria strove
In wealth and luxury. (I, 713)

I feel that here human power, human art, is built up to a great height. The verse seems to drift away into anthropology, geography and primitive religion—Belus and Serapis and all that. Your mind tends to close down, or mine does, and then suddenly you're woken up again by being reminded that this is a model of competition through conspicuous consumption, a vice which is still available to us and well worth satirising.

Lorna Sage: Yes, Pandemonium is very much the symbol of centralised power, isn't it? I think the way Milton deals with it and analyses it shows, by implication, how useful the notion of God's order as abstract actually is to him. Seeing the ultimate order as abstract means that any concrete imitations of that order, any attempts to turn the idea of order into a city state, a hierarchy, a police force or whatever, must be interpreted as mimicries, parodies, apings, of God. I think that's why one instinctively wants to defend Milton from the charge of being authoritarian.

John Broadbent: I would certainly accept that, but I do feel that Milton goes further than we dare to go with him these days. One of the things he does in this section is to attack Pandemonium not only as a tyrannical city and a tyrannical competitive culture but as a place of tyrannical *art*. Even art becomes tyrannical when too much respect is paid to it.

Lorna Sage: Yes, he makes the association between magnificent art and police states, and we spend a lot of our critical energy trying to pull them apart.

John Broadbent: And the reason he puts them together is that they both refuse to acknowledge God. The passage that draws these threads together for me is in Book Eleven. Adam is very pleased at the invention of music and of metal founding (XI, 556-580), but then he sees a scene in which there are beautiful women dancing about and marriages are contracted (XI, 580-602). He turns to Michael, who is showing him this future, and says how wonderful it all is and how happy he is about it. Michael replies that this is all very well, but

studious they appear
Of arts that polish life, inventors rare,
Unmindful of their Maker, though his Spirit
Taught them, but they his gifts acknowledged none. (XI, 609)

This really condemns all human culture which is not "dedicated". Michael goes on, and this is the bit that I'm particularly interested in, to suggest a parallel with the descriptions of Paradise earlier in the poem:

For that fair female troop thou saw'st, that seemed
Of goddesses, so blithe, so smooth, so gay,
Yet empty of all good wherein consists
Woman's domestic honor and chief praise . . . (XI, 614)

We leap to the conclusion that Milton the misogynist is coming on to the stage but then, through Michael, Milton starts talking about the exploitation, in fact the "dollification", of women: these are

Bred only and completed to the taste
Of lustful appetence, to sing, to dance,
To dress, and troll the tongue, and roll the eye. (XI, 618)

Lorna Sage: But perhaps we need to go back a bit here. I don't think we should imply that Milton's irony is all encompassing. We seem to be claiming that Hell, for instance, is a "pseudo-order" from the beginning, but I think this rather falsifies the development of the poem. By putting off the introduction of God to Book Three and suspending judgement of the Fallen Angels Milton invites us to see in them the reflection of a great many human ideals. We are invited to find them pathetic, heroic, to identify with them; for example:

Anon they move
In perfect phalanx to the Dorian mood
Of flutes and soft recorders; such as raised
To highth of noblest temper heroes old
Arming to battle, and instead of rage
Deliberate valor breathed, firm and unmoved
With dread of death to flight or foul retreat,
Nor wanting power to mitigate and swage
With solemn touches troubled thoughts, and chase
Anguish and doubt and fear and sorrow and pain
From mortal or immortal minds. Thus they,
Breathing united force with fixed thought,
Moved on in silence to soft pipes that charmed
Their painful steps o'er the burnt soil. (I, 549)

John Broadbent: Yes, all right, but what I notice most particularly in that passage is the last line and a half. All the emphasis falls on "charmed", and this indicates that any assuagement is purely illusory. It's the same in Book Two with their explorations, their intellectuality, their drugs. You can forget for the moment that you're in Hell if you play pipes enough!

Lorna Sage: Yes, "charm" is a word that recurs. But this has at least a double effect: their attempt to pluck victory out of defeat, to salvage some dignity out of the wreck, is still very recognisable, very moving. In a sense, as long as Satan stays in Hell—he manages to achieve some self confidence, to keep some sense of his own "unfallenness". "The mind is its own place", he says (I, 254). It's only when he gets into Paradise that he has to recognise the irony that surrounds him, the destructiveness and self-destructiveness of anything he can possibly do, the fact that he's lying to himself. I think when he speaks of "such as raised/To highth of noblest temper heroes old" (I, 552) Milton is trying to catch an echo of all the heroic losers there ever were.

John Broadbent: This is very helpful. You're showing me that I have been saying too easily, "That's just heroism, and it's being rejected"; you're saying that I must realize and embrace that heroism.

Lorna Sage: Exactly. It isn't that this is merely false heroism, it's that *all* heroism . . .

John Broadbent: . . . all heroism is false!

Lorna Sage: Yes, all heroism is false. Yet we are being invited here to find a response to it and, I think, a very direct, sympathetic response. There's a lot to be admired here and a lot of the sort of thing that we do admire, as well as narcissism and self-deception.

John Broadbent: But if you take this totalness into Paradise, as you were suggesting just now, it becomes rather more difficult. It's one thing to say that all heroism is false—but to say that all love is false, all naked beauty is false . . . ?

Lorna Sage: Ah, there I think the irony is much more controlled. We're not invited to feel all love is false in Paradise; isn't it rather that *we* are false or corrupt in our *response* to Paradise? Isn't this what Milton is trying to make us feel?

John Broadbent: Well, take this description of Eve:

> She as a veil down to the slender waist
> Her undornèd golden tresses wore
> Disheveled, but in wanton ringlets waved
> As the vine curls her tendrils, which implied
> Subjection, but required with gentle sway,
> And by her yielded, by him best received,
> Yielded with coy submission, modest pride,
> And sweet reluctant amorous delay. (IV, 304)

I find it very difficult to know how to react when we move from that oscillating passage to Milton's own voice in the next line, making a sort of demand upon us in the mythical present: "Nor those mysterious parts were then concealed;/Then was not guilty shame."

Lorna Sage: Yes, isn't it apt that he turns on his reader there? Certainly what happens in my mind when reading about her hair, "Disheveled, but in wanton ringlets waved", is that I feel this description would come better from Sir John Suckling or some Cavalier poet. It doesn't fit in with my ideas of purity, it ought to be more severe, somehow. So I respond to this as a very erotic description and Milton then turns round on me and says, "Look what you've been doing, you've been importing corruption into this; you can't respond to Paradise straightforwardly".

John Broadbent: You mean that these erotic lines are, as it were, unknowingly the vehicle for our corrupt eroticism, and the reality is not corrupt?

Lorna Sage: I think so, yes. Milton refuses to take pleasure out of Paradise just because we associate pleasure with sin. That's a symbol of how fallen we are. I think he knows the effect those lines are going to have.

John Broadbent: Is there then any level at which we are faced with something real and uncorrupt in Paradise?

Lorna Sage: Well, if I'm right about Milton diagnosing the reader's state of mind, he thinks he can only describe purity by indirection, by the sort of description that's already been infected by generations of amorous poets.

John Broadbent: Can I just put one last thing to you about *Paradise Lost*? I notice that while we've been talking about it we haven't once mentioned the great epic similes and the baroque ornament that often attract attention in the poem. I'd like to conclude by saying that, particularly towards the end, the poem is far more realistic than it's often given credit for. Although we can only indirectly see the good that he is writing about we can directly see the bad. In Book Eleven, for example, he writes what is, to my mind, wonderfully compressed history. After the bit about the troop of Goddesses which we referred to earlier there is, in the nature of things, a war; luxurious, decadent civilisation is followed by war. Then he says:

> One way a band select from forage drives
> A herd of beeves, fair oxen and fair kine,
> From a fat meadow ground; or fleecy flock,
> Ewes and their bleating lambs, over the plain,
> Their booty— (XI, 646)

—not their food, their *booty*. This seems to me the language of an exhausted historian, mourning the world.

Lorna Sage: Well, history in the last book seems, doesn't it? to be an accelerating, repeating pattern of tyranny and ravage. Military defeat or military victory, it doesn't matter—both are equally corrupting. History, as Milton reads it, is a pattern of repeated experiences. Apart from the line of lonely people like Milton who stand out against it, history appears dreary, repetitive and miserable, and he's very good at making us recognise this.

John Broadbent: Shall we talk about *Comus* now? People often say that they find it difficult to see why it is a masque.

Lorna Sage: Well, this involves all sorts of difficulties because we don't really have any analogy, any similar convention, in present day drama. Perhaps—since actors started speaking directly to the audience—plays have become a bit more like masques, but we still haven't got any truly analagous situation. And we've certainly got no situation in which some of the actors are actually very respected members of the audience, public figures like Lady Alice, the Lady in Milton's masque. One suspects, incidentally, that this convention must have given the Lady an initial advantage over Comus, who was presumably played by an anonymous actor.

John Broadbent: Does this mean that to some extent the difference between the chaste Lady and the monstrous Comus is a difference of class?

Lorna Sage: Yes, and class is very much an ingredient in the way the masque is arranged. Alice and her brothers, despite their youth, were felt to be fitting representatives of a very old established order. Everything they did, including dancing, was a kind of expression of that order. The Lady's song (lines 230-43), which is about harmony, would be associated by the audience with the kind of social harmony she and her family ideally preside over.

John Broadbent: The truth of the matter is, though, that when I actually read *Comus* I don't find that the social setting and the historical environment and the form of the masque and all that is very much help to me. *Comus* doesn't really seem to be about that.

Lorna Sage: I think it's enough "about that" to prevent Lord Egerton feeling cheated—enough to be a good evening's entertainment for him!

John Broadbent: He shouldn't have felt cheated because surely the one thing you can say about it being a masque is that it's the biggest masque that ever was!

Lorna Sage: Yes, and verbally the biggest, too. The speeches are longer and there's more meat in them than in any other masque, which is why it doesn't really help us with *Comus* to go back and read earlier masques; they are mostly stage directions. In *Comus* there is an awful lot of speech, and speech that matters, arguments that are carried through logically. I suppose this means that *Comus* isn't just a re-enactment of what everybody in the audience already knew—that they all belonged to the best of all possible societies and so on; it's exploratory in a way that other masques aren't. Milton was working something out, and perhaps working something out not in a collective way but in a personal way.

John Broadbent: Yes, I can see that. He's partly working out the form and he's partly working out the social metaphor, but the thing that we're obviously having our attention directed to is the nature of chastity. This seems to be a very difficult thing to talk about. Even the Lady finds it difficult, and this is strange in a work which, as you say, is so full of words.

Lorna Sage: Well, I'm not sure whether the Lady finds it difficult to talk about chastity; what she says is something rather different:

Shall I go on?
Or have I said enough? To him that dares
Arm his profane tongue with contemptuous words
Against the sun-clad power of Chastity,
Fain would I something say, yet to what end?
Thou hast nor ear nor soul to apprehend
The sublime notion and high mystery
That must be uttered to unfold the sage
And serious doctrine of Virginity,
And thou art worthy that thou shouldst not know
More happiness than this thy present lot. (I, 779)

She's hardly saying there that she can't talk about it, she's saying that Comus isn't worthy to hear about it. This may be a very subtle way of combining the difficulty of talking about chastity with a marvellous insult.

John Broadbent: If I can transpose this into contemporary terms, it seems to me possible to look at the treatment of chastity here in two ways. One is to regard it as a metaphor for what we would call integrity or wholeness, so that it loses any particular sexual connotation; the other is to think of it as an example of the kind of attitude which says, in effect, "I've got something you haven't got". This is something I find very offensive in my own life, very unpleasant; it is a denial of communication.

Lorna Sage: Yes, she's saying he wouldn't understand even if she told him, which is a very familiar sort of answer to get! I don't think I can accept, though, those two ways of responding to it. One of them seems to me to dilute it into integrity and the other makes it merely a symbol, a fake, an evasion. I think there is a more positive way of putting the virtues of chastity. We're always finding excuses for compromising ourselves in various ways, but Milton's version of integrity is very demanding and I think virginity in the Lady is a good symbol for it. It isn't just mental integrity, it's total integrity: it implies that your whole way of life physically matters to your state of mind, you can't just retreat into your mind and be yourself there. Admittedly the Lady suggests to Comus that she might retreat in this way (lines 662-5), but she has to be rescued; her integrity must be preserved in her actions in the physical world, not just at some point inside herself. It's an active, militant version of integrity.

John Broadbent: Yes, I see; if you assert the unity of body and soul then you must assert the integrity of the body as well as the soul?

Lorna Sage: Yes, you can't retreat and say, "I let the world have my body"—the Lady isn't a martyr. And martyrdom wouldn't, I think, appeal to Milton.

John Broadbent: But what about Comus, what does it tell us about the Lady, chastity or integrity when we consider the nature of the opponent?

Lorna Sage: People are often bothered that Comus isn't crude enough or isn't evil enough. This is perhaps because his speeches are much more obviously rhetorically inviting than the Lady's and because what he is talking about doesn't seem to be that evil in itself. After all, it's not unlike what Milton talks about as perfectly straightforward pleasure in "L'Allegro".

John Broadbent: Yes.

Lorna Sage: I think this shows that we must define very carefully what Milton means by the threats to chastity. What Comus seems to represent is not some positive evil act so much as a gradual dissipation of oneself, a gradual forgetting of where one belongs and of where one's going, an immersion in the richness, the surface beauty of experience. This is a temptation which his speeches capture very nicely.

John Broadbent: One of the other things that I notice about Comus is that there is a constant political implication behind all his recommendations. His idea is that you should exploit the universe. The Lady picks this up and gives a highly political reply. She opposes Comus' idea of riotous abundance in Nature with Temperance, and adds:

> If every just man that now pines with want
> Had but a moderate and beseeming share
> Of that which lewdly pampered luxury
> Now heaps upon some few with vast excess,
> Nature's full blessings would be well dispensed
> In unsuperfluous even proportion. (I, 768)

And yet this political aspect, although it's interesting, seems rather artificially added on.

Lorna Sage: Perhaps, but it makes Comus a very appropriate kind of threat for the orderly society that the Lady represents. He's not simply an opposite, he's a version of decadence in which the top and bottom of society have grown so far apart that the top is gluttonous and the bottom starving. He represents the sort of intemperance her society could slip into almost without noticing it.

John Broadbent: What about the masks that his victims wear—the animal heads?

Lorna Sage: These represent, don't they?, an inversion of the correct order: the body is taking over from the soul. The symbolism of *Comus* makes clear that the human countenance expresses one's upward, onward, intelligent actions, so beast-headed people are an inversion—the Attendant Spirit says,

> Soon as the potion works, their human count'nance,
> Th'express resemblance of the gods, is changed

Into some brutish form of wolf, or bear . . .   (I, 68)

There is possibly some much more obvious symbolism as well, suggesting that people who are hybrid, made up of grotesquely assorted opposites, symbolise evil, whereas the Lady, in the concern for the purity of her body and so on, wants to be all one thing—all herself.

John Broadbent: Yes, so the animals are a version of non-integrity. But can we return to the question of Comus' attraction and fluency? Isn't this very tempting when it is put up against the Gorgonian rigour, the stony hardness which the Lady and the Elder Brother appeal to in defence of Chastity?

What was that snaky-headed Gorgon shield
That wise Minerva wore, unconquered virgin,
Wherewith she freezed her foes to congealed stone,
But rigid looks of chaste austerity,
And noble grace that dashed brute violence
With sudden adoration and blank awe?   (I, 447)

It's difficult to accept this as an ideal and simultaneously reject that jazzy fluency of Comus.

Lorna Sage: I think what happens when the Lady and Comus meet is that instead of having a conversation, instead of interacting and sympathising with each other, or adopting any of each other's standpoints, they react against each other and polarise each other totally. The Lady closes her ears to what Comus says and tells him he is totally unable to understand her. Rhetorically, in terms of their styles, they bounce off each other: Comus becomes even more sensuous, the Lady even more chaste, pure, austere.

John Broadbent: Yes, so it's the opposite of a relationship.

The world of the epilogue of *Comus*, where Eros "holds his dear Psyche sweet entranced" (line 1005), was not a world Milton minded inhabiting, but he didn't go on inhabiting it. The very obvious shift between *Comus* and *Samson Agonistes* is one of the reasons why people make up myths about Samson and about Milton.

Lorna Sage: Yes. If you try and think about the two together, it's very obvious that in *Comus* Milton is providing the audience with a framework. At the beginning the Spirit arrives in his sky robes and at the end he ascends: there is a visual and ethical frame.

John Broadbent: Whereas in *Samson Agonistes* the virtue of the form seems to be very dubious. I don't really know why Milton used this rather pretentious, perfect, Greek tragic form.

Lorna Sage: Except perhaps that it fits in a negative way with the pre-Christian context, which doesn't have a framework, a heaven, a system for getting from this world to the next.

John Broadbent: So it's a poem about being in a situation where you have no *rite de passage* except to jump off a cliff?

Lorna Sage: Yes. The power of the poem seems to come, curiously, very much from the absence of the reassuring scaffolding that Milton had in *Comus*—the absence of another world to jump off into at the end.

John Broadbent: Then perhaps this accounts for the violence and destructiveness which is apparent even before Samson's end. There's a chorus that I find particularly remarkable for its violence, though this is admittedly directed against a greater violence as in *Paradise Lost*, and an extraordinarily idiosyncratic free verse of a kind never written before or since—at any rate not until *Four Quartets.* This idiosyncracy is again internally directed, I would say, against the formality of the tragedy:

> Oh how comely it is and how reviving
> To the spirits of just men long oppressed,
> When God into the hand of their deliverer
> Puts invincible might
> To quell the mighty of the earth, th'oppressor,
> The brute and boist'rous force of violent men . . . (I, 1268)

And the thing goes on and on like this, with the most unexpected rhythms. But then sometimes it seems to me to contain not just violence and idiosyncracy but actual vulgarity:

> It is not virtue, wisdom, valor, wit,
> Strength, comeliness of shape, or amplest merit
> That woman's love can win or long inherit;
> But what it is, hard is to say,
> Harder to hit,
> (Which way soever men refer it) . . . (I, 1010)

Lorna Sage: You're talking about the sudden very flat descent there into colloquialism; is this what you mean by it being vulgar, the neglect of orderliness, taste, expectation?

John Broadbent: Yes.

Lorna Sage: But it's a kind of challenge to the reader, isn't it? We were talking in *Paradise Lost* about Milton's dislike or questioning of the values of perfect art; here this feeling is much closer to the surface. If you just talked about the verse form you might portray it as a great artistic feat, but in fact what it's used for is to get at, to dislocate, all our notions of taste.

John Broadbent: Ah! Then perhaps this explains why I find *Samson Agonistes* such an extremely difficult work to discuss with students. Perhaps it's because they approach it too cautiously as a set book, a classic, a great work of art, whereas you say that it is in fact a denial of many of the things which we include in the notion of art.

Lorna Sage: Well, if one approaches it with a great deal of reverence and high seriousness, if one simply points to the literal meaning and doesn't say what effect it has—and it's often very brutal and destructive of expectation—then one's not going to get very far. What it seems to me to need is a much brighter, more direct kind of response.

John Broadbent: All right, but do you think that life deserves that blunt, brutal response; is it a balanced response to experience?

Lorna Sage: I think that the conclusion of *Samson Agonistes* manages to persuade one that it's almost the only honest response. The whole play takes place at an extreme point of experience where you've got no time for the surface, the possible beauty, the texture of experience; you're past all that.

John Broadbent: But, you see, I know the puritan view. I find a difficulty here—and I'm surprised Milton didn't find it too: I rather suspect self-dramatisation of the kind that Samson is necessarily engaged in, and I also regard suicide as an indulgence.

Lorna Sage: But Samson's suicide is two things at once, isn't it? In a way it's his ultimate act of self-expression, and so in your terms you'd call it self-indulgence; but it's also an act of self-sacrifice and a very real and practical political act. Regarded like that, isn't it (characteristically of Milton) extremely self-assertive?

John Broadbent: Well, no, I don't think so. I believe that whatever the date may have been when Milton wrote this poem, and we're not altogether sure, it is a poem about being old, or rather feeling old, and—

Lorna Sage: You're saying that one needs to have had a certain sort of experience, or a certain amount of experience, before *Samson* really means much?

John Broadbent: Yes, but I don't think it's a matter of time . . . I think it's a matter of, well, having done enough things to feel sorry for, whatever they may be. I connect it very closely indeed with *Four Quartets*, which again is a poem about old age. Of course, Eliot actually quotes Samson (line 80) in "East Coker": "O dark dark dark. They all go into the dark . . .". Then there's another passage, in "Little Gidding", a scene in which he is accosted during the Blitz and told what it is like when one is old:

Second, the conscious impotence of rage
　　At human folly, and the laceration
　　Of laughter at what ceases to amuse.
And last, the rending pain of re-enactment
　　Of all that you have done, and been; the shame
　　Of motives late revealed, and the awareness
Of things ill done and done to others' harm
　　Which once you took for exercise of virtue.
　　Then fools' approval stings, and honour stains.

I think that's the sort of thing *Samson Agonistes* is about.

Lorna Sage: That sense of shame and of the difficulty, almost the impossibility, of looking back on your life and feeling that it makes any sense, that there is any pattern, any structure. But perhaps Samson's suicide does, retrospectively, make sense of his life and all his earlier failures: he had to fail, to be degraded, in order finally to succeed. Retrospectively, surely, it all falls into place.

John Broadbent: You mean that the play is not really about old age, as I've just been suggesting, but about power? That Samson's difficulty is that he is endowed with more power, more capacity, than he can cope with, and in order to make sense of his life he has to die by giving it up?

Lorna Sage: Yes, the real interest centres on whether the suicide is an act of renunciation or rather a complete exercise of total power. That is what Eliot, I think, is talking about: the power to make sense of everything retrospectively so that it all falls into place. It's a very frightening kind of power.

John Broadbent: So in the end, then, there is "Only the hardly, barely prayable/Prayer of the one Annunciation", as Eliot calls it in "The Dry Salvages": "Be it unto me according to thy will".

Lorna Sage: Yes, except that one of the most amazing things Milton has done is to leave some doubt about just what is God's will. We see no signs, no evidence; Samson, totally isolated, thinks himself into a position where he feels "Some rousing motions in me which dispose/To something extraordinary my thoughts" (lines 1382-3). But there can be no proof, Samson has to intuit God's will as best he can.

Further Reading

Don Cameron Allen, *The Harmonious Vision* (John Hopkins, 1970)
Arthur E. Barker (ed.), *Milton, Modern Essays in Criticism* (Galaxy, 1965)
John Broadbent, *Some Graver Subject* (Chatto, 1960)
Milton: Comus and Samson Agonistes (Arnold, 1961)
Paradise Lost: Introduction (Cambridge, 1972)
David Daiches, *Milton* (Hutchinson, 1957)
John G. Demaray, *Milton and the Masque Tradition* (Harvard, 1968)
William Empson, *Milton's God* (Chatto, 1961)
Stanley E. Fish, *Surprised by Sin* (Macmillan, 1967)
Frank Kermode (ed.), *The Living Milton* (Routledge, 1960)
J.B. Leishman, *Milton's Minor Poems* (Hutchinson, 1969)
Julian Lovelock (ed.), *Milton: Comus and Samson Agonistes* (Macmillan Casebook, 1975)
Louis L. Martz (ed.), *Milton* (Prentice Hall Twentieth Century Views, 1966)
C.A. Patrides, *Milton and the Christian Tradition* (Oxford, 1966)
(ed.), *Milton's Epic Poetry* (Penguin, 1967)
(ed.), *Approaches to Paradise Lost* (Arnold, 1968)
Christopher Ricks, *Milton's Grand Style* (Oxford, 1963)
Alan Rudrum (ed.), *Milton* (Macmillan Modern Judgements, 1968)
Arnold Stein, *Heroic Knowledge* (Minnesota, 1957)
Joseph H. Summers (ed.), *The Lyric and Dramatic Milton* (Columbia, 1965)

V

AUGUSTAN POETRY

Ian Jack, Reader in English Poetry at Pembroke College, Cambridge
Richard Luckett, Lecturer in English at Cambridge University and Fellow of St Catherine's College

Introduction

The Augustan period is usually located between 1660—the Restoration—and around 1750; it includes all the important poetry of Dryden (1631-1700), Pope (1688-1744) and Johnson (1709-1784). The dates are interesting, for they suggest that within the generalizations which enable us to recognize "the Augustan" we might delimit several distinct generations.

Ian Jack and Richard Luckett begin by establishing the common features of Augustan poetry, but then they distinguish sharply between the personal tolerance and political instability Dryden experienced at the court of Charles II and the conditions in which Pope, a Roman Catholic in the reign of Queen Anne, developed his powers. Dryden was the pathfinder and his satire is clever, keen and direct; Pope in his earlier writings especially worked in diverse genres, and in his later satire gained a fine control over an extraordinary range of tones; Johnson absorbed and learnt from Pope but added his own sturdy self-confidence.

The Augustans are the least popular of the major English poets; many people think they are monotonous, complacent, lacking in powerful feeling and trivial in their interests. Jack and Luckett accept that this poetry has its limitations, but they find in it humour, lively intelligence, variety of tone, compassion and a truly moral concern with human life.

AUGUSTAN POETRY

Richard Luckett: I use the word "Augustan" to refer to the period of English Literature which started in the middle of the Seventeenth Century, and lasted until the middle of Dr Johnson's life, around 1750. Can we agree on this?

Ian Jack: I think so. It is difficult to find an exact date for the end of the Augustan period, but easy to fine one for the beginning. In 1660, of course, the monarchy was restored. There are few dates in political history so important that their significance spills over, as it were, into literary history, but this is one of them. If you compare a passage of prose or verse written in the 1660's or 1670's with a piece written twenty or thirty years before you see an enormous difference.

Richard Luckett: The interesting thing is that the Augustans themselves were very conscious of the change and expressed their new sensibility in extraordinary ways. Pope, for example, rewrote Donne so that his numbers flowed more melodiously and corrected the versification. Dr Johnson himself, to whom I suppose we owe the concept of Metaphysical poetry, found the language of the early part of the seventeenth century in many ways grotesque, even uncouth—certainly over-elaborate. He said about Donne in the "Life of Cowley": "Who but Donne would have thought that a good man is a telescope?"

Ian Jack: Yes, that's the kind of image that the Augustans would usually have rejected. A good example of the kind of image which they liked is to be found in a poem which is a particular favourite of mine, Dryden's "To my Honour'd Kinsman, John Driden, of Chesterton" (1700). This John Driden was a country gentleman, with the interests of a country gentleman, so the poet was careful to use images which would make sense to him. He writes, for example,

> The Hare, in Pastures or in Plains is found,
> Emblem of Humane Life, who runs the Round;
> And, after all his wand'ring Ways are done,
> His Circle fills, and ends where he begun,
> Just as the Setting meets the Rising Sun.

As I'm sure you know, a hare has just that peculiar habit. If you startle one walking across a field it will run off very fast in a jinking sort of way, but will then come back in a circle. This is the sort of allusion that a country gentleman would pick up at once.

Richard Luckett: And Donne, of course, would have made that a marvellously complicated image.

Ian Jack: Yes, but in this case it is not complicated. The important thing is that it is *appropriate*—it has what I would call decorum according to audience. In a verse epistle to a scholar it is appropriate, perhaps, to use learned images, as Dryden does in his epistle "To my Honour'd Friend, Dr Charleton, on his learned and useful Works". Writing to a girl then perhaps the Augustan would use some rather fanciful conceit, he would consider that appropriate. This, I think, is the central reason why the Augustans objected to the metaphysical style in love poetry.

Richard Luckett: That's interesting; it's consistent with Dryden's objections to Donne. He complains, "He affects the metaphysics, not only in his satires, but in his amorous verses, where nature only should reign" ("The Original and Progress of Satire", 1692). "The metaphysics" are all right in satires because they have a learned audience, but in love verses this isn't on at all, it's quite improper.

Ian Jack: There are so many changes between the time of the Metaphysicals and of the Augustans that it is very hard to know which changes were significant. Which two or three would you consider most important?

Richard Luckett: The most obvious is the religious change. And, related to that, people were becoming consciously tolerant and, of course, more sceptical as well. Another factor that everybody mentions is the growth of the Royal Society, which was chartered in 1662—Dryden was a member and so were many other men of letters. I think the effect of this, too, was an increase in scepticism. Robert Boyle, for example, wrote a book called *The Sceptical Chymist* (1661). And so moderation becomes a virtue; the remarkable example of this is the case of the Marquis of Halifax. Halifax was called a "trimmer" by his political enemies, a man who trimmed his sails to the wind, but he turned this insult back on his enemies and made it a term which he was proud to own to. He said in *The Character of a Trimmer*, "our *Trimmer* is not asham'd of his Name, and willingly leaveth the bold Champions of either Extream, the Honour of contending with no less Adversaries, than Nature, Religion, Liberty, Prudence, Humanity and Common Sense."

Ian Jack: Yes, *common sense.* It is obvious from the way he finishes where he wants to put the main emphasis. Nothing could be more Augustan than the idea of common sense—Augustans spent so much of their time lamenting that mankind can't live according to common sense!

Richard Luckett: The other key word is "Nature". I found a very interesting example of the use of one concept of Nature in *The Wisdom of God Manifested in the Works of Creation* (1691), a book by a scientist who in his day was as famous as Newton, the biologist John Ray. He has the nerve to assume that he knows what God's purpose was at the Creation: he imagines God as saying that He's placed man in a spacious and well furnished world, endowed him with a capacity for understanding what is beautiful and proportionable and made the earth agreeable and delightful to him. Then God says that He's made all aspects of the world capable of culture and improvement by human industry, that all the animals wait on hand to serve man, and that across the seas there are new lands waiting to be developed by the trader. So the whole Creation is there to supply western man with everything he could possibly need.

Ian Jack: I suppose you could call it an appalling cultural arrogance?

It seems to me very important to see the influence which the character of Charles II had on the literature of his time and on Augustan literature as a whole. I know this is an unfashionable approach at the moment—people would like one to talk about economic forces and the conditions of the working classes and all the rest of it—but in the seventeenth century the court was a cultural centre. There is no understanding shifts of taste at this time in literature or painting or anything else if you forget the character of the king. The same is true, incidentally, of the importance of the character of James VI and I to Metaphysical poetry. James was academic, in fact he was pedantic; he liked learned allusions and talk at table with scholars like George Herbert and Lancelot Andrewes. And this is reflected in the Metaphysical style. The character of Charles II, so very different, throws an equal light, I think, on the nature of early Augustan poetry.

Richard Luckett: Yes, Charles II was a totally different kind of man. You remember the marvellous *Character of King Charles II* by Lord Halifax (published after his death in 1695). Halifax describes Charles' habit of sauntering, ambling easily through rooms never waiting very long in any one place; and his mistresses. He remarks, "His Wit consisted chiefly in the *Quickness* of his *Apprehension.* His Apprehension made him *find Faults*, and that led him to short Sayings upon them, not always equal, but often very good". In fact, Halifax says that Charles talked bawdy—was apt to make "broad allusions". He attributes it to "the Company he kept whilst abroad" and comments, "The Hypocrisy of the former Times inclined Men to think they could not show too great an Aversion to it, and that helped to encourage this unbounded liberty of Talking, without the Restraints of Decency which were before observed. In his more familiar Conversations with the Ladies, even they must be passive, if they would not enter into it."

Ian Jack: I suppose you could call Charles II a natural paperback reader. I don't mean the kind of paperback that is published by the university presses, but the kind you get at railway stations and airports with a nice picture on the cover. He wasn't the sort of person to trouble himself with big books on controversial divinity. With the arrival of Charles II the days of the large folio, the big book with double columns and learned references in the margin were numbered. Once again Halifax put it well in the *Character of Charles*. He said, "In the Library of a young Prince, the solemn Folios are not much rumpled, Books of a lighter Digestion have the Dog's Ears". Charles was genuinely tolerant, wasn't he? In fact, more than tolerant when it came to witty blasphemy or sexual innuendo—he loved them!

Richard Luckett: That toleration extended to people as well. He kept the Earl of Rochester at court despite the fact that he was always publishing lampoons on him as well as exceedingly bawdy poems. If it hadn't been for the character of Charles, Dryden could never have written his extraordinary *Absalom and Achitophel* (1681). I remember being put to read *Absalom* at school, solemnly reading through it, and completely missing the point. I just didn't understand those first ten lines or so at all.

Dryden set himself a difficult task with this poem. He wanted to write a poem against the Earl of Shaftesbury, who was supporting the protestant Duke of Monmouth in his attempt to become heir to the throne in the place of Charles' brother, the Duke of York, who was a Catholic. The problem was that Monmouth was one of Charles' illegitimate children. This is how Dryden deals with the matter of the irregular royal offspring in the opening lines:

In pious times, e'r Priest-craft did begin,
Before *Polygamy* was made a sin;
When man, on many, multiply'd his kind,
E'r one to one was, cursedly, confin'd:
When Nature prompted, and no law deyn'd
Promiscuous use of Concubine and Bride;
Then *Israel's* Monarch, after Heaven's own heart,
His vigorous warmth did, variously, impart
To Wives and Slaves: And, wide as his Command,
Scatter'd his Maker's Image through the Land.

Ian Jack: It's a wonderful passage, isn't it? It could hardly have been written by the Poet Laureate in the reign of Queen Victoria, or indeed in the reign of Elizabeth I or, for that matter, Elizabeth II.

Dryden is clearly the starting point for any consideration of Augustan poetry, although our main concern is with Pope. Dryden was a particularly gifted critic as well as a gifted poet, and for this reason he showed the way to the other Augustans rather as T.S. Eliot showed the way to other modern poets forty or fifty years ago, by precept as well as example. Pope was always explicit and generous in acknowledging his debt to Dryden. He acknowledged, for example, that he learned versification wholly from Dryden.

Richard Luckett: The heroic couplet.

Ian Jack: Yes, it always comes up in text-books, doesn't it? It's used in the poems, certainly, but I don't like the phrase "heroic couplet" because it seems to be telling us something about the style in which a poet is writing, and it doesn't. All it tells us about is the verse form he uses. It just says in old fashioned terms that he is writing in iambic pentameters which rhyme in pairs. But a poet can write in any number of quite different styles in this metrical form and Pope, of course, wrote in a great many styles.

Richard Luckett: The extraordinary thing, though, is that virtually all the best Augustan poetry is written in that verse form. There is a great deal of good Augustan poetry and it is all in heroic couplets. I suppose it was that which led Lytton Strachey to make his famous reply to Matthew Arnold. Matthew Arnold had implied that really there wasn't an "adequate poetic criticism of life" in Pope. Lytton Strachey responded that actually Pope did have a philosophy: the heroic couplet (*Pope*, 1925).

Ian Jack: A very clever lecture that of Lytton Strachey's! He also says that Pope is like a monkey at an upstairs window ladling down molten lead on passers-by whom he doesn't like. In retrospect this seems to apply better to Strachey himself. What he says about Pope's philosophy being the heroic couplet has a very limited validity.

Another thing that occurs to me about the Dryden passage which makes it characteristic of the Augustans is that it deals with contemporary life, admittedly under an allegory, but that scarcely matters. It sometimes seems to me that if one were to generalize one could say that the Augustans wrote about contemporary life while the Romantics and the Victorians wrote about life in the past. Now I know that is only a generalization, but generalizations are like balloons: they have a short life and are easily pricked but they are delightful nonetheless. This one may have some value.

Richard Luckett: It is certainly an accurate observation, but the thing that strikes me first is the fact that Dryden writes about contemporary life wittily, always wittily. One of the extraordinary things about *Absalom and Achitophel* is the way in which the wit is concentrated in the detail, and as well as that in the whole design—in the brilliant series of parallels between Jerusalem and London. You see the one almost through a transparency of the other.

Ian Jack: Yes. Pope learned a good deal, I think, from Dryden in this respect too. Perhaps one should remember at this point, as I notice that we are constantly juxtaposing Dryden and Pope, that there was a very long period between them, almost sixty years. Dryden was born in 1631, Pope in 1688. That's three generations. One is apt to think of them, I think, as being roughly contemporaries, like Corneille and Racine, but they weren't; Pope was proud to claim that as a boy he had seen Dryden. When Pope began writing the social scene had changed completely. It was no longer Charles II on the throne, it was Queen Anne. She couldn't have been addressed in a poem like *Absalom and Achitophel*. She wasn't dissolute, that's no doubt to her credit, but neither was she witty, which was unfortunate. In Pope's time the literary centre was moving away from the court. Patronage was still important, but poets were becoming more independent all the same.

Richard Luckett: Of course Pope was very much to the fore in this. He was born a Roman Catholic and because he stayed a Catholic he never had any hope of official preferment. He was debarred from it. Dryden, on the other hand, spent much of his life fishing for patronage in one form or another. I think that Dryden was in fact more consistent than he's sometimes made out to be, but he was dependent on patronage for jobs. Pope was utterly contemptuous of patronage. It is strange to think, though, that because Pope was a Roman Catholic he couldn't go to university. He really led an extraordinary and isolated life in his early years. One could perhaps call him an outsider; the implications of the term are wrong but it has some truth. He was a natural critic of society. He was also an outsider in another way: he was a hunchback, almost a dwarf, no more than four foot nine . . . .

Ian Jack: Even less I think. Four foot six is a figure I've heard. It is very paradoxical that despite these disadvantages he nonetheless inherited the idea of the poet as the spokesman of his age. All the major Augustans thought in these terms, none of them thought of the poet as "the idle singer of an empty day", as William Morris called him, or as Shelley's lonely nightingale. They all believed in the public nature of a poet's responsibilities.

Richard Luckett: Certainly, though it's interesting that Pope himself could at times have feelings which seem almost romantic. What comes to my mind is the extraordinary fragment he composed "To Mr Gay, Who wrote him a contratulatory Letter on the finishing his House" (1720):

> What are the gay parterre, the chequer'd shade,
> The morning bower, the ev'ning colonade,
> But soft recesses of uneasy minds,
> To sigh unheard in, to the passing winds?
> So the struck deer in some sequester'd part
> Lies down to die, the arrow at his heart;
> There, stretch'd unseen in coverts hid from day,
> Bleeds drop by drop, and pants his life away.

Ian Jack: Yes, that's a passage I'd quite forgotten. The "struck deer" there, I suppose, is the ancestor of those lines in Cowper's *The Task* (1785):

I was a stricken deer, that left the herd
Long since; with many an arrow deep infixt
My panting side was charg'd, when I withdrew
To seek a tranquil death in distant shades. (III, 108)

The Pope passage is interesting, but it does come from a private letter. He had feelings like this and expressed them sometimes, but they've nothing to do with his official public voice.

Richard Luckett: Well, yes, that's fair enough. I think that his official voice seems most obvious to me in a really magnificent passage from the second dialogue of "Epilogue to the Satires":

Yes, I am proud; I must be proud to see
Men not afraid of God, afraid of me:
Safe from the Bar, the Pulpit, and the Throne,
Yet touched and shamed by Ridicule alone.
O sacred weapon! left for Truth's defence,
Sole dread of Folly, Vice, and Insolence!
To all but Heaven-directed hands denied,
The Muse may give thee, but the Gods must guide:
Reverent I touch thee! but with honest zeal;
To rouse the Watchmen of the public Weal,
To Virtue's work provoke the tardy Hall,
And goad the Prelate slumbering in his Stall. (I, 208)

Ian Jack: Yes, this is tremendous satiric verse. How well Pope assessed his own powers when he concentrated on satire in his last years—though one may regret it. It is interesting to remember that he didn't actually set out to be a satirist initially.

Richard Luckett: Any more than Dryden did. In fact, rather like Dryden, Pope wanted to be the great poet, the English Virgil. Is it too fanciful to see this ambition in his work? After all, he started out by writing pastorals just as Virgil did and when he died he was working on an epic, "Brutus"—something quite new for Pope, a blank verse epic.

It is amazing, if one looks at that early collection of poems, the 1717 collection, to see what an extraordinary range it contains. Pope, in fact, was only 29 when it was published. It includes *The Rape of the Lock*, "Eloisa to Abelard", "An Essay on Criticism", "Elegy to the Memory of an Unfortunate Lady", poems which are translations, imitations and even an "Ode on St Cecilia's Day".

Ian Jack: And yet after this, apart from *An Essay on Man*, he wrote satire almost exclusively. At times one feels that this exclusion is regrettable, but the concentration produced some extraordinary work. Think of the *Imitations of Horace* (1733-8). These are highly original poems; there is nothing quite like them, I think, in English literature. According to Pope himself, Bolingbroke came on him one day when he was ill in bed and reading Horace's first satire of the Second Book. He suggested that Pope should write a modern version. Sometimes one finds that the discovery of a new model enables a poet to become a new poet; this happened, for example, with Byron—when he read Frere's *Whistlecraft* and Pulci's *Morgante Maggiore* he was able to write *Beppo* and then *Don Juan*. And it seems to me that the model of Horace was important to Pope. It enabled him to get into his verse some things that hadn't been there before; as if Horace acted as a sort of release for him, he becomes more personal.

Richard Luckett: "Release" or "trigger", I suppose, is the word. He often borrows no more than the merest of hints and then goes on from there. I suppose this reflects one of Pope's most vital qualities, the way in which he took pride in his independence as a poet. This in turn is one of the reasons, of course, for his recurrent satirical attacks on literary contemporaries. He was really assaulting the people whom he saw as the literary serfs, the Grub-street hacks copying away and betraying their vocation. This offers an interesting comparison with Dryden. We remember Dryden as a great satirist and he wrote three great satires. But two of these are political and one is personal. He couldn't really be a *moral* satirist—it just wasn't the thing in the reign of Charles II! On the other hand Pope really does become just that, a moral satirist.

Ian Jack: Indeed. Listen to these lines in *Moral Essay*, II, about women of fashion who are no longer young:

> See how the World its Veterans rewards!
> A Youth of Frolics, an old Age of Cards;
> Fair to no purpose, artful to no end,
> Young without Lovers, old without a Friend;
> A Fop their Passion, but their Prize a Sot;
> Alive, ridiculous, and dead, forgot! (I, 243)

Richard Luckett: There's nothing ambiguous about that! But sometimes of course he does do things rather more subtly, particularly when he starts to dramatize. You remember those marvellous lines on the dying society woman? At that time there was a law for the encouragement of the wool trade that everybody had to have a woollen shroud, and on her death-bed this young woman can only think that her appearance is not all that it might have been:

"Odious! in woollen! 'twould a Saint provoke,"
(Were the last words that poor Narcissa spoke)
"No, let a charming Chintz, and Brussels lace
Wrap my cold limbs, and shade my lifeless face:
One would not, sure, be frightful when one's dead—
And—Betty—give this Cheek a little Red."

(*Moral Essay*, I, 1. 246)

In some ways this is rather like *The Rape of the Lock*. The strange thing about the passage, however, is that although Pope is obviously in the first place a moral satirist, shocked that a woman can be so frivolous on her death-bed, yet at the same time he is almost like an adult looking at a child. Just below the surface there is some spirit of compassion.

Ian Jack: Compassion is a quality one does find in his verse.

Richard Luckett: Pope doesn't have quite the supreme confidence of John Locke, the apostle of toleration throughout Europe. Both in his theory of knowledge and in his theory of education Locke was concerned to tell man that he had the power to shape his own destiny. In effect this was just the sort of power Englishmen had taken upon themselves by throwing out James II and bringing in William of Orange at the Glorious Revolution of 1688. There are moments in the *Essay on Man* when Pope comes very close to this kind of optimism but he was also obsessed by the precariousness of life and achievement, by the fact that civilisation is threatened by fools and pedants and bores and madmen. Pope was also different from people like Locke, Newton and Ray, because they were all more or less puritans, whereas he was a Roman Catholic. I think he saw men as perhaps creating rather than inheriting an ideal order of things. In his own life he tried to create an ideal order with his passion for gardening and for architecture, as Maynard Mack has described so well in his book *The Garden and the City* (1969).

Ian Jack: The classic statement on this is the opening of the second epistle of *An Essay on Man*:

Know then thyself, presume not God to scan;
The proper study of Mankind is Man.
Placed on this isthmus of a middle state,
A Being darkly wise, and rudely great:
With too much knowledge for the Sceptic side,
With too much weakness for the Stoic's pride,
He hangs between; in doubt to act, or rest;
In doubt to deem himself a God, or Beast;
In doubt his Mind or Body to prefer;
Born but to die, and reasoning but to err;
Alike in ignorance, his reason such,
Whether he thinks too little, or too much:
Chaos of Thought and Passion, all confused;
Still by himself abused, or disabused;
Created half to rise, and half to fall;
Great lord of all things, yet a prey to all;
Sole judge of Truth, in endless Error hurled:
The glory, jest, and riddle of the world!

Richard Luckett: Yes, that is an amazing passage; am I right in thinking it originates with Pascal?

Ian Jack: I think so.

Richard Luckett: That's interesting because it shows that the Augustans themselves weren't just an isthmus, a middle state. Here's Pope, not merely using classical tradition, but seventeenth-century tradition as well; and in Byron's admiration for the Augustan one sees something of an on-going tradition. To think of Pope simply as part of a self-contained movement, neatly compartmentalised by the word "Augustan", is really quite wrong.

Ian Jack: Perhaps we should now illustrate the variety and complexity of Augustan poetry by looking at some passages from poems by Dryden, Pope and Johnson. We are taking Dryden as the first major Augustan, the pathfinder as well as a master; Pope as the greatest poet of the Augustans; and Johnson as the last major figure. Let's begin with the opening lines of *Mac Flecknoe*, which was published in 1682.

All humane things are subject to decay,
And, when Fate summons, Monarchs must obey:
This *Fleckno* found, who, like *Augustus*, young

Was call'd to Empire, and had govern'd long:
In Prose and Verse, was own'd, without dispute
Through all the Realms of *Non-sense*, absolute.
This aged Prince now flourishing in Peace,
And blest with issue of a large increase,
Worn out with business, did at length debate
To settle the succession of the State:
And pond'ring which of all his Sons was fit
To Reign, and wage immortal War with Wit;
Cry'd, 'tis resolv'd; for Nature pleads that He
Should onely rule, who most resembles me:
Shadwell alone my perfect image bears,
Mature in dullness from his tender years.
Shadwell alone, of all my Sons, is he
Who stands confirm'd in full stupidity.
The rest to some faint meaning make pretence,
But *Shadwell* never deviates into sense.

That word "deviates" is particularly lethal. The power of satire is terrifying. I remember once meeting a research student who told me that he was going to write a dissertation on Shadwell's plays; I said it was a good idea because he's a good dramatist. I met him again six months later and asked him how he was getting on, and he said, "I've changed my subject". I asked him why and he said he couldn't stand it because whenever he told anybody he was working on Shadwell, they always quoted the opening of *Mac Flecknoe.*

Well, *Mac Flecknoe* is a mock-heroic poem, of course; I think one wants to be clear what this means. It doesn't mean that one is mocking the epic poem, or writing a satire on epic poetry; it would be surprising if it did, because Dryden's great ambition to the end of his life was to write an epic, and Pope had begun an epic when he died. It isn't the epic that's being satirised, it is Shadwell that's being satirised. He's described partly in epic terms, and this makes evident his absurdity.

Richard Luckett: You could say that Dryden is trying to establish the disporportion between the subject and the methods he's using.

Ian Jack: Yes, exactly. It's a matter of dressing a dwarf up in a suit of armour which would be suitable for a giant, and making him ridiculous by doing so. *Mac Flecknoe* is a relatively simple mock-heroic poem; *The Rape of the Lock* (1714) is a very complicated one, and perhaps I might quote a passage from the first canto of

Pope's poem to illustrate this. He's describing a flirtatious young woman being made up, and the imagery is entirely revealing, I think.

And now, unveiled, the Toilet stands displayed,
Each silver Vase in mystic order laid.
First, robed in white, the Nymph intent adores,
With head uncovered, the Cosmetic powers.
A heavenly image in the glass appears,
To that she bends, to that her eyes she rears;
Th'inferior Priestess, at her altar's side,
Trembling, begins the sacred rites of Pride.
Unnumbered treasures ope at once, and here
The various offerings of the world appear;
From each she nicely culls with curious toil,
And decks the Goddess with the glittering spoil.
This casket India's glowing gems unlocks,
And all Arabia breathes from yonder box.
The Tortoise here and Elephant unite,
Transformed to combs, the speckled, and the white.
Here files of pins extend their shining rows,
Puffs, Powders, Patches, Bibles, Billet-doux. (1. 121)

You notice in that last line how the insertion of "Bibles" between the patches and love-letters shows the confusion of values in the midst of which Belinda lives. One notices also the use of imagery of religion here—"heavenly image", "inferior Priestess" and "altar's side". Ben Jonson in a sombre scene at the beginning of *Volpone* makes the evil exploiter pray to gold as if it were a God, but of course Volpone is a wicked man, and that is sombre satire; *The Rape of the Lock* is, appropriately, very much more light-hearted.

Richard Luckett: Yes, Pope's aim wasn't to express the wickedness of anybody in *The Rape of the Lock*. He was trying, or he said he was trying, to effect a reconciliation. Wasn't it Lord Petre who snipped off a lock of Mrs Arabella Fermor's hair? Thus two of the highest Roman Catholic families in the land fell out, but I'm sure Pope was much more interested in the chance it gave him to write a poem.

There is another poem by Pope written at more or less the same time, which also involves a young Lady. It's a far more personal poem: the "Epistle to Miss Blount, on her leaving the Town, after the Coronation", which would have been the cornation of George I in 1714. He imagines the life his friend has gone to from the world of the town—

To muse, and spill her solitary Tea,
Or o'er cold coffee trifle with the spoon,
Count the slow clock, and dine exact at noon;
Divert her eyes with pictures in the fire,
Hum half a tune, tell stories to the squire.

Then he thinks of her lying dreamily on the grass:

In some fair evening, on your elbow laid,
You dream of triumphs in the rural shade;
In pensive thought recall the fancy's scene,
See Coronations rise on ev'ry green;
Before you pass th'imaginary sights
Of Lords, and Earls, and Dukes, and garter'd Knights.

The poem ends, correspondingly, with Pope in London, thinking of her; but then

Streets, chairs, and coxcombs rush upon my sight;
Vext to be still in town, I knit my brow,
Look sow'r, and hum a tune—as you may now.

Ian Jack: It ends beautifully, doesn't it, like so many of Pope's poems? Incidentally, I was recently reading one of the two essays in which Lord Chesterfield tried to get Dr Johnson to dedicate his great dictionary to him. He expressed the hope that Johnson will include some upper-class slang, mentioning as an example the word "flirtation". Chesterfield claims he was present when the word was created: "it fell from the most beautiful lips in Christendom," he says. Johnson of course didn't put it in. "To flirt" in Pope's poem means to do something with your fan, to close it or move it about rapidly; that, I believe, is the derivation of "flirtation".

Richard Luckett: Well, after that I suppose one should look at Pope's later poems. It's very tempting to stay in 1717, because there's so much there. But amongst the later poems obviously *The Dunciad* (1728, 1743) has a preponderant position. *The Dunciad* eventually grew, even if Pope didn't intend it to be so, into his longest and perhaps his most ambitious work.

Ian Jack: Yes, by the end Pope is ironically celebrating the conquest of the world, if not the universe, by Dullness. And Dullness of course meant much more to Pope than the word means now. It's the opposite of wit and wit is intelligence, so Dullness is everything that is an enemy of intelligence.

Lo! thy dread Empire, CHAOS! is restored;
Light dies before thy uncreating word:

Thy hand, great Anarch! lets the curtain fall;
And universal Darkness buries All.

Richard Luckett: That's an extraordinary conclusion, because it's not just mock-epic or mock-heroic: he inverts the whole idea of creation in near blasphemy. *The Dunciad* is obviously a tremendously powerful work, but all the personal allusions make it a difficult poem to come to terms with. Some of the other satires of the late period, the *Imitations of Horace* particularly, have much more general appeal and are in many ways more powerful because Pope was writing more from general principles and less out of literary politics. In the "Epistle to Dr Arbuthnot", where he writes about Addison in the character of Atticus, he manages to elevate the particular to the general in a splendid way—for instance,

Damn with faint praise, assent with civil leer,
And without sneering, teach the rest to sneer;
Willing to wound, and yet afraid to strike,
Just hint a fault, and hesitate dislike. (1. 210)

Ian Jack: Yes, and it's interesting to compare the very different treatment of the character of Sporus, Lord Hervey, in the same poem:

Yet let me flap this bug with gilded wings,
This painted child of dirt, that stinks and stings;
Whose buzz the witty and the fair annoys,
Yet wit ne'er tastes, and beauty ne'er enjoys:
So well-bred spaniels civilly delight
In mumbling of the game they dare not bite.
Eternal smiles his emptiness betray,
As shallow streams run dimpling all the way . . . (1. 309)

Richard Luckett: That is perhaps the most lethal piece of satire ever written in English; the economical use of low language, sliding deliberately between the elevated plane and all those monosyllables.

Ian Jack: Yes, you can hardly get lower diction than "bug, dirt, stinks, stings"—these are the sort of words that some people suppose Pope doesn't use; of course he does, but only when they're decorous or appropriate, as when he's killing Hervey.

Richard Luckett: It's always been an objection to Pope that he is indeed killing, that his satire is a kind of desecration because it is so vindictive. Pope tried to defend himself on this. I'm thinking of that passage in the "Epilogue to the Satires", the beginning of the second dialogue, you remember, where you have Pope and a friend talking:

Friend: Spare then the Person, and expose the Vice.
Pope: How Sir! not damn the Sharper, but the Dice?
Come on then, Satire! general, unconfined,
Spread thy broad wing, and souse [swoop] on all the kind.
Ye Statesmen, Priests, of one Religion all!
Ye Tradesmen, vile, in Army, Court, or Hall!
Ye Reverend Atheists. F: Scandal! name them, Who?
P: Why that's the thing you bid me not to do.
Who starved a Sister, who forswore a Debt,
I never named; the Town's inquiring yet.
The poisoning Dame— F: You mean— P: I don't.— F: You do.
P: See, now I keep the secret, and not you!
The bribing Statesman— F: Hold, too high you go.
P: The bribed Elector— F: There you stoop too low.
P: I fain would please you, if I knew with what;
Tell me, which Knave is lawful Game, which not?

Ian Jack: Yes, Pope is wonderful when he's discussing the ethics of satire. This is rather a vexed subject that we can't say much about now, but clearly if you don't like satire then you won't like the Augustans. Some people don't like satire; I imagine them as being very young, very cheerful and very inexperienced! If you think that life is lovely and that people are very nice and that on the whole everything is splendid then, clearly, you won't like satire. If on the other hand you find that there is much good in the world but also much harm, if you find that there is a great deal of suffering, much of it caused by folly which could easily be avoided, if you think there's a great deal to protest against, then perhaps you will be sympathetic to satire. It seems to me that the literature of the world would be immensely the poorer if Pope hadn't been a great satirist, if Voltaire, Swift, Erasmus and George Orwell had not written satire. It's not too difficult to justify the existence of satire—it's essentially the literature of protest: protest become art is great satire.

Richard Luckett: Yes, and of all periods of great satire there have surely been none in England like the Augustan period. You remember Boswell's observation in his *Life of Johnson* about the publication in 1738 of Johnson's *London, a Poem, in Imitation of the Third Satire of Juvenal*? Boswell says that on the same morning there was the publication of one of Pope's *Imitations*, "so that England had at once its Juvenal and Horace as poetical monitors".

Ian Jack: Yes I remember the passage. I admire Juvenal myself, but nobody is going to persuade me that *The Vanity of Human Wishes* is not greatly superior to its original, to the Tenth Satire of Juvenal. Let me quote one passage, the passage about Wolsey:

In full-blown dignity, see Wolsey stand,
Law in his voice, and fortune in his hand:
To him the church, the realm, their pow'rs consign,
Thro' him the rays of regal bounty shine,
Turn'd by his nod the stream of honour flows,
His smile alone security bestows:
Still to new heights his restless wishes tow'r,
Claim leads to claim, and pow'r advances pow'r.
Till conquest unresisted ceas'd to please,
And rights submitted, left him none to seize.
At length his sov'reign frowns—the train of state
Mark the keen glance, and watch the sign to hate.
Where-e'er he turns he meets a stranger's eye,
His suppliants scorn him, and his followers fly;
At once is lost the pride of aweful state,
The golden canopy, the glitt'ring plate,
The regal palace, the luxurious board,
The liv'ried army, and the menial lord.
With age, with cares, with maladies oppress'd,
He seeks the refuge of monastic rest.
Grief aids disease, remember'd folly stings,
And his last sighs reproach the faith of kings. (1. 99)

This is quite distinct from Pope, but no less powerful.

Richard Luckett: And of course, though not exactly dependent on Pope, Johnson was certainly indebted to Pope. He had read Pope and studied and learned, and this surely gave him something of the sturdy self-confidence that exists behind lines such as those. There are other passages in *The Vanity of Human Wishes* which seem to me equally attractive, and equally remarkable; one of the attributes of the poem is the range within it and the way that it moves over such different subjects. You remember the account of youthful ambition (lines 135-60)?

Ian Jack: Yes indeed. Perhaps finally I could quote one of Johnson's shortest poems, one I particularly admire, the "Epitaph on Hogarth" (1786):

The Hand of Art here torpid lies
  That traced th'essential form of Grace,
Here death has clos'd the curious eyes
  That saw the manners in the face.

If Genius warm thee, Reader, stay,
  If Merit touch thee, shed a tear,
Be Vice and Dulness far away
  Great Hogarth's honour'd Dust is here.

One could make many comments on these simple lines. "Th' essential form of Grace", of course, is a reference to what Hogarth called "the line of beauty", a sort of s-shaped curve that is central in his theory of the beautiful. The word "manners" means much more than in modern English: it means that by looking at somebody's face a great painter like Hogarth can see into the soul. What concerns me at the moment is not this sort of annotation, interesting as it might be, but that this is a characteristically Augustan poem in the passion that one gets beneath an ostensibly quiet surface. I remember A.E. Housman said, in his very romantic lecture on *The Name and Nature of Poetry* (1933), that if a line of good verse came into his mind when he was shaving he cut himself. Well, I have never thought of this poem while shaving, but when I read it I get exactly that *frisson*—the sense that this is a real poem with deep feeling in it. It's particularly revealing that it ends by bracketting "Vice and Dulness". This, again, is peculiarly Augustan: the idea that dullness, which means stupidity, is morally objectionable, is in itself an aspect of vice. Augustans believed in man and in man's intellect. This is just one of many reasons why we can read them with profit as well as great pleasure today.

Further Reading

Louis I. Bredvold, *The Intellectual Milieu of John Dryden* (Michigan University, 1934)
Reuben A. Brower, *Alexander Pope* (Oxford University, 1959)
John Butt, *The Augustan Age* (Hutchinson, 1950)
Thomas R. Edwards, Jr., *This Dark Estate: a Reading of Pope* (California University, 1963)
Boris Ford (ed.), *From Dryden to Johnson* (Penguin, 1957)
Donald J. Greene (ed.), *Samuel Johnson* (Prentice Hall Twentieth Century Views, 1965)
M.J.C. Hodgart, *Samuel Johnson and his Times* (Batsford, 1962)

A.R. Humphries, *The Augustan World* (Metheun, 1954)
Ian Jack, *Augustan Satire* (Oxford University, 1952)
Bruce King (ed.), *Dryden's Mind and Art* (Oliver, 1969)
Maynard Mack, *The Garden and the City* (Toronto University, 1969)
Earl Miner, *Dryden's Poetry* (Indiana University, 1967)
Pat Rogers, *The Augustan Vision* (Weidenfeld, 1974)
James Sutherland, *A Preface to Eighteenth-Century Poetry* (Oxford University, 1948)
W.O.S. Sutherland, Jr., *The Art of the Satirist* (Texas University, 1965)
Geoffrey Tillotson, *Pope and Human Nature* (Oxford University, 1958)
John Wain, *Samuel Johnson* (Macmillan, 1974)
Howard D. Weinbrot, *The Formal Strain* (Chicago University, 1969)
Basil Willey, *The Eighteenth-Century Background* (Chatto, 1940)

VI

WORDSWORTH, COLERIDGE AND KEATS

Christopher Salvesen, Professor of English at Reading University
David Palmer, Senior Lecturer in English at Hull University

Introduction

For many readers today Wordsworth is a very strange poet—not because he uses abstruse ideas or unusual juxtapositions, but because of the unevenness of his inspiration. In the best poems there are lines of stupendous dullness and even the admiring reader may find it hard to perceive exactly where his special quality resides. William Walsh and Christopher Salvesen see him as very original and modern because of his insight into the nature of consciousness, which they relate to his sensuous response to childhood and to an awareness, which he shared with Coleridge, of a luminous, guilty fear in the face of the natural universe. Then they fasten upon the supreme role ascribed to the imagination as the central feature of Romanticism, and elucidate the attitudes of Wordsworth and Coleridge to this mysterious, overwhelming power.

The achievements of the two poets in human sympathy and in the development of language to express it are discussed with detailed attention to "Michael" and Coleridge's "conversation poems"; and finally a comparison is made with the style and humanity of Keats' Odes. We saw how the Metaphysical Poets stimulated quite a sharp debate; Walsh and Salvesen's dialogue is more like a reflective Romantic conversation piece in which they try to capture the tone as well as the essential concepts of these elusive poets.

WORDSWORTH, COLERIDGE AND KEATS

William Walsh: When I think of the Romantics I think first of all of Coleridge, because he seems to me to be in some ways the first modern consciousness. There is a sense in which earlier poets like Chaucer and Pope belong almost to the same world of God, order and clearly defined categories, but in Coleridge we find a nervous, tentative consciousness, whose beliefs are fleeting and without the absolute sanction of the external world.

This individuality or novelty of mind belongs in differing degrees to all the Romantics. Some of them struggled, as Coleridge certainly did, to release themselves and their time from a system of ideas dominated by the theology of Newton and the psychology of Locke. Coleridge, together with most of the Romantics, believed above all, in the activity of the mind, and its capacity to create itself.

Christopher Salvesen: This of course comes out very strongly in Wordsworth too. *The Prelude* is after all subtitled "the growth of a poet's mind", and this was how Wordsworth always thought of it. Do you think Wordsworth is less representative than Coleridge of a modern consciousness, simply because he concentrates more on the business of being a poet?

William Walsh: That's a searching question. There are ways in which Wordsworth is less modern, less contemporary—not less great, but less nervously present than Coleridge. One feels for example that Wordsworth's beliefs were massive, central and, in a very important way, traditional. He, like most of the other first generation Romantics, seems to be very strongly rooted in the eighteenth century.

Christopher Salvesen: Yes, after all, Wordsworth spent thirty years of his life in the eighteenth century. Both stylistically and conceptually, in terms of what he thought or believed about the mind or the cosmos, he is very much a man of the eighteenth century.

But though we can see the tradition there, we can also see that he is very original and modern. This modernity lies primarily in his interest in himself: he himself said that it was a thing unprecedented in literary history that a man should talk so much about himself. He was rather alarmed at the prospect of writing a long poem all about himself. The fact that he mentions literary history is another mark of the modern consciousness in Wordsworth; he sees himself in relation to his predecessors in a slightly different way from Pope or Milton, as part of an ongoing, changing process. But primarily he is interested in himself, both psychologically and as a representative man. Though intensely subjective, he sees himself as someone from whom the rest of the world will learn, as a "prophet of Nature"—this is how he addresses Coleridge at the end of *The Prelude*. In this sort of self-consciousness he is as modern as Coleridge.

William Walsh: Certainly. I think one of the peculiarly modern gifts of Wordsworth is precisely this very nearly unparalled insight into the nature of consciousness. In the first books of *The Prelude* Wordsworth, like Coleridge, but more powerfully and inclusively, registered with extraordinary delicacy and acuteness the rhythms of consciousness itself:

From early days,
Beginning not long after that first time
In which, a Babe, by intercourse of touch
I held mute dialogues with my Mother's heart,
I have endeavoured to display the means
Whereby this infant sensibility,
Great birthright of our being, was in me
Augmented and sustained. (*Prelude*, 1850, II, 265)

Christopher Salvesen: Phrases like "apprehensive habitude" (II, 256 in the 1805 version) may sound a bit awful taken out of context, but this is a semi-clinical childhood. I don't know what "apprehensive habitude" means—it might mean the suckling of the child at the breast—but these psychologically oriented phrases are very much part of Wordsworth's total sensuous response to childhood. It is this sensuous response which makes the opening books of *The Prelude* so vivid.

You mentioned earlier the nervous quality of Coleridge's philosophical sense. His nervousness is rather different in character from Wordsworth's very uncertain sense of his position in the world. This uncertainty preoccupies him in the first book of *The Prelude*. First of all he presents himself as casting around for a subject. He's trying to settle on a theme, but is put off by the vastness of the various subjects that present themselves. Eventually, almost imperceptibly, he starts talking about childhood, about what it was like to be a five-year-old child bathing naked in the sunshine in the little mill-race that he lived near. This sensuous, physiological appreciation of life and of his own subjective mind is very modern and very different from any of the poets who came before.

William Walsh: That's very true. These passages of boating, snaring and so on show the extraordinary sense he had of a boy's early life, in which an unsoiled world meets a clean and naked sensibility. There's nothing to qualify the eagerness of the eye or the exquisite discrimination of the senses—for instance when he describes how "Frost, and the breath of frosty wind, had snapped/The last autumnal crocus" as he went out to snare woodcocks (1850, I, 308).

Christopher Salvesen: But is it as unsoiled as all that, I wonder? He is very aware of guilt; that comes out very strongly, and is a preoccupation which he shares with Coleridge. One of the striking points about the poetry of 1798 and thereabouts is the amount of fear and terror that Wordsworth describes. His is not by any means a pure childhood innocence; instead one has the impression that his childhood was extraordinarily rich in what he calls the "discipline of fear" (*Prelude*, I, 603).

William Walsh: Yes, this word "fear" that you have lighted on is extremely interesting. In the passage about snaring woodcocks, for example, the sensuous delight we've both remarked becomes mixed with an intensifying anxiety:

> Through half the night,
> Scudding away from snare to snare, I plied
> That anxious visitation; — moon and stars
> Were shining o'er my head. I was alone,
> And seemed to be a trouble to the peace
> That dwelt among them. (I, 312)

It's the projection of his belief that his childhood was "Fostered alike by beauty and by fear" (I, 302).

This fear, though it's very hard for us to grasp in an age which is acid with fear, was creative, solitary and disturbing, an intimation of unknown modes of being. It is a voluminous sort of fear, and in a strange and extraordinary way admirable: it's not simply generated by a threat or the approach of danger. It is based on inner guilt, on a kind of participation if not a responsibility. For instance, the act of shooting the albatross in "The Ancient Mariner" has no specific cause; in a sense it simply happens. But it nevertheless represents, in Coleridge's view, a certain deficiency in human nature which is capable of destroying the good. Fear of this kind isn't found in later poets like Shelley or Keats, for various reasons. Indeed, I think this particular luminous fear, this creative reverence towards the universe, is much stronger in the first generation of Romantics, and differentiates them quite clearly from the second.

Christopher Salvesen: The first generation are in fact much more modern in this sense than Keats, Shelley and Byron.

William Walsh: Yes, it comes back to the sense of the activity of consciousness which we mentioned before. This conception of individuality and fear, and the role of imagination, is quite central to the Romantics. It stems from the rejection of Newton and Locke and their purely mechanistic world; it's a return in some ways to Plato's conception of consciousness as creative and constructive, as distinct from the eighteenth century notion that it merely receives impressions in a passive, imitative way.

Christopher Salvesen: Guilt as an aspect of the imagination is also an aspect of Nature; it is Nature which imposes the "discipline of fear" on Wordsworth. This is part of the reciprocal process between man and Nature which both Wordsworth and Coleridge are very keen to make absolutely clear to themselves and to each other. Wordsworth, when he invokes Nature, sees it both as something outside himself, and as something which is experienced totally subjectively, as part of a continuously reciprocal process. When Coleridge says in "Dejection: an Ode", "we receive but what we give,/And in our life alone does Nature live", I think Wordsworth would agree, although he tends to see Nature as slightly more autonomous, and a little bit more outside himself, than Coleridge does.

But it's very hard to pin down exactly what Wordsworth believed. Does he believe in geniuses of the place? Does he really maintain a Greek notion of gods and goddesses inhabiting trees and grottoes and fountains? Or does he see Nature as something much more transcendental, something he sometimes calls God, although he is a semi-atheist, a kind of pantheist?

William Walsh: I think Coleridge believes the same as Wordsworth up to about 1800, doesn't he?

Christopher Salvesen: Well, Coleridge was very much more of an intellectual than Wordsworth. Wordsworth was much more profoundly sagacious, which is I suppose more important in some ways, but Coleridge was almost a professional intellectual. And whether his beliefs are actually the same or not, he certainly shared, or thought he shared at a certain period of his life, a profound harmony of view with Wordsworth. As time went on, differences of temperament tended to make them believe occasionally that they had differences of theory, but one profound belief they certainly had in common was their faith in the remedial and efficacious power of the natural world.

They both also believed in the profoundly creative force of the imagination—that man is not simply a recipient but a doer, a giver and above all a maker. They thought that in the imagination lie the seeds of all moral improvement; that all the forms by which humanity impresses itself on the non-human—sciences, governments and so on—are not simply conclusions from external evidence, but are created essentially from within. This indefinable concept of imagination, which as they use it is almost a description of a certain kind of sensibility, is one of the profoundly unifying Romantic beliefs; we find it in Coleridge, Wordsworth, Keats and many others.

William Walsh: Yes, this is "the holiness of the heart's affections", which Keats talks about in one of his letters. He then goes on to say that imagination is simply another name for the real truth, the transcendental and metaphysical truth (to Bailey, 22 November, 1817). How different this is from Wordsworth's definition of imagination as "Reason in her most exalted mood" (*Prelude*, XIV, 192) I don't know; the latter is possibly just a local definition. It comes towards the end of *The Prelude* at a point where I think Wordsworth is wanting to emphasise the commonsense attributes of his mind. Mostly, though, Wordsworth prefers to see imagination as a mysterious, overwhelming power, something which really does unify all experience and which can't be tamed or in any way pinned down by definitions. I think in this Coleridge agrees with him.

Christopher Salvesen: Yes, and I feel he would have accepted Wordsworth's "Reason in her most exalted mood" as well. One of the fundamental undertakings of the Romantics was the attempt to define, and better still to exercise, a new view of what was rational, as opposed to the narrow, Lockeian, cramped and confined conception of reasoning which was so powerful in the eighteenth century.

William Walsh: There is of course one other aspect that differentiates Wordsworth and Coleridge's sense of imagination from anything that's gone before, and that is the insistence on the importance of Nature. This is the obvious definition of the Romantic as opposed to the classical view of the cosmos. Romanticism takes into account the non-human cosmos; it sees it really as a part of human life. Of course it's different and ultimately less important; or at least, this is the conclusion that Wordsworth reaches right at the end of *The Prelude*. It is the mind of man that interests him primarily, although to begin with he has to develop his sense of the mind of man out of his feelings for nature. Love of nature leads to love of mankind, and to a sense of the mightiness of man's mind.

Christopher Salvesen: This links up with a Romantic principle which has often struck me, namely that the highest function of the poet and the supreme function of the imagination is to arrive at a plane of understanding above that of ordinary rationality, in which the boundaries separating different forms of existence melt, and all modes of being, as Wordsworth says, work mysteriously together.

Whether this happens in practice is of course another matter. Take Wordsworth's "Michael", for instance. It's subtitled "A Pastoral Poem", but what does Wordsworth mean by "pastoral"? It's obviously not an artificial poem on the lines of the typical eighteenth century pastoral. It is, I think, a realistic poem, about a real shepherd. This is the major polemical point of both the volumes known as *Lyrical Ballads*; they contain, Wordsworth claimed in his Preface, poems on "incidents and situations from common life". Michael is a lakeland shepherd, but he is also very nearly a heroic figure, a man of exceptional stature. This is brought out quite strongly:

His bodily frame had been from youth to age
Of an unusual strength: his mind was keen
Intense, and frugal, apt for all affairs,
And in his shepherd's calling he was prompt
And watchful more than ordinary men.

And, of course, he is much older than ordinary men—we're told at one point towards the end of the poem that he's eighty-four. So we have an element of idealisation in the figure of Michael, as well as a realistic presentation. One of the problems in reading the poem is to achieve a balance between this idealisation and the realism.

Obviously the poem should be read in relation to Book Eight of *The Prelude*, where Wordsworth has a good deal to say about the figure of the shepherd. The shepherd represented for him both social man and man in his relation to Nature. "Shepherds," says Wordsworth, "were the men that pleased me first" (VIII, 128). They pleased him because they were solitary, outstanding figures, because he could see them working and taking their place in society, and because he could also see them in relation to Nature, in the hills or in the mists, looking like giants or polar bears, or like

an aerial cross
Stationed alone upon a spiry rock
Of the Chartreuse, for worship. (VIII, 273)

Some of this rubs off on Michael, though primarily he is a realistic figure and it is a simple, realistic tale that Wordsworth is presenting—

Therefore, although it be a history
Homely and rude, I will relate the same
For the delight of a few natural hearts;
And, with yet fonder feeling, for the sake
Of youthful Poets, who among those hills
Will be my second self when I am gone.

There, characteristically, Wordsworth relates the figure of Michael to himself and to the business of being a poet. But "Michael is nevertheless basically a realistic poem. Would you agree?

William Walsh: Yes, indeed; it's founded on a firm sense of actuality. But what strikes me about "Michael" is the way in which moral feeling in Wordsworth can become lyrical without ever seeming in any way absurd. This seems to me a remarkable artistic trend which Wordsworth is often not given sufficient credit for: he combines an extraordinary prodigality of sympathy for very different kinds of men from himself with this severe, austere idiom.

This language is quiet, calm, but capable of extraordinary effects; in this poem, for instance, we can see his capacity to assimilate man to the great mineral forms of life, so that Michael does not just resemble but actually becomes a rock. On one level the poem is realistic; on another it's almost like a French moral tale, with an exquisitely controlled sense of moral discrimination. Then there's a third level, a further orchestration, which represents a much larger, more universal kind of reality. It seems to me that only a great poet could achieve such a balance.

Christopher Salvesen: Yes. I suppose the moral point of "Michael" is summed up in the lines towards the end:

There is a comfort in the strength of love;
'Twill make a thing endurable, which else
Would overset the brain, or break the heart.

Michael still loves his son; even though he has left for the city and gone to the bad, he still loves him and this sustains him. We're told that for another seven years he still goes to build the sheepfold, although he never finishes it.

There's obviously a lot more one could say about the moral tone of "Michael", but perhaps we ought to say a little more about the poetic tone which you mentioned, the evenness and rapidity of the verse which is on the whole very simple but can yet sustain a pretty high level of feeling. Do you think it's a monotonous poem?

William Walsh: That's an interesting question. It's interesting that it should be asked at all; Wordsworth does have this capacity for frankly boring many people. In fact, in my view some of Wordsworth is boring; but there are also parts which certainly don't deserve to be boring but which don't get read with an eye accommodated to that particular object.

Wordsworth's language, as I said, has a kind of bony austerity and severity of contour; it doesn't allow itself billowy outline or outrageous metaphoric life. Yet it does seem to me to have an extraordinary power for revealing the internal moral crisis, and particularly the collision of human sensibility with some fact or event of Nature. It has too an extraordinary capacity for analysis, or if that's too abstract and cerebral a word, for reconstructing a moral problem, showing it in its dimensions. It also conveys a certain depth and serenity, a certain inward power. I am again and again astonishingly surprised by the remarkable range of effect which seems to be possible for what looks like a fairly subdued line.

Coleridge, both as a man and a poet, is really very different. It seems absurd to talk about "the Romantics" when we think of sensibilities so totally different as Wordsworth, Coleridge, Keats, Byron, and Shelley. They are united because they were living in roughly the same period, had some acquaintance with one another and one another's works, and a common background of certain European conceptions worked into the fabric of English intellectual life; but out of this background develops very different sensibilities.

Wordsworth, as we've said, began in the eighteenth century and so of course did Coleridge. Coleridge's first few poems are like everybody else's, evidence of the desire to be a poet rather than to write poems, as Eliot once rather tartly said to a young modern poet. There's all sorts of minor eighteenth-century rambling stretches of boring classical imitation, and couplets which are meant to be like Pope, but are really only lurching imitations. Coleridge wrote an astonishing amount of very feeble verse.

I think Coleridge's two great productions are the preternatural or supernatural poems which everybody knows, and the conversational, reflective poems: "Aeolian Harp", "Frost at Midnight", "Dejection", and others which haven't had due appreciation in his record. Just to think of him as the poet of the supernatural is to distort his real achievement. The extraordinarily supple virtuosity of line which he developed in "This Lime-Tree Bower My Prison", for example, hasn't been appreciated nearly so much as it might have been.

Christopher Salvesen: I agree; I'm not sure I wouldn't take "Frost at Midnight" onto a desert island rather than "The Ancient Mariner"; I think it's one of the most perfectly romantic poems there is. Of course, Wordsworth learned a great deal from these conversation poems. Coleridge himself invented the form, deriving it a bit from Cowper. It was part of his democratic spirit: he wanted to write poetry which would have the quality of good conversation, relaxed and free of poetic diction. Of course, poetic diction is always liable to creep in, even in the conversation poems, but it is their rhythm which is so distinctive. Wordsworth learnt a great deal from them, which comes out in "Tintern Abbey", where he moves gradually from a fairly objective bit of description, a relaxed opening, into a much deeper, meditative tone. That relaxed tone is what gives the conversation poems their character. *The Prelude* too is an extended conversation; it also has this capacity to move from the prosaic and conversational to the profoundly meditative, and back again.

William Walsh: What I find so appealing about these poems is the casual gait and the undressed-up attitude. This very remarkable achievement is very much in keeping with what Coleridge pointed out himself as one of the great themes of his poetry. Describing a small water insect he notes "how the little animal wins its way up against the stream by alternative pulses of active and passive motion, now resisting the current, and now yielding to it in order to gather strength and a momentary *fulcrum* for a further propulsion. This", he says, "is no unapt emblem of the mind's self-experience in the act of thinking" (*Biographia Literaria*, ch. VII). Many of these conversation poems have precisely this as their function, the realising in terms of art of an act of self-experience, of the mind thinking itself—in "The Aeolian Harp", for example:

How exquisite the scents
Snatched from yon bean-field! and the world so hushed!
The stilly murmur of the distant sea
Tells us of silence.

Or in "This Lime-Tree Bower My Prison", when the poet projects himself into the mind and experience of those who are absent from him, but present to the scene. So here we have an extraordinary poem which is concerned with experiences so primary and so ultimate that they can't be described: presence and absence.

Yet this self-experience, the actual experience of his own being and mind, is the theme of so many of Coleridge's poems. A kind of dramatic reconstruction of the actual moment of the experience is united with this superbly casual, unpretentious conversational style, in what seems to me an extraordinary achievement:

Well, they are gone, and here must I remain,
This lime-tree bower my prison! I have lost
Beauties and feelings, such as would have been
Most sweet to my remembrance even when age
Had dimmed mine eyes to blindness!

This apparent absolute, simple spontaneity is of course very carefully organized, but according to the fleeting logic of poetry rather than any external scheme.

I'd like to begin our discussion of Keats with just a few lines from the start of the posthumous "Fall of Hyperion":

Fanatics have their dreams, wherewith they weave
A paradise for a sect; the savage too
From forth the loftiest fashion of his sleep
Guesses at Heaven; pity these have not
Trac'd upon vellum or wild Indian leaf
The shadows of melodious utterance.
But bare of laurel they live, dream, and die.

Now that is not casual in the conversational way of Wordsworth or Coleridge, but it is far from being fake grandeur. I suppose what I mean is that at the end of his life, in his greatest productions, which are of course noble, splendid and palpable, full of the texture of actuality, there is also a very much more inward rhythm, related more closely to the way that the voice proceeds from experience.

Christopher Salvesen: Yes, I think that Keats' Odes are not all that far from the Coleridge conversation poems. They also return on themselves, which everyone notices in "Frost at Midnight", where frost begins the poem and returns at the end, giving you a circular, complete, rhythm. Compare particularly the "Ode to a Nightingale", where Keats starts off by bringing himself onto the stage: "My heart aches, and a drowsy numbness pains/My sense". He describes his feelings and gradually moves into a dream-like state, but his meditation leads him back to reality. He thinks of Ruth, sick for home, standing amid the alien corn; it is the same with the nightingale's song,

that oft-times hath
Charm'd magic casements, opening on the foam
of perilous seas, in faery lands forlorn.

Forlorn! the very word is like a bell
To toll me back from thee to my sole self!
Adieu! the fancy cannot cheat so well
As she is fam'd to do.

He's returned to consciousness of himself, feeling and also thinking. There's a strong meditative element in the "Ode to a Nightingale"; indeed, he's pursuing a kind of meditation in much the same way as Coleridge.

William Walsh: Yes, it's astonishing how Keats' initial cockney vulgarity was in the shortest possible space transformed into work of quite surpassing genius. He kept all the time his richness and his feeling for gorgeous textures, but whereas in his earliest work this is unaccompanied by either an intellectual or moral structure, so that it's a kind of insipid abstraction, it comes to perfection if not in all the Odes certainly in "To Autumn". There the sense of the glow of the material becomes informed with a powerful intellectual passion, and at the same time there is the development of a medium capable of dealing with both. These Odes are like Coleridge's conversation poems in the extraordinary, almost Shakespearian way they use the human voice, perfected and idealised in such a way as to express the density, the totality of the experience. Above all in "Autumn", we have richness which also has in it a sense of Wordsworthian force. Would you agree?

Christopher Salvesen: No, I don't think so. "Autumn" is really quite an artificial poem, for all that one would like to emphasise the juiciness of the apples and the moss on the cottage trees and so forth. The whole of the second stanza, and there's only three of them, is full of figures from pictures:

Who hath not seen thee oft amid thy store?
    Sometimes whoever seeks abroad may find
Thee sitting careless on a granary floor,
    Thy hair soft-lifted by the winnowing wind;
Or on a half-reap'd furrow sound asleep,
    Drows'd with the fune of poppies . . .

It's marvellous, but it's very artistic, and very literary; it doesn't have the sort of reality that a poem like "Michael" has.

William Walsh: Well, if I had to choose between those two realities I wouldn't hesitate for a moment, I'm afraid, before going to Keats. I agree that "Michael" and "To Autumn" are very different, but I don't agree that one is natural and the other artificial. After all, if one wanted to press this, what could be more artificial than this picture of Wordsworth's own identification with the poor, old, bony peasant? Perhaps that's a slight contraction of "Michael"'s moral stature, I don't know. I'm trying to define, probably not precisely enough or rightly, the difference one feels in Keats' later poems. I mentioned Shakespeare, so perhaps I could put it another way; these poems seem to me to have some of the elements of tragedy in them. They represent a much more inclusive, wider kind of human experience, which one wouldn't have thought possible for Keats at the beginning of his career.

Further Reading

M.H. Abrams (ed.), *English Romantic Poets: Modern Essays* (Oxford, 1960)
Walter Jackson Bate (ed.), *Keats* (Prentice Hall Twentieth Century Views, 1964)
Walter Jackson Bate (ed.), *Coleridge* (Weidenfeld, 1969)
F.W. Bateson, *Wordsworth, a Reinterpretation* (Longmans, 1954)
J.B. Beer, *Coleridge the Visionary* (Chatto, 1959)
C.C. Clarke, *Romantic Paradox: Wordsworth* (Routledge, 1962)
Kathleen Coburn (ed.), *Coleridge* (Prentice Hall Twentieth Century Views, 1967)
John F. Danby, *The Simple Wordsworth* (Routledge, 1960)
R.A. Foakes, *The Romantic Assertion* (Methuen, 1958)
Geoffrey H. Hartman, *Wordsworth's Poetry, 1787-1814* (Yale, 1964)
Graham Hough, *The Romantic Poets* (Hutchinson, 1953)
Humphrey House, *Coleridge* (Hart-Davis, 1953)

John Jones, *The Egotistical Sublime* (Chatto, 1954)
John Keats' Dream of Truth (Chatto, 1969)
Kenneth Muir (ed.), *John Keats, a Reassessment* (Liverpool, 1958)
Stephen Prickett, *Coleridge and Wordsworth: The Poetry of Growth* (Cambridge, 1970)
Allan Rodway, *The Romantic Conflict* (Chatto, 1963)
Christopher Salvesen, *The Landscape of Memory* (Arnold, 1965)
William Walsh, *Coleridge, the Work and the Relevance* (Chatto, 1967)
Earl R. Wasserman, *The Finer Tone: Keats' Major Poems* (John Hopkins, 1953)
Donald Wesling, *Wordsworth and the Adequacy of Landscape* (Routledge, 1970)

VII

TENNYSON

John Dixon Hunt, Reader in English at York University
David Palmer, Senior Lecturer in English at Hull University

Introduction

This discussion of Tennyson's poetry starts from the same point as most modern criticism: with the notion that there is a profound gulf between early poems like "Mariana", "The Lady of Shalott", "Ulysses", and much of In Memoriam, *all of which centre on the intense evocation of mood and the struggle for personal and artistic integrity, and the more didactic and public later writings.*

John Dixon Hunt and David Palmer both believe it is wrong to posit any one, simple division in Tennyson's life and work. They give considerable attention to the poems which express a romantic sense of isolation, loss of faith, longing for death, and eventual renewal, but they argue that the reader in these poems is often encouraged to stand a little apart from the emotion, and that Tennyson's concern with public, social issues is evident in all periods of his writing. Maud *is discussed in the same terms and its protagonist identified as one whose psychological peculiarities form a prism through which the light of his materialistic society reaches us.*

The speakers display most fully their determination to see Tennyson whole by devoting a third of their time to the merits of the Arthurian legends, Idylls of the King. *They consider the origins of the poem, the nature of its structure, its oblique narrative techniques and its use of "typology", and treat in detail "The Holy Grail". Tennyson used to say that poetry should be open to a variety of interpretations, "like shot-silk with many glancing colours"; John Dixon Hunt and David Palmer distinguish some of the finer shades.*

John Dixon Hunt: In 1941 W.H. Auden wrote in his *New Year Letter* of "Black *Tennyson*, whose talents were/For an articulate despair". Do you think this emphasis is the right one?

David Palmer: I think it's part of the truth, though it recalls to my mind, an even older view. In 1923 Harold Nicolson published his influential book, *Tennyson: Aspects of his Life, Character and Poetry*, which described Tennyson as having two voices: one of "articulate despair" and one of the public poet, the Victorian Laureate.

John Dixon Hunt: But surely that is an unsatisfactory way of describing a long career? Readers have been worried by Auden's and Nicolson's emphases, so they have been going back to other Victorian writers than Tennyson. This has helped us to get a distinct sense of Tennyson as a more intricate, less divided, personality.

David Palmer: Yes indeed. Nicolson was writing just after the First World War, when there was a reaction against Victorianism, and Tennyson was caught up in this. I also think that Nicolson objected to the notion that a poet can at one and the same time retain his artistic integrity and appeal to a mass readership. Tennyson, like Dickens, was probably the last writer of this stature to have a wide following.

John Dixon Hunt: In fact, in 1875 Henry James said that Tennyson's verse had become part of the civilisation of his day. It is the question of *how* he became part of this civilisation that concerns us. One way to evade Nicolson's dichotomy is to realise that Tennyson, from early on in his poetic career, had certain intense, private recesses of consciousness that he wanted to talk about as a poet. He had constantly to find ways of making these public without betraying their integrity or authority. He was a mystical poet, a visionary—in an early poem, "The Mystic", he talks about

> The imperishable presences serene
> Colossal, without form, or sense, or sound,
> Dim shadows but unwaning presences.

He had to find for these "unwaining presences" forms, senses and sounds. The whole of his career may be seen as a discovery of these vocabularies.

David Palmer: Yes, we have to take seriously Tennyson's claim that he was capable of visionary states of being. It's been called self-hypnosis, but it lies at the root of his attitude to his art, and at the root of his religious faith.

John Dixon Hunt: His faith and his art were so intertwined that, for him, to talk about one was necessarily to talk about the other. The quotation from "The Mystic" suggests his concern not only for the presences themselves, but for a way of making those presences understandable in what Matthew Arnold called the Victorian market-place. All the great writers of their day, Dickens, Tennyson—Arnold wanted to but couldn't—had to go down and talk to the people there.

David Palmer: What we're saying, then, is that there aren't two Tennysons, or one Tennyson, but that he is a poet of enormous range, and a continually experimental poet. For instance, there's considerable support in Tennyson's poetry for the view of some modern critics that he is a forerunner of modern poetry and art—particularly in his use of myth and legend. Some of his earliest critics pointed out Symbolist qualities in his poetry. John Stuart Mill, in a review of the volumes published in 1830 and 1833, described Tennyson as not merely a descriptive writer but a poet who has "the power of *creating* scenery, in keeping with some state of human feeling; so fitted to it as to be the embodied symbol of it, and to summon up the state of feeling itself, with a force not to be surpassed by anything but reality." This is what you find in an early poem like "Mariana". Let me quote the last stanza but one from this poem, which was first published in 1830:

All day within the dreamy house,
    The doors upon their hinges creak'd;
The blue fly sung in the pane; the mouse
    Behind the mouldering wainscot shriek'd,
Or from the crevice peer'd about.
    Old faces glimmer'd thro' the doors,
    Old footsteps trod the upper floors,
Old voices called her from without.
        She only said, "My life is dreary,
            He cometh not," she said;

She said, "I am aweary, aweary,
I would that I were dead!"

John Dixon Hunt: All the landscape images, the images of the house and the moated grange, are designed to lead us into a state of mind or consciousness: they're not there for their own sakes. It's important that Tennyson here as so often uses a character, a persona—what Yeats would call a mask—rather than speak with his own voice. Don't you think we become aware of the fact that this way of looking at the scenery is Mariana's, that she is imposing upon the landscape her own frustrated and tortured soul?

David Palmer: Certainly the two are inseparable. I hadn't looked at the poem in those terms before.

John Dixon Hunt: For instance, in every stanza we're told "she only said", as if to imply that there are other things she could have said.

David Palmer: One of the things which impresses me about this stanza in particular is its evocation of silence. It's not a visual scene; it's the small noises that intensify the apprehension of silence, decay, isolation and imminence of death. This is one of the mystic centres that Tennyson evokes in several poems of this period, a morbid state lingering on the verge of death.

John Dixon Hunt: Yes, but it's all placed sufficiently in Mariana's consciousness for us to look at it objectively, almost as if the poet is offering it in that way. This is very like "The Lady of Shalott", another poem about an isolated lady, though one which is in some ways more complicated with Tennyson's ideas. Here's the beginning of part two:

There she weaves by night and day
A magic web with colours gay.
She has heard a whisper say,
A curse is on her if she stay
To look down to Camelot.
She knows not what the curse may be,
And so she weaveth steadily,
And little other care hath she,
The Lady of Shalott.

It's an image of the isolated person, not just as a morbid psychological state, but as an artist who is dedicated to looking at the outside world through a mirror and recording the reflected images on a tapestry. She neglects the activity, the Victorian work in the fields that the rest of the poem allows us to see—"up and down the people go,/Gazing where the lilies blow"; "heavy barges trail'd/ By slow horses"; "the reaper weary,/Piling sheaves in uplands airy". All this world is apart from her, isn't it?

David Palmer: Yes, but her isolation seems to be a necessary part of her ability to create the tapestry—

John Dixon Hunt: —and when she leaves her isolation at the end of the poem she stops singing:

For ere she reach'd upon the tide
The first house by the water-side,
Singing in her song she died.

The end of art coincides with her approach to the world of everyday living.

David Palmer: It does lend itself to that interpretation. What strikes me too is that Tennyson is reworking the figure of the isolated woman. "The Lady of Shalott" was first published in 1832, two years later than "Mariana", but here he uses narrative. Stagnation is the very essence of Mariana's state, whereas "The Lady of Shalott" moves towards the climactic point when the Lady breaks.

John Dixon Hunt: Tennyson in fact revised the ending of "The Lady of Shalott" when he republished the poem after what's been called his "ten-year silence" between 1832 and 1842. Originally Lancelot bent down and read upon the corpse a woven message:

"The web was woven curiously
The charm is broken utterly,
Draw near and fear not—this is I,
The Lady of Shalott."

We too are drawn in, but the later version has the ambiguity of distance:

But Lancelot mused a little space;
He said, "She has a lovely face;
God in his mercy lend her grace,
The Lady of Shalott."

Surely, this pushes us back further: it doesn't bring us close to read something that gives us a clue, but allows the narrative to be resolved apart from us. We can envisage various different emphases; we're given so many perspectives that innumerable angles of vision are allowed.

David Palmer: Yes, and this poem, more obviously than "Mariana", is concerned with the relationship between the image-world and reality. The Lady comes out of her tower at the end of part three to mingle with reality, but she remains isolated and dies before she reaches Camelot. She's no nearer to attaining the reality of Lancelot at the end of the poem than she was at the beginning.

John Dixon Hunt: No, but I think it's interesting that she leaves her artistic life because of a man. Admittedly the description stresses the emblem on his shield ("A red-cross knight forever kneel'd/To a Lady in his shield") and one might argue, I suppose, that she's moved by the artistic image and not the reality of the love, but she does leave the web and leave the loom and make three paces through the room in order to look out to a particular individual. It suggests that through love we are able to relate our life and our artistic work. To insist on this point would place a slightly partial emphasis on the poem, but it is there and it represents an advance on "Mariana".

David Palmer: The scene recurs in several of the 1832 poems, doesn't it?

John Dixon Hunt: The pictures in "The Palace of Art" are the obvious example to raise here. Like a private art gallery, there is room after room of emblems of some perfect state of soul, each landscape corresponding to some marvellous sensation.

David Palmer: At the same time there is a recognition that this is not sufficient . . .

John Dixon Hunt: Yes, the soul has to leave the Palace, but the awkward thing about this ending is that the "cottage in the vale" to which it withdraws is itself an artistic image. It's not a full contrast.

David Palmer: You mention this awkward ending, and earlier on you were talking about Tennyson's alteration to the the last stanza of "The Lady of Shalott". Is this difficulty in finding a resolution to an ambiguous situation typical? "Mariana" doesn't end at all.

John Dixon Hunt: It's partly that Tennyson is unwilling to venture his own personal voice, neat and uncluttered, in the public market-place. He wants to allow his ideas to emerge indirectly. Perhaps we should turn to "Ulysses", "Tithonus" and "Morte d'Arthur", some of the poems that arose immediately out of the death in 1833 of his great Cambridge friend, Arthur Hallam, to look at Tennyson's "sense of an ending".

David Palmer: Indeed, he felt that the loss of Hallam was itself an ending of one phase of his life. It's remarkable that this death should have triggered off a creative outburst which produced many of his best poems.

John Dixon Hunt: The point I was making, about Tennyson refusing to say things in his own person, is evident in these poems. "Ulysses" is about the need to go forward; its last line is "To strive, to seek, to find, and not to yield". At the same time he writes the draft of "Tithonus", essentially elegiacal and lamenting the things that have no future apart from slowly crumbling into death:

The woods decay, the woods decay and fall,
The vapours weep their burthen to the ground,
Man comes and tills the field and lies beneath,
And after many a summer dies the swan.

David Palmer: Yes, but isn't this the same langorous wish for oblivion that was in "Mariana": "I would that I were dead!"? And, after all, "Mariana", "The Palace of Art" and "The Lady of Shalott", poems which were written before the death of Hallam, also deal with the problem of taking a firm grip on one's life.

John Dixon Hunt: You're saying that Hallam's death was an unhappy accident, but that Tennyson didn't really need it to shape his ideas?

David Palmer: I'd say that it crystallised or focussed things that were happening in Tennyson's poetic development anyway. I feel that Tennyson was predisposed to respond to the loss of Hallam as he did, and this goes some way to account for that tremendous outburst of creativity.

John Dixon Hunt: And for the long years spent on the poem which was published in 1850—*In Memoriam.* "Ulysses" is written in a notebook alongside fragments of *In Memoriam*, so he was thinking about it all together. "Morte d'Arthur" was the death of King

Arthur, but was also the death of Arthur Hallam.

But the way *In Memoriam* uses this particularly personal moment is the aspect that fascinated the Victorians. Almost all the points we debate today were made at the time by the original reviews. Some people thought he'd written a superb philosophical poem that triumphed over the doubt of his age; other people, non-believers themselves, saw *In Memoriam* as the testament of intelligent agnosticism.

David Palmer: We didn't have to wait for T.S. Eliot to tell us in his essay on the poem that one of its remarkable features is the quality of its doubt, more convincing even than the quality of its faith. Yet we have to remember that the poem was published in 1850, before the years we associate with the Victorian crisis of religious faith. If we try to explain why the poem was so immensely popular when it was first published, we have to look at the Victorian attitude to death. To talk of a preoccupation with death is perhaps an overstatement, but compared with modern writers the Victorians were certainly less inhibited in expressing the emotions associated with bereavement. The poet's battle with his tremendous loss is at the heart of *In Memoriam.*

John Dixon Hunt: Yes, and after the death of the Prince Consort Queen Victoria allowed Tennyson to be told that it had been a considerable comfort to her. This preoccupation with death is related to a concern with the deaths and renewals of the world. Evolutionary theories about the way the earth had evolved were used by Tennyson. In sections CXVIII and XXXV he uses the theory of a huge explosion and the rival theory of gradual emergence of the earth as sharp images of different sorts of feeling.

David Palmer: It is interesting to compare *In Memoriam* with the masterpieces of the Romantic poets at the beginning of the century. In many ways the progression of *In Memoriam* is romantic: the decline into spiritual sterility, the loss of faith, and then the renewal, the recovery.

John Dixon Hunt: Yes, we tend to forget that Tennyson became Poet Laureate *after* writing this. It is a young man's romantic poem.

David Palmer: And yet your remarks about his use of up-to-date scientific theories remind me that Tennyson by no means shares Wordsworth's sense of a benevolent nature.

John Dixon Hunt: Yes, the Victorians must have been made aware of this by the publication of *The Prelude* and *In Memoriam* in the same year. It must have been a shock to compare Tennyson's notion of nature, red in tooth and claw, and Wordsworth's sense of the pastoral, vivifying forces of the natural world.

David Palmer: Some of those lyrics in *In Memoriam*—XXXV, LV, LVI—take a bleak view of nature. They sound more like Hardy at the end of the century than the Romantics at the beginning.

John Dixon Hunt: And yet a paper like *The Spectator*, reviewing *In Memoriam* in June of 1850, talked about "pictures of common landscape and daily life, redeemed from triviality by genial feeling and a perception of the lurking beautiful". Tennyson drew upon images and sounds of landscape to focus his own particular feelings of life and death, as he did in "Mariana".

David Palmer: The eventual renewal in *In Memoriam* restates in even more powerful terms the mood which runs through "Morte d'Arthur" and "Ulysses" and so much early Tennyson: the sense of coming to an ending which is also a new beginning. "The old order changeth, yielding place to new", the King says in "Morte d'Arthur". This aspect of Tennyson's imagination aligns him with the earlier Romantics.

John Dixon Hunt: It's in section XCV of *In Memoriam* that the poet has a great experience of renewal out of an old world coming to an end. It originates in the old home which Hallam used to visit and with a re-reading of his letters:

A hunger seized my heart; I read
    Of that glad year which once had been,
    In those fall'n leaves which kept their green,
The noble letters of the dead:

And strangely on the silence broke
    The silent-speaking words, and strange
    Was love's dumb cry defying change
To test his worth.

There is an awareness of a new vocabulary—"silent-speaking words", "love's dumb cry"—and this is continued in the last two stanzas of the section in phrases like "freshlier overhead" and "boundless day":

And gathering freshlier overhead,
    Rock'd the full-foliaged elms, and swung

The heavy-folded rose, and flung
The lilies to and fro, and said

"The dawn, the dawn", and died away;
And East and West, without a breath,
Mixt their dim lights, like life and death,
To broaden into boundless day.

David Palmer: The effect is of a perfectly natural world, and yet it's opened out to evoke the image of "boundless day", evoking in turn something much more significant, eloquent of a larger future.

The other reason why 1833 was a remarkable year in Tennyson's development is that he then began planning that great long poem, *Idylls of the King.*

John Dixon Hunt: Yes. He started making notes on its overall plan and also wrote "Morte d'Arthur". It is in "Morte d'Arthur" in the first speech he gives to the King, that Tennyson hints at a poem about Arthurian society. He seems to see a poem about a civilisation—its founding and sustaining, the contribution to it of private and public life, and eventually its dissolution:

"The sequel of to-day unsolders all
The goodliest fellowship of famous knights
Whereof this world holds record. Such a sleep
They sleep—the men I loved. I think that we
Shall never more, at any future time,
Delight our souls with talk of knightly deeds,
Walking about the gardens and the halls
Of Camelot, as in the days that were."

In that speech of the King the whole project is encapsulated.

David Palmer: At this point we might consider Tennyson's interest in the state of civilisation. His poetry reflects an anxiety for the future of society, particularly in the *Idylls*, where the future involves an eventual decline and decay.

John Dixon Hunt: He was interested in this before he became the public Laureate poet. For example, both the "Locksley Hall" poems look to the present Victorian society and to the future: the first (1842) with enormous confidence and a vision of what could be, and "Locksley Hall Sixty Years After" (1886) with despair that the promise has not been fulfilled.

David Palmer: Yes indeed. I think this gives the lie to Nicolson's view of the two voices.

John Dixon Hunt: —Though one could speculate about whether Tennyson purposely used social themes to bring himself out of the inwardness of private mystical states. *The Princess*, published before *In Memoriam* in 1847, sets out the whole of Tennyson's thinking about how the small family society could be the model of a larger society. It's all handled through the flashback of a legendary world and is a fascinating insight into Tennyson's role as a social commentator.

David Palmer: He used fairy-tale to be very contemporary in his subject matter.

John Dixon Hunt: Nevertheless, one is perfectly aware of the Victorianness of the family life that the Princess has rejected and of the relationship between the Prince and the Princess.

David Palmer: Perhaps Tennyson's most sustained and challenging engagement with the social issues of his day is to be found in *Maud*, the poem published in 1855 at the height of the Crimean War. The poem is concerned with the war and with the state of English society as Tennyson saw it.

John Dixon Hunt: Yet he speaks through the mouthpiece of a strange, maladjusted personality who goes mad at one stage in the poem. As in "Mariana" and "The Lady of Shalott", he's voicing his ideas through a persona whom we can't automatically associate with him.

David Palmer: The poem implies that the abnormality of the hero is a reflection of the sickness in society.

John Dixon Hunt: Yes. The speaker is very aware of the appalling and venal misuses of commercialism that have affected his own family. This sense of a world bound to its money is astonishingly strong in the young man's attitudes towards others, including Maud's family who have supplanted his own in the social structure.

David Palmer: This is a recurrent theme in Tennyson, isn't it? The rejected suitor who sees the woman he loves marrying for money also appears in "Locksley Hall", and no doubt has autobiographical significance for Tennyson. But surely in *Maud* this is not merely a form of self-expression; it's also an indictment of the ethos on which society is based. He speaks of a "civil war" of naked competition.

John Dixon Hunt: "A wounded thing with a rancorous cry,/At war with myself and a wretched race" (I.x.ii), he calls himself. *Maud* is very modern in some ways; one thinks of Eliot's "Love Song of J. Alfred Prufrock". Prufrock, although quite a different character, is also someone whose weaknesses form a prism through which the light of his society comes to us.

David Palmer: Yes, there is a social malaise focussed in the character. I find *Maud* a violent poem, involving murder, madness and war, but the war at the end is presented as a form of release for the hero.

John Dixon Hunt: I think that today we find this difficult to grapple with, but for Tennyson it was a way in which his asocial hero is able at last to find himself a role in society. "I embrace the purpose of God, and the doom assign'd", he says in the last line, so joining the loyal people shouting a battlecry. It's not mere jingoism; it's a way the hero can come through his madness and find the rose that bloomed in the garden for Maud in "The blood-red blossom of war with a heart of fire" (III.I.iv).

David Palmer: Again there's the characteristic progression from despair and alienation towards reintegration and renewal, though to the modern reader it seems odd to talk about a vision of holocaust as a renewal.

John Dixon Hunt: You say we find this ending difficult, but of course his contemporaries did as well and Tennyson was disappointed by the reaction. Sometimes in his Laureate years he wrote directly about the public sphere in the life of his age: the "Ode on the Death of the Duke of Wellington" (1852) was a great Laureate performance and an astonishingly able piece of bravura. Here he addressed himself to public issues in ways that his contemporary readers could accept more easily.

David Palmer: Yes, it's a skilful virtuoso performance as a poem, and it takes up Tennyson's preoccupation with the death of the hero. He thinks of the passing of a heroic age—"The last great Englishman is low"—which also takes us back to *Idylls of the King*.

John Dixon Hunt: The "Ode" is related to another constant image in the *Idylls* when he speaks of "The tides of Music's golden sea/ Setting toward eternity". There is music in the *Idylls* right from the foundation of Camelot at the beginning:

a Fairy King
And Fairy Queens have built the city, son;
They came from out a sacred mountain-cleft
Toward the sunrise, each with harp in hand,
And built it to the music of their harps.

("Gareth and Lynette", I.254)

Art is an image for civilization and order.

David Palmer: *Idylls of the King* is a long poem written over forty years, a collection of episodes written at different times in Tennyson's life. Does it have a unity?

John Dixon Hunt: I think it does, but one must find the unity in its own terms. "Idyll" is a Greek word meaning "a compact form", and the poem is a series of short perspectives upon a central subject. The central idea of civilisation is touched upon in all of them, but it emerges through several angles of vision.

David Palmer: I feel that the poem has a beginning and an end, but no middle. One's constantly recalling, in the different episodes, the creation of Camelot, and one's constantly anticipating its fall. I think it's typical of Tennyson that the first poem he wrote was "Morte d'Arthur": he began with the end. However, whilst the poem points towards an inevitable decline, it is also cyclical and includes the possibility of renewal.

John Dixon Hunt: All this is strongly involved with seasonal imagery, isn't it? There is throughout the poem marvellous evocation of the time of year, and a sense that we move through summer and autumn towards death.

David Palmer: Yes. The technique by which Tennyson built up the poem is interesting. He began with the central characters and an outline of the story—the founding of the kingdom, the coming of Arthur and the eventual fall. Then he filled it in, deciding which episodes from Malory to treat. And all the way through he placed oblique reflections recalling the beginning or anticipating the end, and referring to the central adultery between Lancelot and Guinevere. It is a technique of obliquity, an advanced, experimental form of narrative which doesn't appear in the novel until the end of the century with writers like Conrad and Joyce.

John Dixon Hunt: Tennyson himself, quite late in life, spoke to James Knowles of "what I have always felt even from a boy, and what as a boy I called the 'passion of the past'. And it is so always with me now; it is the distance that charms me in the landscape, the picture and the past, and not the immediate to-day in which I move" (*Nineteenth Century*, XXXIII, 1893, p.170). This was how he saw the *Idylls*: focussing on a distant picture and yet allowing immediate ideas.

David Palmer: I find that a very helpful quotation. It relates Tennyson's sense of the far past and the far future to our previous comments about his use of landscape in poems like "Mariana". It relates the imagery of time to the imagery of space.

John Dixon Hunt: The quotation also illuminates a most interesting structural device in the *Idylls*. It's difficult to explain, but Tennyson uses types or typology. Just as in the Old Testament there were certain characters who pre-figured Christ, so we may think of King Arthur as a type of Christ, and of Arthur Hallam as analogous to King Arthur (at the end of *In Memoriam* Hallam is called "a noble type" of the higher man that is to be). It's not allegory, it works in a curious analogical way; it doesn't tie down one meaning to one image.

David Palmer: You're saying that Tennyson is reviving the lost art of typologies from Medieval theology and Medieval and Renaissance art.

John Dixon Hunt: It was only just being recovered by scholars and antiquarians in the early nineteenth century when Tennyson was beginning to write. Again, it illuminates his experimental qualities.

David Palmer: Indeed. He read comparative mythologies like G.S. Faber's *The Origin of Pagan Idolatry* (1816), didn't he? Tennyson's ability to use legend and reshape it is another aspect of his poetry which seems to anticipate much that has happened since his time.

John Dixon Hunt: His worry as to how he would reshape the legend of the Holy Grail delayed its inclusion in the *Idylls* until 1869 when it was published.

David Palmer: What do you think was the particular problem with "The Holy Grail"?

John Dixon Hunt: Tennyson said he was anxious about incurring a charge of irreverence. That was a public worry; I think the private worry was how to realize the unseen. He told his son, "'The Holy Grail' is one of the most imaginative of my poems. I have expressed there my strong feeling as to the Reality of the Unseen". His solution to the creative problem of finding a language for the unseen was typical: he himself did not comment on the nature of the Holy Grail.

David Palmer: This is the kind of thing I meant by a technique of obliquity: he uses Percivale as the prime narrator.

John Dixon Hunt: Yes, he tells it through Percivale talking with Ambrosius the monk, who is not interested in the mystical question, who prefers to "mingle with our folk" and

> Delight myself with gossip and old wives,
> And ills and aches, and teethings, lyings-in,
> And mirthful sayings, children of the place,
> That have no meaning half a mile away.
>
> ("The Holy Grail", 1.549)

I think it's interesting that, four years before Tennyson's poem, the Pre-Raphaelite painter Rossetti produced a strange watercolour with the long title, "How Sir Galahad, Sir Bors, and Sir Percivale were fed with the Sanc Grael; but Sir Percivale's Sister died by the Way". This painting, in the Tate Gallery in London, is a personal, unmediated vision of three men bent over the communion cup of the Holy Grail, with the dead body of Sir Percivale's sister. When Tennyson comes to this point, he deals with it far more obliquely.

David Palmer: He has Sir Percivale recall a series of events which are already in the remote past, though he modernizes Medieval conventions like the tempting of Sir Percivale in an extraordinarily skilful way.

John Dixon Hunt: Unlike Rossetti, Tennyson was strongly aware of Victorian ideas of activism. One of the themes of "The Holy Grail" is whether you settle down with your visions into a world of contemplation, or whether you dedicate yourself to the society of the Round Table.

David Palmer: It's another version of the old conflict between the claims of the active and the contemplative life. For Tennyson it was an acutely personal conflict.

John Dixon Hunt: One could look at his whole poetic career as a dialogue between the personal existential order of his own being, and the claims upon him of society and the public voice. And yet he doesn't allow the Grail to be completely explicable in terms of Victorian needs. There is a funny Max Beerbohm cartoon of Jowett, one of the great Victorian figures, looking at Rossetti painting his picture and saying, "Well, Mr Rossetti, what will they do with the Grail when they've found it?" Tennyson's Grail just isn't sufficiently material to provoke that kind of demand; Sir Percivale says, "Lo, if I find the Holy Grail itself/And touch it, it will crumble into dust" (1.438). But that doesn't invalidate the ideal, or the energy that will come from finding something for which there is no practical purpose whatever.

David Palmer: Nevertheless, Tennyson seems more interested in the failures then in the saints who have the vision. For me the most powerful passages in "The Holy Grail" are the descriptions of the guilt and neurosis which afflict Percivale and Lancelot.

John Dixon Hunt: Well, this shows our different reactions. The way Galahad moves over that bridge and experiences a vision of the city of the Holy Grail is as strong for me as the disintegration into dust of Percivale's bad dreams.

David Palmer: It's interesting that you should say "vision" in describing that moment; I think it's the proper word to use. Sir Percivale sees Sir Galahad, and that's Sir Percivale's vision, just as Sir Galahad has a vision of the Holy Grail. There is an analogy working through the poem between the spiritual vision and the poetic vision: the poem is itself a vision, for the Arthurian material is visionary and legendary.

John Dixon Hunt: And in the ending of "The Holy Grail" Tennyson allows various visions to comment upon each other in a way which leaves us with them all available, all as possibilities. Shall we end by looking at that last part of "The Holy Grail"? Percivale is relating to Ambrosius how Lancelot told King Arthur's court about the arrival at the Holy Grail, and this experience of seeing the Grail is framed in a series of distancing devices, not unlike the image in "Ulysses" of experience as "an arch wherethro'/Gleams that untravell'd world, whose margin fades/For ever and for ever when I move".

David Palmer: Yes, that's good; it's a set of receding perspectives. First we hear how Lancelot arrived at the castle where he heard the singing of the angels, burst in through the door and swooned, but caught a glimpse:

"O, yet methought I saw the Holy Grail,
All pall'd in crimson samite, and around
Great angels, awful shapes, and wings and eyes.
And but for all my madness and my sin,
And then my swooning, I had sworn I saw
That which I saw; but what I saw was veil'd
And cover'd; and this Quest was not for me." (1. 843)

Then we have Gawain scoffing at the whole idea of the quest—Gawain is the sceptic:

"But by mine eyes and by mine ears I swear,
I will be deafer than the blue-eyed cat,
And thrice as blind as any noonday owl,
To holy virgins in their ecstasies,
Henceforward." (1. 861)

Finally Arthur addresses his knights:

"Deafer," said the blameless King,
"Gawain, and blinder unto holy things
Hope not to make thyself by idle vows,
Being too blind to have desire to see.
But if indeed there came a sign from heaven,
Blessed are Bors, Lancelot and Percivale,
For these have seen according to their sight." (1. 865)

No-one has the right to scoff, says the King, but

"spake I not too truly, O my knights?
Was I too dark a prophet when I said
To those who went upon the Holy Quest,
That most of them would follow wandering fires,
Lost in the quagmire?" (1. 884)

And yet again, even for the King who has responsibilities of state,

"Let visions of the night or of the day
Come, as they will; and many a time they come,
Until this earth he walks on seems not earth,
This light that strikes his eyeball is not light,
This air that smites his forehead is not air
But vision—yea, his very hand and foot—

In moments when he feels he cannot die,
And knows himself no vision to himself,
Nor the high God a vision, nor that One
Who rose again: ye have seen what ye have seen." (l. 906)

Many attitudes are possible, and Sir Percivale can only conclude, "So spake the King: I knew not all he meant".

Further Reading

Jerome H. Buckley, *Tennyson: the Growth of a Poet* (Harvard, 1960)

J. Philip Eggers, *King Arthur's Laureate* (New York University, 1971)

K.W. Gransden, *Tennyson, In Memoriam* (Arnold, 1964)

Ward Hellstrom, *On the Poems of Tennyson* (Florida University, 1972)

John Dixon Hunt (ed.), *Tennyson: In Memoriam* (Macmillan Casebooks, 1970)

E.D.H. Johnson, *The Alien Vision of Victorian Poetry* (Princeton, 1952)

John D. Jump (ed.), *Tennyson, the Critical Heritage* (Routledge, 1967)

John Killham (ed.), *Critical Essays on the Poetry of Tennyson* (Routledge, 1960)

David Palmer (ed.), *Tennyson* (Bell, 1973)

John Pettigrew, *Tennyson: the Early Poems* (Arnold, 1970)

John R. Reed, *Perception and Design in Tennyson's 'Idylls of the King'* (Ohio, 1969)

Christopher Ricks, *Tennyson* (Macmillan, 1972)

John D. Rosenberg, *The Fall of Camelot* (Harvard University, 1973)

Robert H. Ross (ed.), *In Memoriam* (Norton Critical Edition, 1973)

Alan Sinfield, *The Language of Tennyson's 'In Memoriam'* (Blackwells, 1971)

J.B. Steane, *Tennyson* (Evans, 1966)

VIII

READING MODERN POETRY

Laurence Lerner, Professor of English at Sussex University

Introduction

It is an uncomfortable paradox that the poetry which is nearest to us in time and presumably in spirit is often the slowest to stimulate that free-hearted response to structured language, whether elevated or ironical, that for many centuries was the simplest hallmark of good poetry. T.S. Eliot gave the classic explanation in his essay on "The Metaphysical Poets", in which he says that the variety and complexity of modern life must produce various and complex results and that the poet must become more comprehensive, allusive and indirect in order to compel language to express his meaning. Sometimes it seems that this justification is being abused and that the general reader is gratuitously excluded by a kind of "privatism" which delights in personal and literary allusions he is unlikely to recognize. But we should not be too easily disheartened; often only a hit of the direction in which the answer lies is sufficient to spark a uniquely rewarding "explosion into meaning" (Gerard Manley Hopkins' phrase).

In this chapter Laurence Lerner provides an introduction to twentieth-century poetry by talking his way through four important poems: Eliot's "Preludes", Auden's "The Shield of Achilles", Yeats' "Lapis Lazuli" and Stevens' "Of Heaven Considered as a Tomb". He shows how responsiveness to tone and mood, patient attention to detail, and thoughtful common-sense, together with a little specialised knowledge, can afford a rich and unpretentious interpretation. Each poem gives rise to a wider consideration of the work of that poet and of the themes and techniques which characterise twentieth-century poetry—the distress and violence of much modern life, the decline of traditional religion, the role of the artist, Symbolist theory, and the scope for a poetry of direct statement.

READING MODERN POETRY

Laurence Lerner: Eliot's "Preludes" don't really need any introduction; they make their impact directly as descriptive poems with a strong emotional quality about them. They announce their modernity in their subject, the city, and I'll be going on to explain how they announce their modernity in their method as well. The subject is the vast, empty, anonymous monotony of modern city life, and it is clear, quite apart from the way they are written, that the poems are meant to belong very much to the twentieth century. Here is the first one:

The winter evening settles down
With smell of steaks in passageways.
Six o'clock.
The burnt-out ends of smoky days.
And now a gusty shower wraps
The grimy scraps
Of withered leaves about your feet
And newspapers from vacant lots;
The showers beat
On broken blinds and chimney-pots,
And at the corner of the street
A lonely cab-horse steams and stamps.
And then the lighting of the lamps.

I have already implied that these are not just straightforward descriptive poems; they are in fact conveying to us a kind of emotional response to city life. In the opening Prelude we can start by asking ourselves what is this emotional response. There are, after all, one or two details which could sound nostalgic: "A lonely cab-horse steams and stamps" is perhaps the most striking such example, though the same could even apply to the opening lines. But as we read the poem we realise that there is a much stronger and much more unpleasant emotion that it conveys to us—disgust. This is clearest in "The burnt-out ends of smoky days", which compares the end of the day to something used up, dirty and obviously unattractive, like a cigarette end.

I have often noticed that people who read the first Prelude feel that it expresses a kind of gentle nostalgia, but I think the overwhelming emotion is that of disgust at the unpleasantness of city life. I suppose the way to convince people is to go on and read the second Prelude, in which the disgust is much more explicit and more violent; there can be little doubt now what emotion is intended, from the very first line:

The morning comes to consciousness
Of faint stale smells of beer
From the sawdust-trampled street
With all its muddy feet that press
To early coffee-stands.
With the other masquerades
That time resumes,
One thinks of all the hands
That are raising dingy shades
In a thousand furnished rooms.

For a start, "coming to consciousness" seems somehow a less positive, less joyful, almost less alive thing than waking up. It suggests a sort of subdued half-living, and this suggestion is continued through the whole of the second Prelude.

In the third Prelude we find an even more violent disgust but a hint of some kind of fuller consciousness, some further dimension, another way of understanding and responding to the scene. The stronger disgust comes especially at the end:

You tossed a blanket from the bed,
You lay upon your back, and waited;
You dozed, and watched the night revealing
The thousand sordid images
Of which your soul was constituted;
They flickered against the ceiling.
And when all the world came back
And the light crept up between the shutters
And you heard the sparrows in the gutters,
You had such a vision of the street
As the street hardly understands;
Sitting along the bed's edge, where
You curled the papers from your hair,
Or clasped the yellow soles of feet
In the palms of both soiled hands.

This description has the physical unpleasantness which naturally suggests to us a word like "disgust". But what about, "You had such a vision of the street/As the street hardly understands"? These are the most puzzling lines in the third Prelude. They appear to hint at a possibility of some kind of vision, some kind of way of seeing and experiencing the scene that is more profound and involves more understanding, but they tell us nothing whatever about it. So it's possible for us to say only that the lines mean something like "You had the ability to write poems like this one, which express the emptiness of the life of all those who are trampling around the streets, but which they themselves could hardly have written".

In the fourth Prelude the theme that has just begun to appear, the theme of consciousness of the scene, of being able somehow to understand and express it, now becomes more explicit and prominent. Indeed, the poem starts with an almost surrealist image:

His soul stretched tight across the skies
That fade behind a city block,
Or trampled by insistent feet
At four and five and six o'clock;
And short square fingers stuffing pipes,
And evening newspapers, and eyes
Assured of certain certainties,
The conscience of a blackened street
Impatient to assume the world.

I am moved by fancies that are curled
Around these images, and cling:
The notion of some infinitely gentle
Infinitely suffering thing.

Wipe your hand across your mouth, and laugh;
The worlds revolve like ancient women
Gathering fuel in vacant lots.

There is now something unreal about the very matter-of-fact scene that Eliot began by describing: it is unreal because he is now beginning to interest himself not only in the scene itself but in our awareness of the scene. Fed into this fourth poem, as well as the disgust, is a contrasting pity, as often happens in Eliot's early poetry—at the end of "The Hollow Men", for instance, out of the emptiness, the flat despair, comes a kind of vision of humanity. The pity here is in the two really haunting lines about the notion of "some infinitely gentle/Infinitely suffering thing". But the poem is not allowed to end there. It ends with a thoroughly flat movement; we're brought down to earth again, and indeed there's a cynical snarl in the way this image of pity is rejected: "Wipe your hand across your mouth, and laugh".

Now, I've started by going through these poems line by line because, after all, what is really important about them is the quality of their language. To put them in a wider context we can perhaps start with the title, which is a musical term. Eliot also wrote "Rhapsody on a Windy Night", *Four Quartets*, and even "Five Finger Exercises", so we can see that he has deliberately given titles to his poems which stress an analogy with music. This analogy between poetry and music is really central to Modernism or, if we use the term which was taken over from the growth of modern poetry in France, Symbolism. Paul Valéry, who was in a way the theorist of the Symbolist movement, quite explicitly compared poetry to music, saying that what the poet did to the ordinary language of prose was—and he made up the word—to "musicalise" it. Eliot, in this as in so much else, is announcing that he is a follower of modern poetry, because after all Eliot is really the man who first brought Symbolist poetry into English; his contribution was both as a great creative artist and as the acclimatiser of a movement which began in France.

If we look for precedents for the kind of poems that Eliot is writing in "Preludes", however, we don't actually have to go to France; they are very like the poems of the Imagist movement in the early twentieth century. This movement, associated with Ezra Pound and a number of other poets who are now half-forgotten, set an extraordinarily modest aim for poetry by saying that it shouldn't really do much more than present you with a series of clear, sharp images. Eliot has certainly done that in this poem: "muddy feet that press/To early coffee-stands".

But as well as being an Imagist poem this is a Symbolist poem: it rejects the idea that poetry should perform any of the functions that are best performed in prose, such as narrative or argument, and suggests that poetry should confine itself to concrete details and the suggestiveness of metaphoric language. Indeed it often seems to me that in this poem, in a few very simple lines, Eliot has stated the programme of the Symbolist movement, a really very ambitious movement which has produced some very long and very difficult poetry, including Eliot's own *The Waste Land*. The lines I'm thinking of are those in the fourth Prelude, when he says, "I am moved by fancies that are curled/Around these images, and cling". This is almost a technical account of how he has written the poems; he's presented the "images", and clinging around these images are the "fancies" whose emotional impact gives the "Preludes" so much of their quality. So there's a lot of theory lying behind these poems, although they are so vivid, immediate and simple in the impression they make on us.

The second modern poem I'm going to look at is "The Shield of Achilles", by W.H. Auden.

In Book XVIII of the *Iliad* Thetis, the mother of the mighty

Achilles, goes to Hephaestos, the smith of the gods, to ask him to make fresh armour for her son. Hephaestos does this, and Homer gives us a long description of the splendid shield that he makes:

> Adorned all over, it contained scenes of earth, sky and sea. It contained two beautiful cities, one in peace with wedding festivities, banquets and dancing, one in war being attacked by armies. It contained oxen ploughing in the fields, and scenes of hired reapers on a King's estate, among them the King himself standing by in quiet satisfaction. It contained a vineyard, a herd of cattle, a dancing floor. Youths and marriageable maidens were dancing on it with their hands on one another's wrists, the girls in fine linen with lovely garlands on their heads, and the men in closely woven tunics showing the faint gleam of oil, and with daggers of gold hanging from their silver bells.

Now this famous shield of Achilles, one of the great set pieces in Homer's poem, is the starting-point for Auden's poem—the title is the signal. Thetis, who is not named but is clearly the "She" of the first word of the poem, is watching Hephaestos make the armour, but this time it's coming out all wrong:

The Shield of Achilles

She looked over his shoulder
    For vines and olive trees,
Marble well-governed cities
    And ships upon untamed seas,
But there on the shining metal
    His hands had put instead
An artificial wilderness
    And a sky like lead.

A plain without a feature, bare and brown,
    No blade of grass, no sign of neighbourhood,
Nothing to eat and nowhere to sit down,
    Yet, congregated on its blankness, stood
    An unintelligible multitude.
A million eyes, a million boots in line,
Without expression, waiting for a sign.

Out of the air a voice without a face
    Proved by statistics that some cause was just
In tones as dry and level as the place:

No one was cheered and nothing was discussed;
Column by column in a cloud of dust
They marched away enduring a belief
Whose logic brought them, somewhere else, to grief.

She looked over his shoulder
For ritual pieties,
White flower-garlanded heifers,
Libation and sacrifice,
But there on the shining metal
Where the altar should have been,
She saw by his flickering forge-light
Quite another scene.

Barbed wire enclosed an arbitrary spot
Where bored officials lounged (one cracked a joke)
And sentries sweated for the day was hot:
A crowd of ordinary decent folk
Watched from without and neither moved nor spoke
As three pale figures were led forth and bound
To three posts driven upright in the ground.

The mass and majesty of this world, all
That carries weight and always weighs the same
Lay in the hands of others; they were small
And could not hope for help and no help came:
What their foes liked to do was done, their shame
Was all the worst could wish; they lost their pride
And died as men before their bodies died.

She looked over his shoulder
For athletes at their games,
Men and women in a dance
Moving their sweet limbs
Quick, quick, to music,
But there on the shining shield
His hands had set no dancing-floor
But a weed-choked field.

A ragged urchin, aimless and alone,
Loitered about that vacancy, a bird
Flew up to safety from his well-aimed stone:
That girls are raped, that two boys knife a third,
Were axioms to him, who'd never heard
Of any world where promises were kept,
Or one could weep because another wept.

The thin-lipped armourer,
    Hephaestos hobbled away,
Thetis of the shining breasts
    Cried out in dismay
At what the god had wrought
    To please her son, the strong
Iron-hearted man-slaying Achilles
    Who would not live long.

The structure of the poem is an alternating series of stanzas with short lines that describe Thetis looking over the shoulder of Hephaestos and seeing the shield being made, and stanzas in rather longer lines which describe the scene on the shield itself. Auden, in short, has written an anti-heroic poem, the modern version of how he fears the shield of Achilles might come out if some modern smith of the gods were to make it and put contemporary scenes on it.

Most prominent among the scenes that would be put on it is the wilderness, or the desert, one of Auden's favourite symbols for emptiness, spiritual dryness, barrenness and very often modern life itself. Indeed, the scene we are shown is an archetypal modern scene representing the power of the state and of impersonal institutions over the anonymous masses, the sort of theme which Auden had used for comic purposes in, for instance, "The Unknown Citizen". Here he's turning it to something horrible, not comic. There are no place names: none of the details that Homer had so lovingly chronicled when he described his scenes, because this is just a huge, anonymous expanse of land. When the multitude march off they don't go to another place that is named, they just go "somewhere else"; and they march off, you will have noticed, "enduring a belief". I can hardly imagine a more horrible way of showing how what ought to bring us comfort just brings us suffering.

This, of course, is the central contrast of "The Shield of Achilles". Everything that Auden as a poet loves and has always loved—pagan customs, ritual, local piety, and so on—has given place to empty anonymity. Auden has written a lot of poems in which he has celebrated his love of what, for short, we can call paganism—the particularities of local legends, local saints, rituals and ceremonies. His poem "In Praise of Limestone" is, despite its title, not really about landscape and geology so much as culture and ways of life. This poem is a hymn of praise, or perhaps not a hymn so much as a statement, a meditation of praise on the ordinary, everyday quality that pagan culture can have in a simple world, as in its description of

the nude young male who lounges
Against a rock displaying his dildo, never doubting
That for all his faults he is loved, whose works are but
Extensions of his power to charm.

That simple, innocent world has disappeared on the modern shield of Achilles. It has been replaced by impersonality, by a scene that sounds like a description of a concentration camp inhabited, in the eighth stanza, by "A ragged urchin . . . who'd never heard/Of any world where promises were kept".

So the technique of this poem is, after all, rather like the technique of that very different poem, Eliot's *Waste Land*, setting the beauty of the past against the sordidness of the present. But once I've mentioned that comparison you will realise that I am over-simplifying, because in *The Waste Land* Eliot is not really drawing such a simple, nostalgic contrast. He's also suggesting to us that in a way the past, if you really look at it, was as corrupt as the present. I'm not quite sure about "The Shield of Achilles"; I'm not quite sure how much Auden is suggesting to us that it is not just a simple juxtaposition, a simple contrast between the beauty of the pagan past and the corrupt present. In order to settle this question I think we'd have to brood on the stanza which appears to be describing the Crucifixion: "three pale figures were led forth and bound/To three posts driven upright in the ground". If this is in fact about the Crucifixion then it's a hint that somehow or other a new moral dimension is entering into the horror, along with the horror entering into the new world. But it may just be a parody of the Crucifixion.

Still, we can see that this poem is about the end of pagan innocence and the end of the pagan world; it ends with Thetis crying out in dismay

At what the god had wrought
To please her son, the strong
Iron-hearted man-slaying Achilles
Who would not live long.

We realise that Achilles is not going to live long because in the *Iliad* itself he is doomed; Homer frequently mentions the fact that he is not going to live much longer. But also Achilles is not going to live long because the whole world that he belongs to is not going to live long; it is the doom of the pagan world as well as that of an individual that is being evoked.

I must say something about the style of this poem, because you must have been struck by the extraordinarily powerful simplicity and directness with which it is written. Certainly it has very little of Auden's usual fireworks, the extravagant displays of wit, linguistic ingenuity, and out-of-the-way words that he so loves. Compare the landscape of "The Shield of Achilles" with the landscape of "Vespers", the other really brilliant poem in the same volume, which begins:

> If the hill overlooking our city has always been known as
> Adam's Grave, only at dusk can you see the recumbent
> giant, his head turned to the west, his right arm resting for
> ever on Eve's haunch.

You can see how much more loving particularity there is in "Vespers"; it also deals with a kind of Arcadian civilisation, but not in such a despairing way.

Here, however, Auden has deliberately written with austerity and directness. Perhaps that's surprising, because Auden has himself said that he doesn't believe directness is possible any more in writing. Here are a few lines from the prefatory poem to Auden's previous volume, *Nones*:

> But, pawed-at and gossiped-over
> By the promiscuous crowd,
> Concocted by editors
> Into spells to befuddle the crowd,
> All words like peace and love,
> All sane affirmative speech,
> Had been soiled, profaned, debased
> To a horrid mechanical screech:
> No civil style survived
> That pandaemonium
> But the wry, the sotto-voce,
> Ironic and monochrome.

Now Auden is not the only poet to have said that he feels that in the twentieth century some of the more traditional orthodox, dignified and heroic forms of language are no longer feasible. He felt that the only way you can write with honesty, if you are expressing your conviction, is to be ironic, indirect and bitter; to be, as he puts it, "wry" and "sotto-voce". Yet he seems to have contradicted his own formula when he wrote "The Shield of Achilles". The answer, I suppose, is that there is one emotion for which, with a poet like Auden, direct speech is still possible, and that is anger. "The Shield of Achilles" is a poem which expresses a kind of moral fury at what has happened to the world; and that, it appears, can still be expressed directly.

Finally I should say that this poem, in a volume published in the mid-Fifties, is in some ways like the Auden of the Thirties. The most frequently made remark about Auden's career is that he turned from a political poet in the 1930's into a religious and academic poet in the Fifties and Sixties. This is true, or rather it's partly true, for Auden has himself pointed out that there is a kind of psychological interest common to all his work and running right through it. Therefore it is particularly interesting to find that the later Auden is still writing the sort of poem that the earlier, committed, political Auden of the Thirties might have written, but it's now given a new historical dimension: it's put in the framework of a re-working of the Homeric shield of Achilles. That reminds us of the different kind of historical consciousness, the new academic approach that sometimes makes the later Auden surprisingly impersonal and dry. But in a poem like this it makes him richer and more powerful, even when he deals with his old themes.

My third poem, Yeats' "Lapis Lazuli", is about art; indeed it offers us a theory of art, so perhaps we had better start by trying to say what sort of theories of art exist. In order to be very simple we'll divide them simply into two, which I'll call "committed" and "aesthetic". Committed art aims to have some kind of lasting effect upon the reader, to change him, perhaps permanently; it even aims to change the world. We can contrast this committed art with the theory that aesthetic experience is self-contained—that reading a poem, seeing a painting or hearing music is a unique experience which can't be translated into anything else. Value resides in the aesthetic experience itself, not in any kind of human, moral, social, let alone political, spin-off or consequences.

Of these two views, the committed and the aesthetic, there's no doubt where Yeats belongs: he always held the second view, and always attacked the idea that art was important because of its human or moral consequences. In "Lapis Lazuli" he sets out to state his aesthetic creed.

Lapis Lazuli

I have heard that hysterical women say
They are sick of the palette and fiddle-bow,
Of poets that are always gay,
For everybody knows or else should know
That if nothing drastic is done
Aeroplane and Zeppelin will come out,

Pitch like King Billy bomb-balls in
Until the town lie beaten flat.

All perform their tragic play,
There struts Hamlet, there is Lear,
That's Ophelia, that Cordelia;
Yet they, should the last scene be there,
The great stage curtain about to drop,
If worthy their prominent part in the play,
Do not break up their lines to weep.
They know that Hamlet and Lear are gay;
Gaiety transfiguring all that dread.
All men have aimed at, found and lost;
Black out; Heaven blazing into the head:
Tragedy wrought to its uttermost.
Though Hamlet rambles and Lear rages,
And all the drop-scenes drop at once
Upon a hundred thousand stages,
It cannot grow by an inch or an ounce.

On their own feet they came, or on shipboard,
Camel-back, horse-back, ass-back, mule-back,
Old civilisations put to the sword.
Then they and their wisdom went to rack:
No handiwork of Callimachus,
Who handled marble as if it were bronze,
Made draperies that seemed to rise
When sea-wind swept the corner, stands;
His long lamp-chimney shaped like the stem
Of a slender palm, stood but a day;
All things fall and are built again,
And those that build them again are gay.

Two Chinamen, behind them a third,
Are carved in lapis lazuli,
Over them flies a long-legged bird,
A symbol of longevity;
The third, doubtless a serving-man,
Carries a musical instrument.

Every discoloration of the stone,
Every accidental crack or dent,
Seems a water-course of an avalanche,
Or lofty slope where it still snows
Though doubtless plum or cherry-branch
Sweetens the little half-way house

Those Chinamen climb towards, and I
Delight to imagine them seated there;
There, on the mountain and the sky,
On all the tragic scene they stare.
One asks for mournful melodies;
Accomplished fingers begin to play.
Their eyes mid many wrinkles, their eyes,
Their ancient, glittering eyes, are gay.

The first section of the poem sets out to attack the idea of committed art, or *littérature engagée*. Yeats slips in a slightly mischievous piece of local learning: "King Billy" is William of Orange, hero of the Ulsterman, who is still celebrated for his victory at the Battle of the Boyne in Northern Ireland. The serious purpose of these lines is to say we mustn't dismiss the poets who are always gay. I think the "hysterical women" that Yeats is here pouring scorn upon had been reading the poets of the Thirties—Auden, Stephen Spender, Cecil Day Lewis and other committed poets—who felt that because the world was in such a desperate mess they must give to their poetry a purpose, and do something about the mess. Yeats has no wish to deny that the world is in a mess. Indeed the poem that comes just before "Lapis Lazuli" in his collected works, "The Gyres", tells us that "Irrational streams of blood are staining earth". But it also tells us: "We that look on but laugh in tragic joy"; that is to say, the response to the terrible state of the world that Yeats is here suggesting to us is almost—though it sounds outrageous—one of enjoyment.

For the expansion of this idea we should look at the second section of "Lapis Lazuli", which is about tragedy. We recall the age-old paradox about tragedy: why does the greatest aesthetic delight come from the contemplation of the expression of human suffering? Yeats is here reminding us that the great tragic poet doesn't react immediately to suffering by trying to do something about it, or by weeping in sympathy. If an actor were to weep in sympathy he wouldn't be able to speak his lines: Ophelia and Cordelia, "If worthy their prominent part in the play,/Do not break up their lines to weep". "Worthy" is a very important word, because it suggests a kind of craftsmanship and loyalty to the act of expressing the tragic subject matter as splendidly as possible. In order to do this you have to write as a poet, because the aim of tragedy is to work to its uttermost all these terrible happenings, "All men have aimed at, found and lost". And once the tragedy is written you must be loyal to the beauty of what has been done: "It cannot grow by an inch or an ounce".

In order to express the full force of the paradox Yeats uses a word that will shock us. Instead of saying "Tragedy gives us a profound aesthetic experience", or "Tragedy gives us something of beauty and permanent value", he says that what tragedy offers us is *gaiety*. "Lapis Lazuli" is not the only poem in which Yeats says something like this. Many years before he'd written a little lyric called "Tom O'Roughley" in which the homely philosopher of the title says, "Wisdom is a butterfly/And not a gloomy bird of prey", and is made to end his song by saying, "And if my dearest friend were dead/I'd dance a measure on his grave". It's even more shocking, in a sense, when Tom O'Roughley says it, because he is talking about personal grief.

I can offer a parallel to "Lapis Lazuli" in a little known poem by Wailace Stevens called "Mozart, 1935". It's an apparently trivial little poem in which Stevens talks to the poet, telling him to sit down at the piano and to go on playing:

If they throw stones upon the roof
While you practise arpeggios,
It is because they carry down the stairs
A body in rags.
Be seated at the piano.

That seems to me exactly the situation that the first section of "Lapis Lazuli" is dealing with: the poet is surrounded by suffering, but he is told to get on with his job of writing. "Be thou the voice", says Stevens, "Not you" (presumably the "you" were the people who were throwing stones on the roof); he tells the poet to get on with his job of composing:

Be thou the voice,
Not you. Be thou, be thou
The voice of angry fear,
The voice of this besieging pain.

Like Yeats, Stevens is saying that the most important job is to turn the tragedy into art. For Yeats, I think, this is not only a theory of art but a theory of living. For instance in a famous little poem written during the First World War, "The Irish Airman Foresees His Death", Yeats seems to feel that all sorts of experiences, even the experiences of flying and fighting in aeroplanes in the First World War, are really worthwhile, not because of what they achieve but because of the actual experience itself. The airman says,

Nor law, nor duty bade me fight,
Nor public men, nor cheering crowds,
A lonely impulse of delight
Drove to this tumult in the clouds.

Well, that seems to me the central point of "Lapis Lazuli". But the poem doesn't end there, and we must say a few words about the last three sections. Yeats is not always explicit about the structure of his arguments, and we should notice that he now goes on to say quite explicitly that works of art perish: as he puts it in the third section, which deals with the rise and fall of civilisations, "All things fall and are built again". The answer, however, is that though the individual works of art might be destroyed the creating of art goes on, "And those that build them again are gay".

Then the poem ends on a single example, the one that provides the title. Here's one work of art which has survived from the very distant past, a carving in the bright blue stone, lapis lazuli, in which we see "Two Chinamen, behind them a third". These two Chinamen have the total detachment of pure artists. They clearly belong to a civilisation which is hierarchical and ceremonial. They climb up in order to survey the landscape and when they look down they see a "tragic scene". Of course, we now realise that they're not going to respond by helpless fits of weeping; instead, in a way that might seem almost frighteningly impersonal, they're going to make it into the subject matter of art. They therefore ask their serving-man (for they belong to a hierarchical culture) to play to them with his "Accomplished fingers"—"accomplished" makes the same kind of point as "worthy" did in the section about tragedy. Here is someone who doesn't break up his lines, but gets on with the act of expression; and the little old Chinamen listen:

On all the tragic scene they stare.
One asks for mournful melodies;.
Accomplished fingers begin to play.
Their eyes mid many wrinkles, their eyes,
Their ancient, glittering eyes, are gay.

After discussing three poems by the three central and most important modern English poets I want to introduce you to perhaps the strangest, the most difficult and the most enchanting of all modern poets, the American, Wallace Stevens, who died in 1955. It's not easy to introduce him by means of a single poem, for he has a special kind of difficulty. It's not that there are particular knotty details in his poems, so that after you've worked through them what was unclear becomes clear; it's much more that the same poem, and certainly this is my experience, can seem crystal clear one day and totally obscure the next, as if the total message of what it is saying adds up or doesn't add up according to the reader's mood and the reader's response.

Well, I have chosen a fairly straightforward poem, short and marvellously impressive, "Of Heaven Considered as a Tomb":

What word have you, interpreters, of men
Who in the tomb of heaven walk by night,
The darkened ghosts of our old comedy?
Do they believe they range the gusty cold,
With lanterns borne aloft to light the way,
Freemen of death, about and still about
To find whatever it is they seek? Or does
That burial, pillared up each day as porte
And spiritous passage into nothingness,
Foretell each night the one abysmal night,
When the host shall no more wander, nor the light
Of the steadfast lanterns creep across the dark?
Make hue among the dark comedians,
Halloo them in the topmost distances
For answer from their icy Élysée.

The title is, for once, rather helpful. Stevens enjoyed giving nonsense titles to his poems, almost out of sheer quirkiness, but here we've got a title which really announces what the poem is about. What happens to the dead, "The darkened ghosts of our old comedy"?—that's clearly the subject of this poem. The Greek stories of the Elysian Fields differ from the Christian idea of Heaven in a lot of ways, of course, particularly in the belief the Greeks seemed to hold that although there was a life after death it was a pale, uninteresting feeble shadow of this life. The Christian tradition, on the other hand, believing in life after death, tells us that in heaven our happiness will be of an immeasurably purer and finer quality. But a Christian would hardly describe life on earth as a "comedy", though of course Dante considered it a comedy, if you added on the happy ending in Heaven. To speak of the dead, then, as having escaped from this "comedy" (and later in the poem they're actually called "comedians") and to speak of them as "darkened ghosts", is to suggest that if there is any kind of life after death it's a half-hearted, unattractive version of the really full-blooded life on earth.

The poem is addressed to "interpreters"; we're not told who

they are, but since their job is apparently to tell us what happens after death we can assume that they are priests, theologians, and possibly even poets. They are asked to choose between two alternatives. The first is that the dead have set out on a new and exciting journey:

With lanterns borne aloft to light the way,
Freemen of death, about and still about
To find whatever it is they seek.

It's an exciting journey, but the poet thinks that there is something futile about it, that perhaps there isn't anything that they're looking for. The second alternative that the interpreters might bring to us is that the death of each man leads to nothingness, that indeed the death of each man foretells the death of all,

the one abysmal night,
When the host shall no more wander, nor the light
Of the steadfast lanterns creep across the dark.

It's true that there was a procession of the dead with lanterns mentioned earlier, but at this point in the poem it may well be the procession of the living. So this second alternative may be saying quite simply that entering this gate into nothingness foretells the time when humanity will no longer be processing over the earth in this way.

When discussing Yeats I drew a parallel with Stevens; so, when discussing Stevens, I am going to draw a parallel with Yeats. The Yeats poem I want to mention is "Mohini Chatterjee", a poem he wrote in 1928 about a Brahmin who had come to Dublin to preach reincarnation. The poet seems fascinated at the idea of reincarnation, and at the thought that he ought to say to himself every night in bed, "I have been a king,/I have been a slave". The idea of reincarnation seems to be for him the expression of a continuing faith in humanity, the belief that mankind is going to go on and on, somehow or other, still carrying on its "old comedy", if we can use Stevens' phrase. Perhaps the most impressive moment in Yeats' poem is when he says, "Over the blackened earth/The old troops parade". These two, almost tired lines of Yeats say something very similar to the much more exhilarated lines of Stevens, "the light/Of the steadfast lanterns creep across the dark". And if I am right in seeing this as the procession of humanity going through human history then the two poets are using the image in a very similar way.

Well, Stevens ends with three ringing, mocking lines to the interpreters:

Make hue among the dark comedians,

Halloo them in the topmost distances
For answer from their icy Élysée.

Where are the dead? "Élysée"—in the Elysian Fields, I take it, which are icy because they are in the icy cold of outer space. Indeed, there's a strong feeling in these lines that the dead don't seem to be answering, isn't there? "The dark comedians": does this suggestive phrase mean that they are human actors who have now gone into the dark? Or does it mean that they are now performing in some kind of dark comedy, some mocking echo of what human life was like?

That, as it seems to me, is the outline of what Stevens is saying in this poem. There are several things that are very striking about it. First, its agnosticism: Stevens is, I suppose, the great agnostic poet of the twentieth century, the poet who has most marvellously expressed the feeling that this life is probably all, and that certainly nothing can be known about any other life.

The honey of heaven may or may not come,
But that of earth both comes and goes at once—

in these two haunting lines, which come from "Le Monocle de mon Oncle", a poem with a comic title but a very serious poem in itself, Stevens is expressing the agnostic position. It is central to his creed that beauty depends on transitoriness, on time and change, and therefore what is most honeyed is at the same time most obviously departing from us.

Then, in "Of Heaven Considered as A Tomb" there are a few touches of preciousness that you may have noticed. He breaks into French occasionally, saying "Élysée" for Elysian Fields. He talks about the "porte" and "spiritous passage into nothingness". Really he just means gate when he says "porte". These are one or two slight touches of what is very prominent in other poems of Stevens, showing how he enjoys the arbitrariness and what he himself once called the essential "gaudiness" of poetry. Sometimes he even writes nonsense verse, enjoying the writing of it but in a sense rejecting it because he was so haunted by the idea that poetry should describe the world exactly as it is.

Finally, there is the marvellous blank verse movement of the poem. No other modern poet can write blank verse like Stevens. Even when he is mocking, as he is in this poem to some extent, the splendour of his rhythm is still there. As a parallel I'd like to quote some lines from Stevens' poem "Sunday Morning", which is an even more direct and far more eloquent statement of agnosticism than this small poem.

Is there no change of death in paradise?
Does ripe fruit never fall? Or do the boughs
Hang always heavy in that perfect sky,
Unchanging, yet so like our perishing earth,
With rivers like our own that seek for seas
They never find, the same receding shores
That never touch with inarticulate pang?
Why set the pear upon those river-banks
Or spice the shores with odours of the plum?
Alas, that they should wear our colours there,
The silken weavings of our afternoons,
And pick the strings of our insipid lutes!
Death is the mother of beauty, mystical,
Within whose burning bosom we devise
Our earthly mothers waiting, sleeplessly.

Death is the mother of beauty because beauty is the product of process, growth, maturity, change, and therefore dying. So the very idea of paradise is a contradiction: how can there be a paradise in which ripe fruit never falls? Of course, Stevens is not the first to express this kind of view and the whole stanza, as I'm sure you'll feel, is rich with the influence of Keats. We can see that Stevens' agnosticism, both in little poems like "Of Heaven Considered as a Tomb" and in much more ambitious poems like "Sunday Morning", is not necessarily a pessimistic creed. It's a love of earth, an acceptance of transience rather than a horror of it, which enables him to write so eloquently on this subject.

Further Reading

A. Alvarez, *The Shaping Spirit* (Chatto, 1967)
Thomas Blackburn, *The Price of an Eye* (Longmans, 1961)
Geoffrey Bullough, *The Trend of Modern Poetry* (Oliver, 1934)
David Daiches, *Poetry and the Modern World* (Chicago, 1940)
G.S. Fraser, *Vision and Rhetoric* (Faber, 1959)
F.R. Leavis, *New Bearings in English Poetry* (Chatto, 1932)
J. Hillis Miller, *Poets of Reality* (Harvard, 1966)
Laura Riding and Robert Graves, *A Survey of Modernist Poetry* (Heinemann, 1929)
C.K. Stead, *The New Poetic* (Hutchinson, 1964)
Anthony Thwaite, *Contemporary English Poetry* (Heinemann, 1959)

IX

W.B. YEATS

Richard Ellmann, Professor of English at Oxford University
with **Peter Wilson**

Introduction

"Between extremities Man runs his course", Yeats wrote in "Vacillation". Escape and engagement, aristocrat and common man, passion and intellect, beauty and terror, action and ideals, time and eternity, body and soul, youth and age, life and art—it is characteristically around such opposites that Yeats organized his poetry. From occult science, the turbulence of Irish politics and his often frustrating relations with women he forged a complex and continually changing philosophy. He expressed it systematically in a prose work, A Vision, *but with far more flexibility and response to the actual circumstances of life in his poetry.*

Here Richard Ellmann, interviewed by Peter Wilson, considers Yeats' dialectic of extremes and outlines some of his principal themes and attitudes. Then they take three poems: the famous, early "Lake Isle of Innisfree", full of Romantic nostalgia; "Sailing to Byzantium", in which a difficult subject turns out to be even more paradoxical than one might have supposed; and "Crazy Jane Talks with the Bishop", where Yeats' spokeswoman argues for an acceptance of opposites, foul and fair, body and soul, in a totality of experience. Yeats' complexities and eccentricities are shown as all contributing to a structure of argument and imagery in the poems, creating a fascinating union of the concrete and the abstract.

Richard Ellmann: Yeats had the great good fortune to live through a good part of two centuries and two very different poetic periods. He began with the Pre-Raphaelites and he ended with the most modern of modern poets. That gave him the possibility, which so few poets have ever realised, of developing out of one personality into another. To a considerable extent that's what he succeeded in doing. He began largely in the Pre-Raphaelite tradition but with certain tendencies of his own, chiefly towards the making of a systematic symbolism. In *The Wind Among the Reeds* (1899) he developed a thorough-going system of symbolism in which the rose and cross, the four elements and the like had very distinct places. The covers of his books of that period feature large designs in gilt showing a tree of life with a rose blossoming from a cross, and two faces—a man and a woman—kissing, and a skeleton at the bottom to signify death.

But at the end of the nineteenth century he realised that this system was too self enclosed and that he was excluding too much from it, and so at the beginning of the century Years tries to become much more athletic, as he said, and muscular. He changes his rhythms: instead of slowing them down he hastens them; he has abruptnesses; he has sudden things occurring at the beginnings of poems and often at the ends.

Peter Wilson: Is this the lyric poet sacrificing Tennysonian diction, but not the thing Yeats has all his life, beautiful imagery, the sense of a mind working through the poems? How much does he sacrifice of the earlier mode when he moves into the new mode at the beginning of the twentieth century?

Richard Ellmann: Well, there has been a difference of opinion about that. Some people have felt that Yeats split himself in two in about 1912, but clearly that isn't possible. He seems rather to have been gradually exfoliating throughout his life and taking in more and more material as he proceeded. At the end of his life he was writing with more animation and vigour than he had ever shown earlier. So I would say that Yeats did not split himself in two, but into a great many parts. He had a kind of internal dialectic by which he'd place something he'd done before against something he might do now, and then place the two against each other and get something else. Very often he deals with similar themes but in completely new ways; there was a constant dialectic process by which his poetry came to be written.

Peter Wilson: This dialectic of extremes always seems very interesting. I was thinking of a particular poem, "All Things Can Tempt Me":

When I was young,
I had not given a penny for a song
Did not the poet sing it with such airs
That one believed he had a sword upstairs;
Yet would be now, could I but have my wish,
Colder and dumber and deafer than a fish.

He talks about coldness, deafness and dumbness, but he didn't actually want that, he never really achieved the coldness of a fish. Nor did he ever get to the point at which he was waving a sword and leaping on the tables. He posits one thing and then posits the other extreme, but in fact what he chooses is something in between. So through these extremes isn't Yeats trying out things, taking them as far as he can possibly mention them, but in fact withdrawing from them?

Richard Ellmann: Well I don't think there is any timidity about the way he handles these themes. It is simply that there are various ways of conceiving of them. For example, it was true that in the Nineties one of the great themes was life versus art. But if one really considers what that means it is very difficult to keep that antithesis going, because after all art is one of the impulses which people who are alive have. But at the same time it is a very useful antithesis because in fact we all know that there are moments when we want to immerse ourselves totally in experience, and there are other moments when we would like to draw ourselves back and contemplate rather than be involved. And I think Yeats was aware of both withdrawal and return and that he saturates his poetry with both impulses, depending upon the particular context.

As Yeats said of his poems when he was preparing a collected edition in 1932, "The swordsman throughout repudiates the saint, but not without vacillation". I think he was very fond of the notion that one ought to vacillate a little: one should recognise that the saint has a great deal to be said for him, but in fact he hever quite accepts what the saint has to offer, a complete removal from this world. He father once said that what you want really is this world made better, not some other world. His father was a very astute man.

Peter Wilson: Can we talk, then, about what there is that makes Yeats' poetry a unity—major themes, preoccupations—for instance with nature or with physicality or with politics? What is there among these themes that makes Yeats' poetry a whole?

Richard Ellmann: What gives Yeats his unity is, I suppose, the sense that he is dealing with the same themes but gradually making them richer and richer as he proceeds, and rejecting easy solutions in every case. One feels that essentially the poems are not decisions for one kind of conduct or another, but instead a kind of "densification", you might say, of the materials for decision. It is not that necessarily his last poems are better than his poems of the middle period. Some are and some aren't. But we have a sense of all things being considered—of a man who even at the moment of decision can look backwards and see what he is leaving behind, and keep that in mind as well.

It brings him, I think, into a different kind of lyrical mode from that to which we are often accustomed. He seems to be able to bring passion and philosophy together in a quite extraordinary way so that when names such as Plato or Plotinus are invoked, as they often are, they are invoked in a way which brings them into touch with the most ordinary drives of human consciousness. That, I think, is the great quality in Yeats' work. He himself felt that poetry should not be merely emotional but intellectual as well, and that it then somehow entered into the procession of what he called "Monuments of unageing intellect" ("Sailing to Byzantium").

Peter Wilson: What are Yeats' concerns?

Richard Ellmann: Yeats begins and ends as a love poet. And a great many of his poems are devoted to his hopeless or almost hopeless love affair with Maud Gonne, the beautiful Irish patriot who was six feet tall and walked around the countryside with a great dane, and who caught Yeats' imagination in 1889 when she came to his house and spoke in favour of war—war in general, not war for any specific purpose. And he wasn't able to forget her after her marriage in 1903 either, because she soon separated from her husband. Her husband was executed in the Easter Rebellion in 1916 and after that Yeats asked her to marry him. By this time he was not so eager: he stipulated that she should give up her interest in politics, a condition which he knew would be unacceptable to her.

Peter Wilson: And he proposed to her daughter as well?

Richard Ellmann: Yes, he was interested in her daughter, he had known her for some time. He had decided to get married—he was over 50. Fortunately, because I think the daughter was almost as difficult as her mother, she also refused him and he then married the woman with whom he lived for the rest of his life and through whom in part he was able to write the poetry by which we most remember him.

Yeats' other great interest was Irish politics. He insisted that his poetry must be conceived of as having a political ambition—not usually anything immediate or direct, but essentially to make the country better. He wanted to give it a kind of culture which would make it impregnable against the cheapening effects of the culture of other countries.

Peter Wilson: Isn't this a desire to write national poetry rather than political poetry? Rather like the African nations now, he wanted to exploit this vast backlog of myth, Cuchulain and so on, particularly in the plays. He brings it all to bear on problems of modern Ireland, partly in order to work out, I think, intellectual problems of his own, but also to give Ireland the sense of a history, a culture.

Richard Ellmann: In *A Portrait of the Artist as a Young Man* James Joyce has Stephen think that no one has yet been able to draw a line of beauty through Irish myth, but in fact Yeats had started to do that, as Joyce was probably already aware, and Yeats did make it part of his life-long work to deal with the history of Cuchulain in particular as a possible type for Irish heroism of the future.

He was also a great poet for occasions. The death of O'Leary in 1913 made him write "September 1913" in which he said "Romantic Ireland's dead and gone,/It's with O'Leary in the grave", but three years later the Easter Rebellion came and to his astonishment these people who he had known as quite ordinary people coming from their ordinary houses suddenly turned out to be quite extraordinary ones. The man who had married Maud Gonne he had thought "A drunken, vainglorious lout", but he like the others was "changed, changed utterly:/A terrible beauty is born". Yeats has clearly taken the imagery of rebirth that goes with Easter and aligned it to the notion of the rebirth of his own country—Ireland.

Peter Wilson: Yes, and the way Yeats develops the image of the stone is characteristic, isn't it? At first "Hearts with one purpose alone" seem only "To trouble the living stream", but after a dozen lines they take on an essential power: others live "Minute by minute", only "The stone's in the midst of all". This is the "terrible beauty": in a sense these people are hard, unflinching, awful in a monumental way, because they are unapproachable and inhuman, and yet they are beautiful and they are constant, they do stand up for unchanging abstracts, ideals.

Richard Ellmann: Yes. In the Twenties he uses a related image in "Meditations in Time of Civil War". He envies "An affable Irregular,/A heavily-built Falstaffian man" who comes to his house:

> I count those feathered balls of soot
> The moor-hen guides upon the stream,
> To silence the envy in my thought;
> And turn towards my chamber, caught
> In the cold snows of a dream.

He fears that the imaginative life may after all be less than the life of the man of action, though one feels that this is only the attitude that he will have in that poem. In his later work, Yeats returned to political themes; he wrote ballads as he had not done very often since his very earliest work, ballads for Roger Casement, some marching songs which were originally intended to be sung by General O'Duffy's Blue Shirts.

Peter Wilson: Do you think Yeats was a fascist?

Richard Ellmann: Those who have attacked him for being fascistic usually bring up O'Duffy, but the evidence is really very slight. It seems that Yeats was interested in him for a few months and then gave him up. Some people say that he gave him up only after O'Duffy had more or less gone under anyway, but that I don't think is quite true. But even if it were true, it seems clear that Yeats was anxious especially in his later years to keep from simply becoming senile, and therefore he tried various political possibilities, never I think, without reservations.

Peter Wilson: How much do you think the reader needs to know of Yeats' private philosophy to get value out of his good poems?

Richard Ellmann: Well, in later life, after various kinds of interest in occult philosophy, but also in Platonism and Neo-platonism, and I must say in the philosophical tradition in general, Yeats evolved his own book, *A Vision*, as he called it, which came out in two editions, the first in 1925 and the second in 1937; the second was much improved over the first. But both of them were attempts at a mature symbology as distinguished from that symbology I described about the rose and cross. They were attempts to give a mythical view of history, to see certain elements of myth as constantly operative in human life, to avoid the chronicle kind of history and to see a mode of stylisation in all human behaviour, as if we were all wittingly or unwittingly artists. So he wrote the book which embodied this; he said it was for his school-fellows only, meaning that it was primarily for people who were going to study his poems very closely. *A Vision* goes along with his poetry, sometimes coinciding with it and sometimes diverging from it. Occasionally a line in *A Vision* will illuminate a poem, but sometimes the poem seems to break away from *A Vision* as if Yeats had decided that the poem was much more important than the symbology. In general his letters afford more direct commentary on what he means in any given instance.

Peter Wilson: Well, perhaps we should look closely at a few poems.

Richard Ellmann: Yes. The one I thought we might begin with is "The Lake Isle of Innisfree". It was written when Yeats was twenty-five years old and he said of it that it was his first lyric with anything in its rhythm of his own music. It's clear that some of that rhythm consists in slowing down the action as much as possible, and that seems to suit the rather stylised diction which he employs.

I will arise and go now, and go to Innisfree,
And a small cabin build there, of clay and wattles made:
Nine bean-rows will I have there, a hive for the honey-bee,
And live alone in the bee-loud glade.

And I shall have some peace there, for peace comes dropping slow,
Dropping from the veils of the morning to where the cricket sings;
There midnight's all a glimmer, and noon a purple glow,
And evening full of the linnet's wings.

I will arise and go now, for always night and day
I hear lake water lapping with low sounds by the shore;

While I stand on the roadway, or on the pavements grey,
I hear it in the deep heart's core.

The poem begins with the rhythms and the phrase from the Book of Common Prayer, "I will arise and go now", and that is repeated in the last stanza. It's a rather curious way of announcing an intention to go, even in the late nineteenth century, and I suppose the poem really dwells more upon the idea of going than it gives you the sense that he's actually booked a passage back to Ireland (as "pavements grey" suggest, the poem was written in London). The repetition of "and go" seems to be deliberately hypnotic and part of the slowing-up effect that I mentioned. And similarly the repetition of "there" in the next two lines, and the general sense of one phrase heaping-up on top of another; and then we're arrested by the extremely long vowel sound, "bee-loud glade".

In the second stanza he describes what seems to be a natural scene, but in such stylised terms that it becomes almost an artistic landscape. You'll notice that in the first stanza he's talked about earth, clay and wattles; and in this stanza he speaks of water "Dropping from the veils of the morning", then of midnight "all a glimmer, and noon a purple glow" (imagery of fire), and then of "evening full of the linnet's wings" (imagery of air). Yeats seems to feel that the conjunction of the four elements of earh, fire, air and water is like an image of perfection and that, I think, is why he elaborates it in that way. You'll notice also that we have morning, midnight, noon and evening: he seems deliberately to vary the conventional time sequence as if to suggest that this is almost outside of time.

Peter Wilson: In this context, it's interesting that in the first stanza he says "I *will* arise", and that "will" carries right through the stanza, whereas in the second stanza he says "I *shall* have", which is more like wishing to have, and the "shall" doesn't carry through to subsequent verbs. So the second stanza is in a lingering present tense, and this abnormality of the time scale allows him to go into the future and the past and not to be too specific about exactly when it all happens.

Richard Ellmann: Well, I think there is a deliberate effort to be as timeless as possible and although he seems to be giving the language of decision in the first stanza, the fact that he repeats it in the last indicates that he hasn't arisen and hasn't gone yet, and the "now" becomes increasingly vague as we proceed in the poem. All these tenses seem to be part of a kind of dream rather than an actual description of intention. And at the end of the poem he doesn't dwell upon that intention to depart, rather it's simply his delight in the image: "I hear it in the deep heart's core".

Peter Wilson: Yes—he hears the lake water while he stands on the roadway, so he doesn't have to make the trip in order to be in the world of Innisfree.

Richard Ellmann: Exactly, he can stay right in London.

Peter Wilson: This is the romantic.

Richard Ellmann: Yes, it is the romantic, it's a little like Hamlet losing the power of action in the energy of resolve, as Coleridge puts it; it's clear that this young man is more devoted to dreaming of a voyage than to actually taking it.

Let's look now at "Sailing to Byzantium". This poem was written thirty-one years later than the other and it also is a trip, in this case to Byzantium, the capital of the old Eastern Empire. But the poem does not begin by describing Byzantium but by describing Ireland:

That is no country for old men. The young
In one another's arms, birds in the trees
—Those dying generations—at their song,
The salmon-falls, the mackerel-crowded seas,
Fish, flesh, or fowl, commend all summer long
Whatever is begotten, born, and dies.
Caught in that sensual music all neglect
Monuments of unageing intellect.

The old man who is speaking feels that he no longer has a place in the world of Ireland, that he should be devoting himself to "Monuments of unageing intellect". He's not rejecting Ireland completely because the salmon-falls and the mackerel-crowded seas, even if there is a slight sense of pushing among the mackerel, give a very beatific picture. If he were rejecting Ireland completely he obviously could find different images to use. But these "dying generations" are caught up entirely in the cycle of time: it's rather beautiful but it's only the cycle of time, it's only a "sensual music" and it involves a neglect of "Monuments of unageing intellect".

Peter Wilson: And in the way he speaks about the Irish scene—the almost after-thought of "Those dying generations"—he seems slightly beguiled by the young in one another's arms and the sensual music.

Richard Ellmann: Yes, it's not only sensual music to them; in a way his description of it becomes sensual music too. In the second stanza he takes up his own plight more directly:

An aged man is but a paltry thing,
A tattered coat upon a stick, unless
Soul clap its hands and sing, and lounder sing
For every tatter in its mortal dress,
Nor is there singing school but studying
Monuments of its own magnificence;
And therefore have I sailed the seas and come
To the holy city of Byzantium.

It's rather grand, but what he's describing is how pitiful old age is, how an old man is only a scarecrow unless "Soul clap its hands and sing". William Blake said that he had seen the soul of his dead brother Robert rising to heaven clapping its hands for joy and Yeats clearly has this in mind, but he makes it his own. He opposes the soul to the body: the soul compensates by its ecstasy for all the dishevellment of its moral frame. And there is no singing school except the study of monuments of the soul's own magnificence, so it's to do this that he has "sailed the seas and come/To the holy city of Byzantium".

Peter Walker: What strikes me as particularly clever about this second stanza is the way it sets up an argument. We have statement, "An aged man is . . .", then counterstatement, "Nor is there singing school but . . .", and then, "*therefore* I have sailed . . .". There is a true logical progression, but without any sacrifice of the lyricism of the imagery. So he gets very rapidly from the aged man to Byzantium through a combination of images and logical process.

Richard Ellmann: Yes, up to a point it seems quite logical, but I think that the logic shifts as we proceed in it until at the end it's no longer simply the parts of a syllogism. He's clearly saying something much more dense than originally appeared, and that comes out in the last two stanzas. In the third he salutes the saints, whom he prefers to call sages because this is a holy city of the imagination rather than a spiritual one—he doesn't believe in Eastern Christianity or perhaps in Christianity at all. He says,

O sages standing in God's holy fire
As in the gold mosaic of a wall,

Come from the holy fire, perne in a gyre,
And be the singing-masters of my soul.
Consume my heart away; sick with desire
And fastened to a dying animal
It knows not what it is; and gather me
Into the artifice of eternity.

As he looks at the mosaics in Byzantium and sees the sages there he feels that they are standing in God's holy fire as if in the gold mosaic of a wall—or *vice versa*, the two parts of the metaphor are interchangeable, for they are fused in his imagination. He asks the sages to "perne in a gyre". Now this is a special Yeatsian phrase. He pronounced it "gyre" rather than "jyre", and "perne" is an old Irish dialect word meaning to wind or unwind as on a bobbin of thread. So he asks the sages to whirl down from their point in the timelessness to his point in time in a gyrating motion, and then he asks them to be the singing-masters of his soul, to be his musers, as it were. He particularly delights in them because they seem to be themselves works of art and a part of the immortality of works of art. The last phrase of the stanza is so strange that before we examine it we should read the last stanza:

Once out of nature I shall never take
My bodily form from any natural thing,
But such a form as Grecian goldsmiths make
Of hammered gold and gold enamelling
To keep a drowsy Emperor awake;
Or set upon a golden bough to sing
To lords and ladies of Byzantium
Of what is past, or passing, or to come.

There's a wonderful sense of the soul going on long after one has stopped reading the poem, as if its reverberations were still in the air. Returning to "the artifice of eternity", in one sense it is sublime for eternity to be an artifice, like a work of art, because clearly then it will not be subject to mortal conditions; and yet there is a very curious shift in the last stanza when he imagines what it would be like to be completely out of the world of nature. He begins to pull back a little, and we realise that there is reason for describing Ireland so pleasantly in the first stanza. The Emperor of Byzantium did have golden birds which were marvellously ingenious, but they still are rather mechanical toys. It is extraordinary that this poet, looking for the highest aspiration possible, should wish to be changed into so small and so artificial a thing as a golden bird.

Peter Wilson: Artificial and trivial as well.

Richard Ellmann: And trivial yes. But I think it begins to show how complicated his attitude is throughout the poem. What he will do once he is completely in Byzantium, once he has lost his bodily form and become completely soul, is sing—not of the world of eternity, there's nothing to sing of there—no, he's going to sing "Of what is past, or passing, or to come"! In other words, he will continue to sing of the world of time even when he is become an immortal bird in Byzantium! I think that this is the movement of the whole poem then: Yeats begins with the most attractive picture of the world which he is renouncing and a statement that he must renounce it because it doesn't suit him anymore; then he imagines what life would be like if he could live entirely in the imagination, but once he has brought himself to conceive of his transformation into an imaginative bird, pure imagination presumably, it turns out that all the bird can sing about is the world of time. So the worlds of eternity and time seem to coalesce and interpenetrate, and the poet who seems to be asking to be removed from the world of time actually remains a part of it even when he gets to eternity.

Of course, not all Yeats' poems are about voyages whether imaginative or actual. There are poems in which the emphasis seems to be not on moving away from the present situation but on accepting it, on saturation in life rather than a shifting or purging of it. An example of this kind of poem is "Crazy Jane Talks with the Bishop". Crazy Jane was based on an actual woman whom Yeats had heard of in the west of Ireland whose real name was "Cracked Mary", but like the fool in a play of Shakespeare she's not so cracked, not so mad as she seems to be, and that is what Yeats is driving at. I think that we have to assume that she is the spokesman for Yeats, yet he tries to set up an adequate debate and against Crazy Jane he has the Bishop who admonishes her for the life she has been leading and points out that she, like the old man of Byzantium, is too old for love. She begins and then he speaks:

I met the Bishop on the road
And much said he and I.
"Those breasts are flat and fallen now,
Those veins must soon be dry;
Live in a heavenly mansion,
Not in some foul sty."

"Fair and foul are near of kin,
And fair needs foul," I cried.

"My friends are gone, but that's a truth
Nor grave nor bed denied,
Learned in bodily lowliness
And in the heart's pride.

"A woman can be proud and stiff
When on love intent;
But Love has pitched his mansion in
The place of excrement;
For nothing can be sole or whole
That has not been rent."

Crazy Jane defends herself and says that in fact one cannot have what is fine without having also what is foul, that the two opposites require each other and that if she were to devote herself only to a heavenly mansion she would lose a great deal of her experience. She takes up the Bishop's suggestion that her lovers have left her: she says she knew her friends would leave her either through death or because sexual intercourse can only last for a brief time; the bed as well as the grave made her recognise that love was transitory.

Peter Wilson: So she learned "in bodily lowliness"—the foul—and "in the heart's pride"—the fair.

Richard Ellmann: Yes, that life is a matter of acceptance of both opposites, fair and foul, not an attempt to separate one from the other. And then the last stanza re-asserts this in quite extraordinary language, doesn't it? The organs of love are connected with the organs of excretion and only through an acceptance of these opposites can we achieve genuine wholeness—a kind of secular or lay sanctity, a kind of "Profane perfection of mankind", as Yeats calls it in his last poem, "Under Ben Bulben". It's at this point I think that Yeats really ends. It's not simply an acceptance of the body; what Crazy Jane says is that one must accept the heart and the body *together*. Against the mere cultivation of the soul which is offered by the Bishop he offers the totality of experience.

Further Reading

Daniel Albright, *The Myth against Myth* (Oxford, 1972)
Harold Bloom, *Yeats* (Oxford, 1970)
Denis Donoghue, *Yeats* (Fontana Modern Masters, 1971)
Richard Ellmann, *Yeats: the Man and the Masks* (Faber, 1949)
The Identity of Yeats (Faber, 1954)
James Hall and Martin Steinman (eds.), *The Permanence of Yeats* (Macmillan, 1950)

T.R. Henn, *The Lonely Tower* (Methuen, 1965)
A. Norman Jeffares, *The Poetry of W.B. Yeats* (Arnold, 1961)
A Commentary on the Collected Poems (Macmillan, 1968)
Frank Kermode, *Romantic Image* (Routledge, 1957)
Giorgio Melchiori, *The Whole Mystery of Art* (Routledge, 1960)
William H. Pritchard (ed.), *W.B. Yeats* (Penguin Critical Anthologies, 1972)
John Stallworthy, *Between the Lines: Yeats' Poetry in the Making* (Oxford, 1963)
John Stallworthy, *Vision and Revision in Yeats' Last Poems* (Oxford, 1969)
John Unterecker (ed.), *Yeats* (Prentice Hall Twentieth Century Views, 1963)
W.B. Yeats, *Selected Criticism*, ed. A.N. Jeffares (Macmillan, 1964)

X

EZRA POUND AND T.S. ELIOT

M.L. Rosenthal, Professor of English at New York University

Introduction

The literary relationship between Ezra Pound and T.S. Eliot parallels in significance that between Coleridge and Wordsworth. In London during the First World War Pound encouraged and influenced Eliot's development as a poet, culminating in his surgery upon the manuscript of The Waste Land.

In this chapter M.L. Rosenthal seeks to define the qualities of each writer. By concentrating on three short poems ("The Study in Aesthetics", "Ballatetta" and "The Return") he shows the kind of poetry Pound was writing when Eliot came upon his work: he brings out Pound's method of using images to create focal points of concrete attention, the combination of the formal and the colloquial in his tone, his attitude to the poetic tradition and his continual experimentation.

But Eliot in The Waste Land *is equally individual, for he developed a dramatic technique involving shifts of intensity and a centring upon moments of realization of the inner self. For many modern readers the sense of futility and desolation they perceive in "Prufrock" and* The Waste Land *is more attractive than the Christian commitment of later poems, but Professor Rosenthal distinguishes a very personal and characteristically modern theme which he traces in "Prufrock", "Rhapsody on a Windy Night",* The Waste Land, *"Gerontion" and* Four Quartets.

EZRA POUND AND T.S. ELIOT

M.L. Rosenthal: Perhaps I should begin talking about Ezra Pound by discussing his relation to the Imagist movement and to the other literary figures and movements he affected in the early part of this century. All these basic facts, however, can be found in any literary history. The books show the importance of his early connection with *Poetry* magazine, the Chicago periodical that advocated and printed much of the most interesting new poetry of the century, and his encouragement of and alliance with T.S. Eliot. They describe his association with William Carlos Williams, whom he met when both were students at the University of Pennsylvania; with Yeats and Ford Maddox Ford; and with Wyndham Lewis as co-editor of the Vorticist magazine *BLAST*. They also show the effect of his explorations of Chinese poetry and Japanese drama. His own critical ideas about poetry can be found in his *Literary Essays*. What you will not find in most literary histories or critical studies is a simple consideration of Pound's poems in their own right. What I want to do is simply to look at some of these poems and comment on them briefly.

The first of these poems Pound wrote in his mid-twenties: "The Study in Aesthetics" (1910).

The very small children in patched clothing,
Being smitten with an unusual wisdom,
Stopped in their play as she passed them
And cried up from their cobbles:

Guarda! Ahi, guarda! ch'è be'a!

But three years after this
I heard the young Dante, whose last name I do not know—
For there are, in Sirmione, twenty-eight young Dantes and
thirty-four Catulli;
And there has been a great catch of sardines,
And his elders
Were packing them in the great wooden boxes
For the market in Brescia, and he
Leapt about, snatching at the bright fish
And getting in both of their ways;
And in vain they commanded him to *sta fermo!*
And when they would not let him arrange

The fish in the boxes
He stroked those which were already arranged,
Murmuring for his own satisfaction
This identical phrase:

Ch'è be'a.

And at this I was mildly abashed.

The title of the poem shows us that the recognition and understanding of beauty are Pound's theme, but when we get into the poem we see that there are certain points of concrete attention, two or three moments of sensuous focussing, that embody this recognition and understanding. They also show us that this aesthetic awareness is not just a matter of the abstract knowledge of a tradition of the worship of beauty such as the children inadvertently express when they see the beautiful girl passing by. They look up at her as if they were medieval Provençal troubadours and exclaim at her beauty, and that's one point of sensuous focus, but the appreciation of the bright appearance and touch of the fish by the little boy, that's another, and it teaches the poet a lesson. The conclusion—'And at this I was mildly abashed'—puts the whole thing in perspective.

What is Pound's achievement as a poet in this apparently simple poem? He uses natural speech, rather humorous speech: "I heard the young Dante, whose last name I do not know—/For there are, in Sirmione, twenty-eight young Dantes and thirty-four Catulli". And he combines this direct, straightforward, simple speech with a chivalric or courtly tone—

Being smitten with an unusual wisdom,
Stopped in their play as she passed them
And cried up from their cobbles.

That sounds like one of the great Provençal love poems. His humorous description of the Italians is a counterpoint to his use as a refrain of the Italian phrases, "Guarda! Ahi, guarda! ch'è be'a!" ("Hey, look! She's a beauty!"). And of course, the fact that they're named Dante and Catullus and cry out this beautiful thought suggests an innate poetic sense. The ordinary people responding in their lovely language out of the whole tradition which makes them all Dantes and Catulli, are examples to him of how the poet should respond to any manifestation of beauty.

The union of sense, intelligence and feeling through the use of an image (which he defined as "an intellectual and emotional complex in an instant of time") can be seen in many of Pound's early poems. You don't need to wait for his most famous work, the *Cantos*, or his most unified long work, *Hugh Selwyn Mauberley*, to see the enormous originality combined with a rich sense of traditional poetic structure.

Another early poem, "Ballatetta", is in the model of the Provençal poets of the late Middle Ages:

The light became her grace and dwelt among
Blind eyes and shadows that are formed as men;
Lo, how the light doth melt us into song:

The broken sunlight for a healm she beareth
Who hath my heart in jurisdiction.
In wild-wood never fawn nor fallow fareth
So silent light; no gossamer is spun
So delicate as she is, when the sun
Drives the clear emeralds from the bended grasses
Lest they should parch too swiftly, where she passes.

Here the speaker is responding to his Courtly-Love beauty just like the little children looking up and crying, "Ch'è be'a!". Notice again the sensuous emphasis; the beauty's appearance among men makes them break into song: "Lo, how the light" (an aureole around her because she appears like a goddess) "doth melt us into song". Then, speaking for the mere men to whom her beauty appears, the poet gives us the song into which we are melted: "The broken sunlight for a healm she beareth", he begins, a pure image for the aureole about her head as she moves through the air; and he ends with the notion that she might wither the grass, a metaphor expressing the extraordinary intensity of her presence and the effect of that intensity on all of nature, not simply on the lover who's singing about her.

This brings us naturally to one of Pound's great interests. The key to his entire poetic theory was the principle that tradition is a living presence from the past in our own time. He believed that there is a continuous body of literature going back, by way of all sorts of touchstones, to the ancient Greeks. This tradition consists of the lessons, usable lessons, that are absorbed by the poet through the ages and it is combined with whatever the modern sensibility needs to pierce the furthest into what it has to say, how it feels. The whole ambiance of our own life is considered as the point which human feeling has reached in the course of its long progress through the ages; it's a continuing process, broken perhaps, but nevertheless gathering more means of relating to the external world as it goes.

An apparently simple poem called "The Return" (1912) harks back to the scene in Homer's *Odyssey* (Book XI) where the dead appear to Odysseus after he has performed the proper rites. This poem, "The Return", was used by Yeats in his book *A Vision* to clarify the presence of images, motifs, values from the past at the moments of creative repossession of the past in our own lives, the moments when we wish to pierce the present as sharply as possible. To summon up into full life the ghosts of the past, the ancients had rituals. Homer shows Odysseus doing the proper ritual: the dead come hesitantly, he feeds them blood, they speak to him, then they fade away. In similar manner the person who is deeply involved with the greatest literature of the past will have a sense of his mind being populated by innumerable voices and figures from the past, just as his mind and spirit are more obviously populated by numerous voices and figures from his own life and the world around him. The problem is to select and reorientate the different voices, meanings, passions, that crowd against one another like the mobs of the dead trying to get Odysseus to pay attention to them in Homer's *Odyssey.* Here is Pound's poem:

See, they return; ah, see the tentative
        Movements, and the slow feet,
        The trouble in the pace and the uncertain
        Wavering!

See, they return, one, and by one,
With fear, as half-awakened;
As if the snow should hesitate
And murmur in the wind,
                and half turn back;
These were the "Wing'd-with-Awe",
                Inviolable.

Gods of the winged shoe!
With them the silver hounds,
                sniffing the trace of air!

Haie! Haie!
        These were the swift to harry;
These the keen-scented;
These were the souls of blood.

Slow on the leash,
                pallid the leash-men!

This extraordinary poem is itself a perfect example of the fact that Pound's deep sense of tradition is inseparable from his talent for genuine experimentation with form. The tentative quality of the spiritual figures, the shades of the past, as they move forward toward the immediacy of the present that the speaker desires—because in a way the poem is an incantation to bring them into the foreground of his awareness—is presented to us by way of improvised, rhythmic line structures and stanzaic structures. You can't find a regular form of stanza, line length or rhyme. What you do find is a slow or hesitant movement which gradually becomes more and more swift and firm until there is a shout of ecstatic affirmation; then at the end of the poem the slow receding movement returns. Pound had studied his Homer, but he's not trying to adapt Homer's long hexameter line. Instead he's trying to catch the feeling of Homer, and put it into a modern English verse form improvised to fit the actual development and recession of the apparitions themselves.

I haven't much more space to talk about the many-faceted Ezra Pound; perhaps the best thing I can do is refer the reader to the *Hugh Selwyn Mauberley* sequence which appeared in two sections after the Second War. There we see Pound's extraordinary gift for improvisation, for variety within a relatively set form: we see also his clear exposition of an aesthetic view of the problems of modern society and modern war. This view led Pound into all sorts of trouble and established him as an independent figure who took the risk of committing himself on the basis of what his knowledge happened to be at a given point in history. I am referring to his move to Mussolini's Italy and his rather abstruse broadcasts on Rome Radio to American troops, which most people couldn't understand; nor could they understand the perspective from which he spoke. In *Mauberley* you will find Pound's larger point of view and some exquisitely modulated instances of the purity and the far-reaching quality of his technique.

The principal poem which emerged from the period when Pound influenced T.S. Eliot was, of course *The Waste Land* (1922). I want to quote a passage from the second section. There are two speakers. One is a hysterical woman whose life, despite her wealth, has reached an empty state; she and her husband have come to a point of complete absence of communication. She speaks to him, but there is no response, and in her distraction she seems entirely lost. However, there are answers from another speaker—the poet himself. He is the one who answers with such hard irony: "I think we are in rats' alley/Where the dead men lost their bones"; and it is he who comments, in the jazzy idiom and rhythm of the Twenties, on the modern loss of the tragic and romantic vision of Shakespeare.

"My nerves are bad to-night. Yes, bad. Stay with me.
"Speak to me. Why do you never speak. Speak.
"What are you thinking of? What thinking? What?
"I never know what you are thinking. Think."

I think we are in rats' alley
Where the dead men lost their bones.

"What is that noise?"
The wind under the door.
"What is that noise now? What is the wind doing?"
Nothing again nothing.
"Do
"You know nothing? Do you see nothing? Do you remember
"Nothing?"

I remember
Those are pearls that were his eyes.
"Are you alive, or not? Is there nothing in your head?"
But
O O O O that Shakespeherian Rag—
It's so elegant
So intelligent
"What shall I do now? What shall I do?
"I shall rush out as I am, and walk the street
"With my hair down, so. What shall we do tomorrow?
"What shall we ever do?"

This sounds a little bit like Pound in its emphasis on hard, concrete centres of dramatic or imagistic attention, but not entirely. Eliot, like Pound, omits direct comment by the poet in this particular scene; he focuses on the dramatic presentation of characters defined only by what they say in crisis. But he's actually far more of a dramatist than Pound: he gives himself far more to the projection of whatever has to be said, in what should really be conceived of as a truncated dramatic scene. It projects not so much direct communication as the inability to communicate—in that respect Eliot is a true ancestor of Harold Pinter, Beckett and such other contemporary dramatists. The dynamic shifts of intensity between the hysterical question, the silence that follows it, the sardonic, bitter and self-distancing comment by the ultimate speaker, the poet, and the open forum which enables the poet to shift suddenly into a completely new perspective are like the later discoveries of Pound in his *Cantos*, but they are far more economical and in the long run far less intellectually oriented. They are centred on moments of intense inward realisation of a type that Pound's method usually avoids.

The whole career of Eliot may be viewed in the light of this passage. It suggests a modern sense of the violence that has been done to the private self and of an inexpressible anguish compounded of fear, anxiety and güilt, leading to a kind of moral paralysis like that of Prufrock in "The Love Song of J. Alfred Prufrock". Despite the irony, the compassion of the poet is very real. He's haunted, as he says in "Preludes", by "The notion of some infinitely gentle/Infinitely suffering thing", and by the feeling that somehow we are deprived of the means of making our deepest emotions and needs clear. Perhaps it's a heightened psychological awareness, or the natural result of two centuries or more of the growth of technology and a commerce-minded, impersonal civilisation.

Eliot did not discover this malaise; you can find it everywhere in the last century—in Dickens' novel *Bleak House*, for example. In Eliot's early poem, "The Love Song of J. Alfred Prufrock" (1917), we find a very depressed sense of the modern city near the very beginning of the poem:

Let us go, through certain half-deserted streets,
The muttering retreats
Of restless nights in one-night cheap hotels
And sawdust restaurants with oyster-shells:
Streets that follow like a tedious argument
Of insidious intent.

Or take "Rhapsody on a Windy Night", another early piece, perhaps his best of that period: the whole poem is a vision of terror at the heart of things, which the poet catches with dismay. The fourth stanza is typical:

Half-past two,
The street-lamp said,
"Remark the cat which flattens itself in the gutter,
Slips out its tongue
And devours a morsel of rancid butter."
So the hand of the child, automatic,
Slipped out and pocketed a toy that was running along the quay.
I could see nothing behind that child's eye.
I have seen eyes in the street

Trying to peer through lighted shutters,
And a crab one afternoon in a pool,
An old crab with barnacles on his back,
Gripped the end of a stick which I held him.

Here we see the feeling that all life is a bleak, mindless automatic, snatching, unspeakably and grossly tenacious force. It isn't just a quality of the society, or the present state of our religious attitudes, or whatever—but simply a sense that there is nothing commensurable in nature with what we, in our dearest dreams of what life should be, conceive.

Eliot never justifies this oppressive feeling of impersonal cruelty and alienation of the sensitive spirit. In his early work he presents it sadly and bitterly. Then, in the poetry of his mid-thirties, he wrestles with it in various ways. After the First War "Gerontion" and *The Waste Land* place it in the perspectives of the whole character of Western civilisation today and its historical background, of Christian faith. Then in the poetry of later years, in "Marina" and *Four Quartets*, the emphasis shifts to the problems of spiritual and religious affirmation in the face of the kind of insight expressed in the earlier poetry. So even in the later phases of his career the bleakness and emptiness projected in "Prufrock" and "Rhapsody on a Windy Night" remain critical points of attention, if only because the poet strives so intently to overcome them.

Consider, for instance, the view of the world given us in "Gerontion" (1920). This poem was originally intended as a companion piece to *The Waste Land*, or at least Eliot entertained the idea. The speaker is a shrunken old man (that is what his name means) and he tells us that he is feeble and almost blind. He is without memory of any heroic or personal past, and is in fact the embodiment of a society grown foul and stale by substituting a gross commercialism for every other human meaning. The decayed house he says he lives in is associated with the great European centres of commerce that emerged in the late Middle Ages, and the land about it is infertile—"Rocks, moss, stonecrop, iron, merds". The world he represents has perverted and denatured everything by which man surpasses his animal nature—love, art, religion—and, ironically, has in the process deprived the senses themselves of their primal freshness. He longs for redemption, but believes it is impossible because of his long immersion in cynical secularism. He cannot identify himself with the Passion, the suffering of Christ, because of this self-betrayal; nor can he recapture a state of innocence in which he could come freshly to faith:

I have lost my passion: why should I need to keep it
Since what is kept must be adulterated?
I have lost my sight, smell, hearing, taste and touch:
How should I use them for your closer contact?

Many years later, in "Burnt Norton", the first of the *Four Quartets*, we have another version of the meaningless modern world, this time symbolised by the atmosphere of the London Underground—what we Americans call the subway system. As he does so often, Eliot here echoes Dante's "Inferno", presenting the modern, big-city hell:

Tumid apathy with no concentration
Men and bits of paper, whirled by the cold wind
That blows before and after time,
Wind in and out of unwholesome lungs
Time before and time after.
Eructation of unhealthy souls
Into the faded air, the torpid
Driven on the wind that sweeps the gloomy hills of London.
(1. 103)

But how does Eliot escape being maudlin and tiresome and purely subjective in all this poetry of sensibility, describing the private suffering and confusion of modern man's betrayed spirit? He does it through the fact that his method is not subjective, but objective. Emotion is never just stated abstractly; rather it is evoked by concrete images, dramatic scenes, echoes of speech, comic effects. Remember the social comedy of poor, balding Prufrock among the elegant ladies, or the evocation of his loneliness and fear in his allusion to "lonely men in shirt-sleeves, leaning out of windows", and in his sudden, pathetic outcry: "I should have been a pair of ragged claws/Scuttling across the floors of silent seas". In his essay on *Hamlet* Eliot called the method of evoking the right sense of emotion by such objective means the use of an "objective correlative". At first he used it for relatively short lyrical and dramatic poems, but in *The Waste Land* he deployed it on a much larger scale, showing the most extraordinary virtuosity of any poet of our age. In *Four Quartets* he continues the same technique but more calmly and philosophically, though not always less intensely.

What cannot be shown in a brief presentation is the intricate weaving of sensuous perception, wit and humour, meditative tone and elusive moments of barely contained feeling which makes Eliot's poetry so unique. He cannot be caught in any sort of dogmatic, religious or theoretical net. The object, as with all the greatest poetry of our age, is to penetrate to a sense of balance within a volatile structure in a way that reflects both our desire for permanent meanings and our sense of human insecurity within chaotic reality. I shall end with a passage near the end of *The Waste Land* that creates a note of gaiety and hope to hold and check the accumulated doubt, anguish and despair of most of what has gone before it:

The boat responded
Gaily, to the hand expert with sail and oar
The sea was calm, your heart would have responded
Gaily, when invited, beating obedient
To controlling hands.

Further Reading

Bernard Bergonzi, *T.S. Eliot* (Macmillan, 1972)
Christine Brooke-Rose, *A ZBC to Ezra Pound's 'Personae'* (University of California, 1969)
Donald Davie, *Ezra Pound* (Routledge, 1965)
G.S. Fraser, *Ezra Pound* (Oliver, 1960)
Northrop Frye, *T.S. Eliot* (Oliver, 1963)
Helen Gardner, *The Art of T.S. Eliot* (Cresset, 1949)
Thomas H. Jackson, *The Early Poetry of Ezra Pound* (Harvard, 1968)
Hugh Kenner, *The Invisible Poet: T.S. Eliot* (Allen, 1960)
(ed.), *T.S. Eliot* (Prentice Hall Twentieth Century Views, 1962)
D.E.S. Maxwell, *The Poetry of T.S. Eliot* (Routledge, 1952)
F.O. Matthiessen, *The Achievement of T.S. Eliot* (Oxford, 1947)
Eustace Mullins, *This Difficult Individual, Ezra Pound* (Fleet, 1961)
Charles Norman, *Ezra Pound* (Macmillan, 1960)
William Van O'Connor, *A Casebook on Ezra Pound* (Cromwell, 1959)
Michael Reck, *Ezra Pound: a Close Up* (Hart-Davis, 1968)
M.L. Rosenthal, *A Primer of Ezra Pound* (Macmillan, 1960)
Grover Smith, *T.S. Eliot's Poetry and Plays* (Chicago, 1956)
B.C. Southam, *A Student's Guide to the Selected Poems of Eliot* (Faber, 1968)
Noel Stock, *Poet in Exile: Ezra Pound* (Manchester, 1964)
(ed.), *Ezra Pound: Perspectives* (Regnery, 1965)
Walter Sutton (ed.), *Ezra Pound* (Prentice Hall Twentiety Century Views, 1963)
Allen Tate (ed.), *T.S. Eliot* (Chatto, 1967)
George Williamson, *A Reader's Guide to T.S. Eliot* (Thames, 1967)

George T. Wright, *The Poet in the Poem* (University of California, 1960)

XI

THE THIRTIES

Cyril Connolly, editor of the literary journal *Horizon* throughout the Forties and regular critic for *The Sunday Times* until his death in 1974
Stephen Spender, Professor of English at University College, London
David Daiches, Professor of English at Sussex University
Laurence Lerner, Professor of English at Sussex University

Introduction

As we approach the present day the prospect appears of direct discussion with prominent literary figures about movements of which they are or have been a part. In May 1971 at the University of Sussex an all-day seminar was held in which a number of writers and critics associated with the poetry of the Thirties described and analysed that period of political excitement and literary achievement. At moments it was moving to see men, advanced in years and part of the Anglo-American cultural establishment, appealing to others, whom they now meet only occasionally as their lives have diverged, for confirmation of the facts or the mood of youthful experiences which they shared as close companions in literary experiment, political endeavour or the dangers of warfare.

Four personal statements from the seminar are printed here. The late Cyril Connolly, for forty years a central figure in the London literary world, places the principal writers of the Thirties with a series of pointed reminiscences, rising to a vivid description of the atmosphere in the International Brigade in Spain. Secondly, Stephen Spender explains how the apolitical literary scene of the Twenties developed into the several kinds of engagement which characterised the Thirties, and analyses the problems of artistic and personal integrity this created for poets like Auden and himself. Then David Daiches talks mainly about the period as one of exciting poetic innovation—Auden's half-rhyme, slang and wistful tone, Spender's capacity to express feeling and to domicile industrial imagery. Finally in a postscript Laurence Lerner compares the Thirties with society and poetry of the present time.

THE THIRTIES

Cyril Connolly: All literary periods are open-ended, but I suppose the Thirties with a capital T did overlap to some extent with the thirties with a small t. They were over by 1941 and they began about 1927-8 when Auden, Day Lewis and MacNeice were at Oxford and took over Oxford poetry. Spender was there too, and of course John Betjeman.

I belonged to the tail end of the Twenties myself; my contemporaries were a little older—Evelyn Waugh, Graham Greene, Kenneth Clarke. Empson was then at Cambridge and I was taken to see him when I went over. He was already regarded as a prodigy. His poetry emerged fully-fledged in little magazines; it was as good as all the rest of his poetry, with nothing adolescent about it. He could be terribly rude—Cambridge intellectuals were ruder than Oxford ones, more withering!

We can date the Thirties by Auden's *Poems*, which came out in 1930, and we can end them with his *Another Time* and his famous "September 1, 1939":

I sit in one of the dives
On Fifty-second Street
Uncertain and afraid
As the clever hopes expire
Of a low dishonest decade . . .

But only the politicians seemed low and dishonest, and it was in reality a tragic decade in which the urban youth of its galaxy of young creative artists was matched by the ebbing of peace and human values. Just as the period before the First World War seemed to end with the sinking of "The Titanic", the Thirties expired with the sinking of "The Thetis", the British submarine that foundered on the seabed while the crew were asphyxiated. So the air seemed to be drawn out of our lives as Hitler ranted, drawn out from the squares of Bloomsbury, the pubs of Soho, the cafés of Montparnasse, the beaches of Provence.

But the real capital was London, as Paris had been for the Twenties and New York was to be. Antnony Powell, another novelist of the Thirties, then a resolutely non-political humourist, has always attached importance to how and where his characters met, however insignificant they may prove to be. My memory is like an old mattress with feathers flying from a thousand cuts, but I search it and remember Spender. I reviewed a book of his, *The Destructive*

Element (1936), and got a long letter back from Yugoslavia, which I can't find; all good letters go to the University of Texas when they die and it may be there! This led to a meeting, and so to one with Isherwood; it must have been Isherwood who gave me a verbal introduction to Auden, then in Barcelona, and I suppose MacNeice came bumbling after. Very soon I knew the whole group and went to their parties and the first nights of their plays. Perhaps I was some use to them as a critic on the *New Statesman*, but I think we were destined to be friends. My need was greater than theirs, but they too needed something. Perhaps my American wife's sympathy and French cooking. They gave me a small part in the bandwagon.

What were they like? Auden was quite captivating. My wife always called him "Uncle Whiz", although he was under thirty. He had a long, pale face, the Mediterranean on his lips and the Arctic in his eyes. One longed to please him and one pleased him by following his advice, which was sometimes disastrous. I did not see eye to eye with my father who thought we should give Germany back her colonies and once said to me, "Things are looking better in France, I see Blum was hissed at the races". Auden thought I was much too nice to him, and after a few Freudian home truths on the virtues of parricide he insisted that next time I gave my father lunch (he was an *edenté gourmet*) I should not ask him back to our flat in Chelsea but speed him on to his hotel. When my father, lame from arthritis with his two cherry-wood sticks with rubber ferrules beside him in the taxi, was told that he would not be coming in, he said nothing, and two tears rolled down into his grey moustache. Never again. In Spain we used to play chess with Auden, and one night in the hotel in Barcelona we went to bed leaving a game unfinished; in the morning it had progressed by several moves for which he had no explanation . . .

Spender has written so much about himself that I cannot disentangle what he was like from what he has told us he was like. He loved to laugh and was merrier than the others. Perhaps by virtue of his juniority he was much more of a success with older people; he was a friend of the Woolfs and E.M. Forster and he had a special relationship with Rosamond Lehmann, whose brother John was the creative editor of the period, though the expression had not yet been coined. Isherwood was slightly apart as always, a steely, dominating will masked by an almost ingratiating friendliness. He disapproved of sitting over meals, and would not come to our luncheons or dinners. But no one can resist discerning admiration of their work, and I particularly liked the memorial in *Lions and Shadows*. He also gave advice with a smile and a quiet "Well, I think you should . . ." followed by a preposterous suggestion. It was wearing my tails that Auden went to receive his King's Medal for Poetry. Perhaps that is symptomatic: how much rather I would have been mentioned in one of them!

At that time I was a kind of Clapham Junction where various literary lines crossed, partly through my work on the *New Statesman*, partly through my eclectic temperament and my position as a renegade from the Sitwellian aesthetes trying to pass as one of the "Pylon Boys", though it was I who named them that. There were other important groups—Evelyn Waugh, Elizabeth Bowen, the Powells, Henry Green, William Plomer, the Lehmanns, John and Penelope Betjeman, the international left-wing writers round *New Writing*, the poets round Geoffrey Grigson's *New Verse*. There was also the outsider George Orwell, who entered the literary scene under his new name. I have been asked so many times to tell everything I knew about Orwell, for it's the opening gambit of every visiting American critic, that I am coming to dream the name. "You were at school with George Orwell, weren't you, can you recollect . . . ?" I now answer, "No, he was at school with me". In the Thirties you won fame as a reporter rather than as a novelist, and I still think the non-tractarian parts of *Homage to Catalonia* the best thing written about the Spanish War.

The Spanish War was the great "good cause" which brought so many writers into intimate relationships. It seemed that right must be certain to prevail, and the course of the war and non-intervention gave everyone a terrible lesson in what the world was really like. There were bad things in the good cause and there may have been some good things in the bad cause, though we did not see them, to produce this stalemate. Without Russian help, since British and French aid was withheld, the Republic could not win, and Russian help meant conditions which unmanned the defenders—the suppression of the Anarchists and the spread of forced propaganda. Finally the liquidators were recalled themselves to be liquidated, and Hitler's war became inevitable.

Many who had been in Spain took several years to adjust. I still think the best poems about the Spanish War were John Cornford's and after him Spender's. In my copy of Auden's "Spain" he has written after the last lines, "History to the defeated/May say alas but cannot help or pardon", "This is a lie". I prefer Spender's "Port-Bou", where all Spanish journies started. Armed with safe-conducts from Kingsley Martin, the Spanish Embassy and Harry

Pollitt and perhaps a note to an anarchist, one arrived on the platform overlooking the little bay where the yellowing vines grew down the hillside past the garish villa of some returned emigrant. The train to Barcelona was painted with slogans, Anarchists' black and red, hammers and sickles, Catalan green, marching men and sheaves of corn; the troops hung out of the windows. In spite of shortages, blackouts, wear-and-tear of everything and the total absence of priests, bourgeois women and businessmen, of anything but Anarchist pamphlets on the book-stalls, there was an elation utterly unlike anything to be felt across the French border. War and revolution had become the same thing and everyone who clenched a fist was our friend. This atmosphere changed from month to month and then from day to day and grew more and more suspicious. The goodwill with which the Anarchists had begun their revolution turned to violence, Valencia closed down on Barcelona, Franco closed down on Valencia. Ministers in whose ante-rooms one had waited ended up among the stench of the camps at Aguilas; generals who had joked at Albacete vanished and were not heard of again.

Stephen Spender: I want to go back a little bit further. The period between 1918 and 1930 was, amongst the intellectuals and the writers, a period of very great disillusionment. If you think of the literature of that period—D.H. Lawrence, Eliot's *The Waste Land*, Virginia Woolf, Aldous Huxley—there is very little politics in it at all. It is about a society the premises of which are accepted with a kind of political despair, and on top of this political despair you try to lead a significant personal life, you cultivate personal relationships and aesthetic values. The more you are aware of the despair, the more you are likely to produce an impression of a complete social and moral void.

The Waste Land was certainly the poem that impressed us most, and also the essays of Eliot which were published in *The Sacred Wood.* It is very difficult to be sure of being accurate because one has so much hindsight, but I should say that when we first read *The Waste Land* it didn't seem to us the tremendous intellectual puzzle which it became later on when people started to elucidate it and to explain it. It was to me a tremendous shock when I first read it; the key lines were something like "The awful daring of a moment's surrender/Which an age of prudence can never retract". Then a bit later on it seemed a poem of despair; as I was saying, it meant for us a completely negative, non-political attitude towards the civilisation in which we were living, an acceptance that no action could be taken because this was the condition in which we found ourselves. Nevertheless, when a friend of mine read the poem as a schoolboy at Stowe, he instantly became a Communist because he thought it was about the decay of capitalist society. But we thought it was about the decay of the whole society.

Then when I was at Oxford and we talked about poetry or literature, we considered that politics was absolute anathema to literature. Auden went much further than this and thought that no opinions at all should be expressed. Coming from a rather opinionated person this was strange, but as a matter of fact if you look at very early poems like "This Lunar Beauty" (1930) you do get the impression of something very close to pure poetry, in which all the opinion has been extracted:

This lunar beauty
Has no history,
Is complete and early;
If beauty later
Bear any feature
It had a lover
And is another.

At the same time of course, buried deep down in Auden there was an ideologist waiting to get out. The General Strike of 1926, when we were schoolboys, had made us for the moment think about politics. Auden drove an ambulance for the T.U.C. (but then he has an explanation for that) and my brother, who was at school with Auden, actually drove a steam engine. Auden has astutely observed that the working class did not realise how the middle class was always longing to drive trains and so loved the General Strike, because this was a great opportunity to do such things. But on the whole, even when we were school boys, if there was a choice we always called ourselves socialists and were for the strikers rather than for our parents' society.

However, the Slump in 1929 suddenly sliced this society down the middle and brought about a confrontation of oppressors and victims. So instead of just accepting that one belonged to this and couldn't possibly do anything about it, one was suddenly faced with the possibility of taking the side of the victims, and that is what we did. And then the Slump was compounded by Fascism, which was a further split right down the society. Fascism presented us with the choice of either continuing to write a "silver age" kind of poetry in a society which might collapse so that you wouldn't even be able to carry on any task of literature, or fighting against Fascism. So we resisted Fascism.

But once we had got in this position there were further pressures, the most fundamental of which was the fact that we were really in a frivolous position. I really think this was true—I'm not just saying it for effect. About five years ago I said to Isaiah Berlin, "You know, I think we were a frivolous generation", and he looked rather upset; but then the next morning he rang me and said, "You know, I have been thinking about it: you are quite right, we were in a sort of frivolous position". Well, I will tell you why.

At this point you can divide the Thirties into three groups. One group is the serious ideologists, the Communists—and let's forget all about Stalinism and the actual results of Communism—the people who seriously said, This society is finished, it is incapable of maintaining itself and we have to have another kind of society in order to have full employment; for what could be more proof of the complete decay of a capitalist society than its inability to go on employing people? Then it followed that we must fight Hitler, and if you are going to fight Hitler seriously you must if necessary combat his propaganda with our propaganda, his lies with our lies. So the ideologists rubbed our noses in the dirt and said, We have analysed this social system, we know the answer and if you are really seriously going to support Communism you have to accept our directives, even if your ideals are going to suffer.

There was a second group of people whom I would call "the Saints", that is to say people who didn't actually become Communists but who did go over to the working class. They reduced their standard of living to that of the working class; they lived amongst the workers, although they maintained a completely free attitude as regards their opinions. Simone Weil, for instance went to Spain and lived the life not of an intellectual, like myself or those of us who went to Spain and attended congresses and so on, but of a Spanish worker. And George Orwell went to Wigan during the Slump and lived with a working class family. He wrote his book *The Road to Wigan Pier*, and then worked as a dishwasher in Paris and wrote *Down and Out in London and Paris.*

Thirdly, there were people who combined both of these things, who were both Saints and Communists, like John Cornford, Christopher Caldwell and so on. There were also people like Dylan Thomas and Empson who were very critical of us on perfectly justified grounds. But at the same time we didn't doubt at all that they were in some way on our side, we didn't have any doubts about their moral and political judgement.

People often wonder why Auden withdrew "Spain". Orwell

wrote an essay in which he attacked this poem as being absolutely typical of the attitude of someone who, to use the phrase that came in during the Second World War, swans his way through a revolution. He took the lines "Today the deliberate increase in the chances of death,/The conscious acceptance of guilt in the necessary murder", and he said that no one who had actually seen a political murder, of which I suppose Orwell had seen heaps, would or could write lines of this kind. Of course, Auden pointed out that he was simply stating the situation, which was that if you joined you did have to accept murder and propaganda, but he felt very challenged and started taking it out of his poems. You see, although Auden wrote some deeply moving poems, like "Refugee Blues", about this situation, communism also appealed to something in him just as an idea to play around with. So "Spain" is really a sort of Marxist model of a poem—thesis, the past; antithesis, the present struggle; synthesis, the future. Eventually he came to realise he wasn't truly a Marxist, and he felt critical of himself for having written like that, and it was for this reason that he didn't want such poems to be printed. Ideology was very attractive to him—one could say that his development has been from Freud through Marx to Christian theology. It's the same with "September 1, 1939", which contains the line, "We must love one another or die". I asked him why he suppressed that poem, whether it was because we aren't going to love one another and so it is only a rhetorical statement. He said, "No, it is because we are going to die anyway, so it is perfectly meaningless". Of course, he knows perfectly well that these poems will be dug up; suppressing them is a kind of game.

A turning point for me was a congress in Madrid in 1937. Anti-Fascists were very split then because André Gide had just written his book, *Retour de l'U.R.S.S.*, in which he told various unpleasant facts about Russia. There were people, some of whom I admired very much, who got up and said, "It isn't that we think everything Gide has written is untrue, but this pamphlet is giving solace and comfort to the people who at this moment are dropping shells on us" (though it wasn't more than one or two shells that got anywhere near us). Well, I found myself very much on the side of Gide in this; it was a sort of test case. When I came home through Paris I left a note for Gide saying that I supported him, and then after that I had a conversation with Auden and he said, "Yes, in whatever circumstances of revolution we cannot give way to the idea that you have to tell lies and do things simply out of the exigence of the revolution". So that was a turning point.

Editor: In the discussion which followed there was a question about Germany:

Stephen Spender: Well, personally I am half German on my mother's side, although the family has been in England for a long time. The extraordinary thing is how one was made to feel if one wasn't completely English and one hadn't been to a public school. I went to University College School where the head-master used to tell us that if we behaved like public school boys, that was the real test, but I don't think we did. One reason for the Germanism of the Thirties was the reaction against Bloomsbury and its irritating way of trotting out French all the time—French painting, French everything, French culture. The tremendous air of superiority of the Francophile annoyed us very much, and we preferred the Germans, whom I suppose we regarded at that time as a bit down-trodden. Of course, Berlin was exceedingly interesting politically; you really did feel that you were at the centre of some ghastly kind of drama, rather like you do in America now. I asked Stuart Hampshire when he left America, "What do you regret most about leaving?" and he said, "Well, it is like leaving a crime story half way through, one would rather like to be there to read on to the end". There was that kind of feeling about Germany. Also there was an extraordinary openness about it; I mean Berlin is a vulgar place, in fact I think it has always been the most classless town in the world. Maybe there was a sort of upper class hidden away somewhere, but I never met them; Christopher Isherwood describes them a bit in one or two of his stories. But otherwise it was a place where you felt you knew everything about everybody, because they told you their whole life-stories almost the moment you met them; perhaps it was partly because of a lack of subtlety in the Germans—they had nothing very much to withhold!

David Daiches: I'd like to say something about the particular kind of excitement and torment which we felt in the Thirties, in spite of our sense of doom as Hitler marched into the Rhineland and seized Czechoslovakia. It looked as though war was inevitable, and we all saw the Spanish Civil War as a rehearsal for that war. But as I say, in spite of that sense of doom there was a sense of excitement, almost comparable to the excitement that Wordsworth felt in the French Revolution: "Bliss was it in that dawn to be alive". It seemed that in spite of all the horrors that were on the horizon there was a brave new world coming. It was a very strange mixture, that. We felt that the war was inevitable, and that it was going to be absolutely horrible—much worse, in fact, than it actually was, though God knows it was bad enough, because we were brought up on the anti-war books from the First World War, the Wellsian Apocalyptic vision of *The War of the Worlds*, and that sort of thing. We really thought that on the first day of the war London would be wiped out, and it was an enormous surprise and relief when it wasn't. I remember, to be quite personal about it, marrying when I was only twenty-four because my wife and I agreed that we probably wouldn't survive and certainly our children wouldn't, so we might as well get what we could out of the world before it was too late. Curiously, my children experienced this same kind of excitement when they went on Aldermaston marches; the sense of doom and the sense of solidarity went together. It was exciting and it was enjoyable, and yet it was doom-laden at the same time. In spite of everything there was a feeling of gaiety and solidarity which made this time much happier than it may sound in retrospect.

But I want to talk about the poetry rather than the politics. In 1934 Cecil Day Lewis produced a book called *A Hope for Poetry*, which was an account of the new poetry, that is to say mostly Auden, Spender and himself (MacNeice was a rather different kind of person and wasn't really associated in that trilogy). We know now, of course, that those three poets were very different and went very different ways eventually, but at that time they were associated for various personal reasons; they were friends. What Cecil Day Lewis tried to do in that book was to explain the influences on his generation of poets, and those influences were Hopkins, Wilfred Owen, Walt Whitman and to some extent Eliot, but I don't think he made a great fuss about Eliot.

The point I want to make now is that these poems were full of verbal excitement, quite apart from the politics. All the time what I noticed in *Poems* (1930) was Auden's use of para-rhymes: "Since you are going to begin today/Let us consider what it is you do". I traced that right through the poem, and wrote a little note on the bottom, trying to explain to myself how those lines fall on the ear, and how the para-rhyme adds to the rhetorical effect of the poem. This was a great linguistic excitement. Again,

> The Spring unsettles sleeping partnerships,
> Foundries improve their casting process, shops
> Open a further wing on credit till
> The winter. In summer boys grow tall . . .

That half-rhyme of "ships" and "shops", and "till" and "tall", is what I noticed; the fact that this is a poem about the decline and destruction of the capitalist system is not something that caught my immediate attention. I was also interested in Auden's use of slang, though I wasn't particularly happy about such poems as:

It's no use raising a shout.
No, Honey, you can cut that right out.
I don't want any more hugs;
Make me some fresh tea, fetch me some rugs.
Here am I, here are you:
But what does it mean? What are we going to do?

That is the refrain of the poem: "what does it mean? What are we going to do?" I didn't think that was a terribly successful poem, but I was interested in the American-style slang, as we considered it to be.

In the volume called *Look, Stranger!* (1936) I was especially impressed by a new emergent quality, a sense of sadness that the foundations of civilisation were not collapsing with a thunderous bang, but somehow slowly and sadly ebbing away. Auden gets this effect in generalised retrospective poems about the unhappy story of man: "Our hunting fathers told the story/Of the sadness of the creatures"—I have always found and still find that a very moving poem. And those poems which he wrote when he was teaching at a school in Helensburgh in Scotland, looking out over the loch on evenings, meditating about his sleeping pupils in the little town below his window and the water, and thinking back about his past, his parents and his destiny, are very remarkable. I just want to quote two stanzas from two different poems. One is from "To a Writer"—Christopher Isherwood—"on His Birthday", which comes to a slow meditative stop as he leans out of the window, looking out over the water, trying to hold the moment of history in his hand and to understand its meaning:

This then my birthday wish for you, as now
From the narrow window of my fourth floor room
I smoke into the night, and watch reflections
Stretch in the harbour. In the houses
The little pianos are closed, and a clock strikes.
And all sway forward on the dangerous flood
Of history that never sleeps or dies.
And, held one moment, burns the hand.

The other stanzas I want to quote come from "The earth turns over, our side feels the cold":

Language of moderation cannot hide;
My sea is empty and the waves are rough:
Gone from the map the shore where childhood played

Tight-fisted as a peasant, eating love;
Lost in my wake the archipelago,
Islands of self through which I sailed all day,
Planting a pirate's flag, a generous boy;
And lost the way to action and to you.

Lost if I steer. Gale of desire may blow
Sailor and ship past the illusive reef,
And I yet land to celebrate with you
Birth of a natural order and of love;
With you enjoy the untransfigured scene,
My father down the garden in his gaiters,
My mother at her bureau writing letters,
Free to our favours, all our titles gone.

It is a remarkable last line, with that pun on "titles" meaning that our inheritance, our legal right to the past, and all our social pretensions are gone, with an organic human relationship replacing the artificial ones.

Similarly, in the Thirties what impressed us most about Stephen Spender's poems was his lyrical quality. His poems were much more open-worked than Auden's. They were less obviously intellectual and sometimes less gimmicky, because Auden tended to throw the book at you; he tried absolutely everything, and if it didn't work he tried something else. One had the feeling about Spender that he was a simpler soul, if I could say so without offence; I don't mean it in any bad sense at all. One felt that he was perhaps less interested in language than in his feelings, and was trying to get the language right so that he could get the feelings right, whereas it sometimes appears to be the other way round with Auden. Spender's other striking quality was his capacity to domicile industrial imagery in a lyrical nature poem, which I suppose led to the "Pylon Poets" name that Cyril Connolly invented. In fact he has a poem called "The Pylons":

Now over these small hills they have built the concrete
That trails black wire:
Pylons, those pillars
Bare like nude, giant girls that have no secret.

And in that fine poem, "The Landscape near an Aerodrome" he again tries to domicile industrial and technological imagery in a nature landscape; there are also the poems like "Oh young men oh young comrades", which is in the simple rhetorical tradition of left-wing exhortation. They were more interesting then than now, I think. There is also that strange poem, often quoted since, illustrative of the attempt to find out what history was about and how we established continuity with a tradition of people rather than of things, beginning "I think continually of those who were truly great". It has always stuck in my mind, as I think it has stuck in the minds of most people in the Thirties, as indicative of an almost anguished search for a human condition across the years.

So I hope I have redressed the balance a little; a lot of these poems were interesting just as poems, as uses of language, as developments in new poetic techniques, in the domiciling of new kinds of imagery into traditional patterns, in the developing of new kinds of rhetoric, and in the synthesising of new kinds of comic gaiety. This was all very exciting, and it wasn't all political; a lot of it was literary excitement.

Laurence Lerner: We so often hear nowadays, and I am sure we say it ourselves, that the young are very unhistorical, because they are so interested in the present and the future and subordinate the past. I have been struck by the fact that everybody here has been talking about the Thirties in an historical and almost antiquarian spirit, because I half expected people to offer comparisons between the Thirties and the situation today, to ask how much we have got back to the situation of the Thirties and how much we have completely moved away from it. I would like to suggest one or two points of comparison.

No one has said absolutely explicitly, though I suppose we might have assumed it, that a lot of the reaction against the Thirties took place in the Fifties. But now, as we look back on the Thirties, we see them as a decade that was absolutely frightened stiff of being annihilated. Almost all the political stances of the decade seemed to spring from two things, a fear of Communism and fear of annihilation. In the Fifties the one really popular political movement that sprang up in Britain was CND, which was also about fear of annihilation; but now that has gone, hasn't it? The bombs are just as likely, scientifically, to blow us up, but they do not seem to be dominating people's thoughts in the same way. Then in the late Sixties, when all the student revolts broke out, I remember wondering whether we were returning to the nineteenth-century situation when people could march through the streets waving banners, uninhibited by a fear that they might disturb a frozen situation and unleash a war of some kind. So it is obviously interesting to ask in what sense this has taken us back to the position of the Thirties and in what sense it hasn't.

Here one is speculating wildly, but the one thought that has struck me is that in the Thirties, as many people have been saying, there was this one big, obviously evil, external threat of Fascism, and therefore you directed your political antagonism towards that. In the Seventies this threat doesn't exist in the same way: there is not this great big shadow of Hitler looming. Therefore people turn round and direct their attacks on what, to many older people, seems the normal way of life, on all sorts of institutions which their parents have normally lived with. Of course you can take two attitudes to this: you either say it is an irrational attack on authority, or else you say it is the result of a much subtler analysis, which can detect the more insidious repressive factors because the obvious ones have gone.

Moving to a literary perspective, my own, over-simplified view of twentieth-century poetry is that the strict forms used in earlier times seem to have been no longer tolerable to poets. Almost every serious poet has felt that, because he was a man who spoke ordinary speech and his personal feelings were unique, he must in some way break the traditional forms and seem obviously to defy them. This fight between traditional forms and a wish to throw them off has had all sorts of results which are typified by MacNeice's poems in which he deliberately writes colloquial verse which does not quite scan but has the ghost of a metrical scheme in it. Sometimes I think half-rhymes are the absolutely essential feature of twentieth-century poetry: you have the form and then you defy it.

There was a lot of this in the Sixties and there is a lot now, but it has recently become very unfashionable. It seems that the thing to do now is not to break form but to ignore it. This is poetically very sad. Just as it would seem wrong to me for a modern poet to write totally in traditional form, so to write as if no one had ever used traditional metres and rhymes and formal devices is to cut yourself off from the really exciting creative battle of twentieth-century poetry, which Auden fought—the battle inside the poem between the form and the speech, the traditional and the individual.

Further Reading

Ronald Blythe, *Age of Illusion* (Houghton Mifflin, 1964)

Noreen Branson and Margot Heinemann, *Britain in the 1930s* (Weidenfeld, 1971)

David Daiches, *Poetry and the Modern World* (Chicago University, 1940)

Robert Graves and Alan Hodge, *The Long Week-End* (Faber, 1940)

Christopher Isherwood, *Mr Norris Changes Trains* (Woolf, 1935)

Lions and Shadows (Hogarth, 1938)

Christopher Isherwood, *Goodbye to Berlin* (Hogarth, 1939)
C. Day Lewis, *The Buried Day* (Chatto, 1969)
D.E.S. Maxwell, *Poets of the Thirties* (Routledge, 1969)
Charles L. Mowat, *Britain Between the Wars* (Methuen, 1955)
Malcolm Muggeridge, *The Thirties* (Hamilton, 1940)
George Orwell, *The Road to Wigan Pier* (Gollancz, 1937)
Homage to Catalonia (Secker, 1938)
Stephen Spender, *World Within World* (Hamilton, 1951)
Julian Symons, *The Thirties* (Cresset, 1960)
Hugh Thomas, *The Spanish Civil War* (Eyre, 1961)

XII

DYLAN THOMAS

John Wain, Professor of Poetry at the University of Oxford

Introduction

Dylan Thomas' fame after the Second World War derived as much from stories about his wild life as from the notorious obscurity of some of his poems and the highly charged lyricism of others. Since then his work has paid the penalty of fashionable success, for it was eclipsed for many in the Fifties and Sixties by the determinedly unpretentious good sense and controlled tone of poets like Philip Larkin. A. Alvarez has suggested that Larkin's attitude is summed up in the opening of "Church-going"—"Hatless, I take off/My cycle-clips in awkward reverence"—and this is certainly a total contrast with the impassioned eloquence of lines like "And death shall have no dominion" and "Do not go gentle into that good night".

John Wain, who came to prominence as a novelist and poet in the early Fifties, recalls that Thomas' "bardic exultation" suited exactly the deep emotions of the War Years. He traces this bardic quality to Thomas' Welsh background, telling us enough about the life to illuminate the main stages in his poetic development. Mr Wain recognizes and accounts for the unevenness of Thomas' achievement, but argues that there is enduring value in the superb orchestration of the verse and in the feeling for ordinary people which is expressed in the short stories and the later poems.

John Wain: There is a preliminary hesitation in speaking of Dylan Thomas caused simply by the pronunciation of his name: whether is should be the English "Dillon", which he used most often, or the original Welsh "Dullon". This hesitation on the threshold is symptomatic, because the Welshness of this poet is a characteristic that people have difficulty in grasping and coming to terms with. In my opinion an appreciation of Dylan Thomas really begins and ends with an appreciation of his Welshness—it saves one from all manner of false emphases.

Let us begin, though, by looking at a few lines that occur near the beginning of his poem "After the Funeral (in memory of Ann Jones)". This is one of the early poems, though not the earliest. It contains these lines:

In a room with a stuffed fox and a stale fern,
I stand, for this memorial's sake, alone
In the snivelling hours with dead, humped Ann
Whose hooded, fountain heart once fell in puddles
Round the parched worlds of Wales and drowned each sun
(Though this for her is a monstrous image blindly
Magnified out of praise; her death was a still drop;
She would not have me sinking in the holy
Flood of her heart's fame; she would lie dumb and deep
And need no druid of her broken body).
But I, Ann's bard on a raised hearth, call all
The seas to service that her wood-tongued virtue
Babble like a bellbuoy over the hymning heads,
Bow down the walls of the ferned and foxy woods
That her love sing and swing through a brown chapel,
Bless her bent spirit with four, crossing birds.

The expression "I, Ann's bard on a raised hearth" is the kind of double exposure one finds so very often in modern literature. The raised hearth is primarily and physically the cold, tiled hearth in the horrible little front room where the young man has gone to get away from the other people at the funeral. In the Thirties, all houses of the respectable lower-middle or artisan classes had in the front of the house a "best room". This front room was usually cold, stiff and extremely miserable—quite unlike the lived-in room next door with a fire burning, a dog lying asleep on the hearth, deep armchairs, a smell of cooking, and people bustling about. The best room, where important visitors were shown, was a sheer waste of space for ordinary living purposes, but it was very important for ritual purposes. In the front room of this poem, where the poet is meditating over his dead relative, Ann Jones, there is a stuffed fox, and a fern under a glass dome: dead ornaments. Everything in the room is dead.

But also, of course, "Ann's bard on a raised hearth" is the poet on his rostrum, the bard on his platform. In a tribal society where the poet is the bard, the bard is brought out at ceremonial occasions, occasions of rejoicing, of significance for the whole people. On his dais he utters his lofty song to memorialise great events and praise the heroes of the nation; he is listened to by the entire people from the highest to the lowest; he is their memory, their collective voice. The craft of bardic poetry takes many years to master and in every society in which we have record of a bard it was a part of ordinary people's education to know the rules and the general ground plan of bardic poetry and what kind of effect the bard was aiming at. So when the youthful Dylan Thomas says, "I, Ann's bard on a raised hearth", he is pointing to an element in his poetry that it is very important not to miss.

To this day Welsh poetry has retained some of the bardic atmosphere and conventions. The poetry written in Welsh itself makes use of conventions that have remained unbroken since the Middle Ages. I have attended a competition for poets at the National Eistedfodd. The form of the competition was that half-a-dozen poets came on to the platform and the master of ceremonies read out the first three lines of a quatrain written according to the traditional rules of Welsh versification. The poets were given ten minutes, at the end of which they had to recite the quatrain with their own last lines. Unable to follow the language, I watched my fellow auditors. It was wonderful to see the feelings that ran through them: when a poet had provided a witty line they all laughed delightedly, when it was something grave and serious they listened solemnly. It was obviously a very deep experience for them all yet, as far as I could see, they didn't come from any one particular social class—there were farmers, bank employees, the man in front of me was a miner with coal scars on his neck. This atmosphere, where a whole people is interested in the poetic craft and knows about it, must spill over, even into the work of a poet who has no Welsh.

Dylan Thomas came from a background which had been rural

and Welsh-speaking until the generation of his parents. Both the parents had come to Swansea, where he grew up, from the rural hinterland of Caernarvonshire. One of his great uncles on his father's side was an acknowledged poet in Welsh—his bardic name was Gwilym Marles, and that's where Dylan's middle name came from: he was called Dylan Marlais Thomas. This poet was part of the ancestral presence, the rest was made up of country people, Welsh-speaking rurals, small farmers. However, Dylan's father, D.J. Thomas, had made a more or less conscious rejection of the Welsh side of his being. He sent Dylan and his sister to an elocutionist to learn to rid themselves of their sing-song Welsh accent and to speak with what Dylan himself called a "cut-glass" English accent. Furthermore, he indoctrinated Dylan very early into classical English literature, particularly by reading Shakespeare to him. I feel sure it was of great value to the developing poetic mind to have Shakespeare read by a man who, whoever he may have wished to get away from it, was a Welshman, who would put plenty of rhetorical fire into his reading. So Welshness came seeping through into the essentially English trained sensibility of the boy. He attended Swansea Grammar School where his father was an English teacher; he didn't do very much work there, but I think he took from it what he needed. He left school at sixteen and lived at home until the age of twenty. He then went to London.

The London literary scene in which the young Dylan Thomas arrived was dominated by a kind of verse that was, in the best sense, almost journalistic. It dealt with the events and issues of the time. Poets wrote about international unrest, war, unemployment; they brought social realities into their verse. The worst of that socially committed Thirties verse is very poor, like rather clumsy journalism. The best, as in the early poems of Auden, is very interesting, very discursive, very alert, very informed and bright, sometimes rather brittle. It wasn't the kind of poetry that Dylan Thomas was good at writing. He always knew himself well enough to realise that his greatest strength was for a poetry very highly charged with emotion, exploring the complexities of feeling and aware of the deep underlying currents of life, the merging of the physical and the spiritual within the human consciousness. It was a poetry which was highly rhetorical, very crafted—very *bardic*, when all is said and done. It had no truck with the "social reality" verse which was dominant at the time he went to London. It's not that he was himself indifferent to politics; he was a left-wing socialist with the same kind of views as the young men who were writing the socially conscious left-wing poems that appeared in magazines like *New Signatures* at that time, but these views didn't get into his work. What got into his work was the deep underlying instinctual basic presences of life.

A typical early Dylan Thomas poem from the volume that he published when he was twenty called *18 Poems* is this poem of identification with nature:

The force that through the green fuse drives the flower
Drives my green age; that blasts the roots of trees
Is my destroyer.
And I am dumb to tell the crooked rose
My youth is bent by the same wintry fever.

The force that drives the water through the rocks
Drives my red blood; that dries the mouthing streams
Turns mine to wax.
And I am dumb to mouth unto my veins
How at the mountain spring the same mouth sucks.

The hand that whirls the water in the pool
Stirs the quicksand; that ropes the blowing wind
Hauls my shroud sail.
And I am dumb to tell the hanging man
How of my clay is made the hangman's lime.

The lips of time leech to the fountain head;
Love drips and gathers, but the fallen blood
Shall calm her sores.
And I am dumb to tell a weather's wind
How time has ticked a heaven round the stars.

And I am dumb to tell the lover's tomb
How at my sheet goes the same crooked worm.

Now that is remarkable poetry for a boy in his teens to write. It's highly theatrical, in some respects it's exaggerated and overstated, but it's beautifully strong and very rhythmic. Here we have one of Dylan Thomas' enduring strengths: his poetry is very strongly rhythmic. He usually invents his own stanzaic forms, rather than borrowing from other poets, and once he has invented the form he makes each stanza revolve on its axis in a wonderful way. He knew how to do that even at the very beginning. Thus he communicates a very strong sense of the huge importance of what he is saying.

18 Poems, which Thomas published in 1934, established his

reputation as a poet at the age of twenty. Obviously he was under pressure to produce another book of poems as soon as possible, and after a couple of years he brought out his second book. *Twenty-five Poems* is not, on the whole, as good as *18 Poems*. The poems are less powerful and thrusting, less purposive, more confused and confusing, more clotted; they have too much language, too many images.

Years ago, when I was first reading Thomas, before there was such a thing as a collected edition, I bought the individual volumes and I was always puzzled by the fact that he started so well with *18 Poems* and that *Twenty-five Poems* were on the whole not as interesting. All that has been cleared up since scholars got to work on editing his papers after his death. It has been established that he was drawing on notebooks full of poems that he'd written whilst living in Swansea between the ages of sixteen and twenty. There are 250 poems that he thought good enough to be copied carefully as finished drafts, and these fuelled him for the rest of his life. Almost half of his poetic output is already in the notebooks that he'd written before he was twenty. Sometimes the poems are slightly altered, sometimes they are reworked so completely that they are barely recognizable, but the basic idea or impulse is already there in the notebooks. Naturally, he creamed the notebooks, brought out all the best, for his first book. But when he had to bring out his second book his London life, which was far less tranquil than his mother's cossetting in Swansea, didn't leave him with enough time to work patiently. The imaginative impetus was—not exactly dying down—but it was certainly more interrupted, more hindered. He had no choice but to go back over the notebooks and take, as it were, the second cream from them.

Most of the poems in *Twenty-five Poems* are extremely obscure, and a word is in place here, I think, about the whole question of Thomas as a difficult poet. I must say that it has been my experience in thirty years of reading him that the poems that satisfy me best are the ones that I don't have to struggle with too much. This is not the case with every poet. Some poets are naturally difficult, their minds inhabit ideas very subtly; they are deep thinkers, or agile, acute thinkers, and when they express themselves in a way that takes a lot of working out it is usually very well worth the effort. A naturally difficult poet like Thomas' friend William Empson is very accustomed to handling ideas, since he deals with them in his analytical, critical work. When Empson is difficult it is always a good plan to dig hard at that point. But when Thomas is at his most difficult digging hard at that point very often doesn't produce very much. The obscurity usually occurs when he's throwing in too much language, piling one thing on top of another before he's perfectly satisfied with what he's got to say. On the whole, from the start to the finish, the simpler poems of Thomas are the best.

I know that people have performed miracles of brilliant exegesis on Thomas' work. They have explained why every word is where it is in his most obscure poems—but then, of course, that is a very simple thing to do! If you sit down and cover a sheet of paper with words, a clever person will always be able to provide a meaning for those words, so it doesn't really matter that Professor this and Professor that have explained the difficult poems. What matters is whether the poems themselves live with you, whether after repeated readings you win through to something that you can take away and keep as a permanent possession. I can always do that with the simpler poems of Thomas, the ones that come to me, but the ones that I have to go after have not, on the whole, proved worth it. This is a personal judgement, and one I would not wish to force on anybody, but the more obscure he is the less his poems seem to live in my mind and this, as I say, is not the case with all poets.

The *Twenty-five Poems* of 1936 also come from the period in which Thomas was associated in the public mind with Surrealism. That, in my opinion, was simply a mistake. In the poetic, literary and artistic culture of the Thirties the only alternative centre, so to speak, to the socially conscious left-wing school represented by Auden and his followers was that offered by the Surrealists, who were preoccupied with the Unconscious—the exposing of those things which are usually covered up and disguised by the conscious mind. If you were not a socially conscious, clever poet then you were probably a Surrealist, or so people thought. And quite understandably, as a young man ready to go along with anything and to join in with anything that promised a bit of fun, Thomas associated himself with the Surrealists. At the gigantic Surrealist exhibition in 1936 there were a number of Surrealist poetry readings and Thomas took part in one. He also attended a reception, at which he circulated with a dish of boiled pieces of string, politely offering them as refreshments—a typical Surrealist joke. He enjoyed all that kind of thing. I think he rather misled his admirers, though, and they spent a long time looking for Surrealist virtues in his work, when what they actually had on their hands was a Welsh bard.

During these years Thomas was also writing short stories. As a writer of fiction he had no very strong narrative drive; his method was to cluster the action about a place and a set of characters. When he wrote fiction it was not narrative, it was what the Elizabethans would have called an "anatomy". Right from the beginning he was busy with the idea of describing a Welsh community. He wanted to write a series of stories that would link up into a long episodic novel about what he called "the Jarvis valley"—his name for the area that he knew in South Wales.

The stories that survive from the early and middle Thirties are almost Grand Guignol, full of blood, full of death, full of a sick distaste for life which seems to have welled up from I don't quite know where in this rather overprotected boy. Certainly his attitude at that time towards ordinary, common life as he observed it was very often one of rejection and disgust. There's a letter of 20th May 1934 to Pamela Hansford Johnson in which he talks about watching women digging for cockles on the sands at Laugharne in South Wales: "These women are sweating the oil of life out of the pores of their stupid bodies, and sweating away what brains they had so that their children might eat, be married, and ravished, conceive in their wombs that are stamped with the herring, and, themselves, bring up another race of thick-hipped fools to sweat their strengths away on these unutterably deadly sands." The very young Thomas, in other words, combined two attitudes that are very common among youthful radicals. On the one hand he had extreme anarchistic socialist views; on the other he seems to have had a distaste and revulsion for ordinary people. In theory socialism ought to go with a liking and admiration for ordinary people but, as we actually know, youthful revolutionaries seldom have any difficulty in reconciling these two logically quite irreconcilable positions, and he was no exception.

One of the things that happened to Thomas in the years just before the war was that quite suddenly he seemed to outgrow this revulsion against ordinary people. Quite suddenly common humanity, common, unremarkable life, came to seem to him something beautiful. In 1940 he brought out a group of ten stories about his growing up in Swansea, called *Portrait of the Artist as a Young Dog*. They are very beautiful—I think the finest thing he did outside his ten or a dozen supremely finest poems. They have all the quality of adolescence, of discovering oneself; they cast a very shrewd and humorous, but also a loving and accepting eye on average humanity. Typical of this is the story called "Patricia, Edith, and Arnold", about two servant-girls who are in love with the same young man. It's full of compassion and humour; in fact the whole book is irradiated with these qualities.

1940 was a very important year for Dylan Thomas in other ways. When the War began the effect on literary culture was that the popularity of Auden's kind of critical debating poetry suddenly crumbled. When war begins, when fighting actually breaks out, nobody has time to argue the toss any more. People are left with the basic realities of life—death, suffering, loneliness, and also, of course, joy. A time of disaster brings terrible miseries, but it also brings joys which are more intense than the joys of everyday placid life; the joy of people reunited for twenty-four hours before being separated again burns very fiercely. Auden, of course, left for America, and the person who stepped into the centre of the stage, without any doubt, was Dylan Thomas. The War period in Thomas' writing mingles with my personal memories. This is when I first began to read him, and I can certainly testify that those of us who were young at that time and were thinking of ourselves as trying to write poetry admired him more than anybody else. He was not so much older than ourselves that he was impossibly removed from our generation, and he wrote the sort of poetry we would like to write. The strength, the bardic exaltation with which he used language made him absolutely the right poet to celebrate those years. He is certainly, I think, the greatest poet of the Second World War.

Thomas was turned down for war service because of weak lungs (I should think he had that and a number of other things wrong with him by that time because he was drinking very heavily). He spent the War with the Crown Film Unit, the Government documentary film agency, and he identified with the life of the civilian population. With 40,000 people killed in the London Blitz the civilian was just as much involved in death as the serviceman except during the very heaviest fighting, and there are no finer utterances than the poems that were prompted by the suffering and death. Here is "A Refusal to Mourn the Death, by Fire, of a Child in London":

Never until the manking making
Bird beast and flower
Fathering and all humbling darkness
Tells with silence the last light breaking
And the still hour

Is come of the sea tumbling in harness

And I must enter again the round
Zion of the water bead
And the synagogue of the ear of corn
Shall I let pray the shadow of a sound
Or sow my salt seed
In the least valley of sackcloth to mourn

The majesty and burning of the child's death.
I shall not murder
The mankind of her going with a grave truth
Nor blaspheme down the stations of the breath
With any further
Elegy of innocence and youth.

Deep with the first dead lies London's daughter,
Robed in the long friends,
The grains beyond age, the dark veins of her mother,
Secret by the unmourning water
Of the riding Thames.
After the first death, there is no other.

The language here is as lofty, as far from colloquial syntax as always. The apparent difficulty of the poem is really only that it is constructed in very large syntactical bridges. For example, it's not until the end of the third line that we reach "darkness", the subject of the opening sentence, and there isn't a main verb until "Shall I let pray" in line ten. Briefly, he's saying that never until everything is over and life returns again to its elements will he involve himself in mourning because it is the process of continuing life which is taking the child. Notice an obvious example of a common cause of difficulty with Thomas' verse, his pivoting of his poems on puns: "The mankind of her going with a *grave* truth". Observe also the characteristic strategy of taking a form of words that is expected and then slipping in an unexpected word: "Shall I let *pray* the shadow of a sound", where one would normally expect "let fall".

The poem is superbly orchestrated: "the still hour/Is come of the sea tumbling in harness". That kind of internal rhyme—*come . . . tumbling*—occurs everywhere in these poems; it may derive from the echoing of sounds which in classical Welsh poetry is known as *cynghanedd*. "The Conversation of Prayer" was written at about the same time. It begins like this:

The conversation of prayers about to be said

By the child going to bed and the man on the stairs
Who climbs to his dying love in her high room,
The one not caring to whom in his sleep he will move
And the other full of tears that she will be dead . . .

Every line not only takes its place in a rhyme scheme but is broken, or broken and joined, by internal rhyme. This quality of orchestration marks all Thomas' work. It also points to the difference between his poetry and the work that has become fashionable in the Seventies. Although I'm sure it is temporary, for these things come and go, most poets have ceased to orchestrate, to care very much about verbal music. Thomas cared very greatly.

The poems of this period were printed in the volume *Deaths and Entrances*, which came out at the very end of the War. They had been printed in the literary periodicals, and I remember how one watched for them and waited for them; it was always an event. This was, I think, his supreme moment of ascendancy; he really did have a tremendous number of devoted readers.

The poems of *Deaths and Entrances* are not only about the War—its suffering and exaltation—they are also about the moments when those feelings lifted and allowed time for memories. Thomas' memories were always of his childhood, of the Caernarvonshire countryside, the farm, Fern Hill, where he went to stay with his Uncle Jack and Aunt Annie. One of the most famous of those poems is "Fern Hill", which is such a classic that it is practically a chestnut. Nonetheless it has an extraordinary quality of tenderness in recollection:

Nothing I cared, in the lamb white days, that time would
        take me
Up to the swallow thronged loft by the shadow of my hand,
    In the moon that is always rising,
        Nor that riding to sleep
    I should hear him fly with the high fields
And wake to the farm forever fled from the childless land.
Oh as I was young and easy in the mercy of his means,
        Time held me green and dying
    Though I sang in my chains like the sea.

The grandeur of those lines! That closing metaphor is something that one might almost find in Shakespeare—the mighty power of the sea which is nevertheless controlled, as in chains, because the tied moves it to and fro. It's a superb metaphor for the gathering power of the human being growing to maturity. And "Time held me green and dying", that is superbly strong and felicitous, poetic language very highly charged, and of a kind that the poets now, in the Seventies, are not really giving us. I expect the next chahge of taste will bring it back.

This was Thomas' greatest achievement, these were his greatest years. In 1952 he published his *Collected Poems*, which had a tremendous success. They sold 30,000 copies straight-away—which must have meant that virtually every reader of poetry in the British Isles bought a copy. Thomas was now a very successful, very dominant poet, but his personal problems were getting worse and worse. He could not be described in his later years as a happy man. In some ways he was always looking for those early years again, for a life where he was protected and had no responsibility. Although he was a husband and father and a famous literary man, he continued to behave like a child, a nice child very often, but always like a child. He never really knew what to do about life. He made a lot of money going on very exhausting tours in America, but when he had his pockets full of money he somehow managed to spend it all in a few hours. The problems returned and the bills returned and he retreated into drink; his health became worse and worse and, of course, he didn't live very long, he died at the age of 38.

During those last years he was working on a radio play called *Under Milk Wood*. Here he deals in his familiar way with a set of characters and a setting; once again, it is not so much a narrative as an anatomy of a little town. It might be Laugharne, where he spent some of the happiest and most tranquil parts of his last years, or it might be Newquay which he also knew. Anyway, he took a little seaport town and dwelt lovingly, but to my mind a little sentimentally on the characters there. All the qualities which I think are freshly and beautifully expressed in *Portrait of the Artist as a Young Dog* recur in *Under Milk Wood* in, to my way of thinking, a slightly squashy form. It doesn't seem to me such a good work as the early stories, but that is a personal opinion. Nevertheless, we see here Thomas' craftsmanship as a writer; whenever he was able to get down to work he was always deeply conscientious. With every form that he practised he showed very great respect for the laws of its being—not artificial literary conventions but the laws by which the form existed and flourished. *Under Milk Wood* is a showcase example of a radio play, whatever else it is.

How, then, should we estimate Dylan Thomas' achievement? Some of it, as in the work of every writer, will wash away, but some things will remain as rocks in a landscape. Personally I think we will remember the superb orchestration, the way his poems sing, the wonderful, let me say it, *bardic* craftsmanship of his work. The other quality that will remain is the way he won through—not, I think, without some spiritual toil—to the acceptance of ordinary people, to the liking and admiration for them which is so strong in *Deaths and Entrances.* This is powerful in the poem "The Hunchback in the Park", where the "solitary mister" who sleeps in a dog kennel and is teased by truant children dreams of

A woman figure without fault
Straight as a young elm
Straight and tall from his crooked bones
That she might stand in the night
After the locks and chains

All night in the unmade park
After the railings and shrubberies
The birds the grass the trees the lake
And the wild boys innocent as strawberries
Had followed the hunchback
To his kennel in the dark.

Further Reading

John Ackerman, *Dylan Thomas* (Oxford, 1964)
John M. Brinnin (ed.), *A Casebook on Dylan Thomas* (Cromwell, 1960)
Walford Davies (ed.), *Dylan Thomas, New Critical Essays* (Dent, 1972)
Clark Emery, *The World of Dylan Thomas* (Dent, 1971)
David Holbrook, *Llareggub Revisited* (Bowes, 1962)
Dylan Thomas (Athlone, 1972)
T.H. Jones, *Dylan Thomas* (Oliver, 1973)
Ralph Maud, *Poet in the Making: the Notebooks of Thomas* (Dent, 1965)
Ralph Maud, *Entrances to Dylan Thomas' Poetry* (Pittsburgh University, 1963)
William T. Moynihan, *The Craft and Art of Dylan Thomas* (Cornell, 1966)
Elder Olson, *The Poetry of Dylan Thomas* (Chicago, 1961)
E.W. Tedlock (ed.), *Dylan Thomas: the Legend and the Poet* (Heinemann, 1960)

XIII
WRITING POETRY

Ted Walker

Introduction

It is obviously appropriate to conclude a volume such as this with a contemporary poet's account of his own art. Ted Walker was born in 1934 and has published five books of poems, the first in 1964. His writing is marked by concrete and precisely detailed imagery, mostly of natural creatures and objects, but that is rarely all he seeks to do. Either by allowing his mind meditatively to build upon the observed scene or by describing it with heightened intensity he leads the reader to consider the deeper springs of human action. He makes a particularly free and vivid use of the relationship between clause structure and line and stanza length to wind his way into his themes and to alert the reader to the sharp turns in his meaning.

In his talk Ted Walker explains in engaging personal terms how he came to write three poems: "Father's gloves", "Founder" and "Easter Poem". He distinguishes the writing of "a proper poem", which he calls "a voyage of discovery", from the poem which is put together from a preconceived scheme. We see how the proper poem develops through inspiration out of experience, but that does not mean that it flows easily from any trivial event or through the first words that come to mind; a lot of strenuous imaginative work is required before the full significance of the poem emerges. Above all, perhaps, we see that the poet must be his own severest critic: the most important critical dialogue is that of the poet with himself.

Ted Walker: A poet depends to a very large extent for his craft on the accidents of his everyday life: poems come to him and he can't go in search of poems. So it's quite understandable that a long time might elapse without a poem coming to him at all, and this is distressing, because a poet who is not writing poems is suddenly not a poet any more. Although he's looking at life with the same sort of eyes that he always uses, he sees nothing that particularly inspires him to write. So what can he do about this? One thing is to do other sorts of writing—translations and so on—which will keep him going in the meantime, or perhaps, as I sometimes do with friends of mine, he can pick up the phone and say, Give me a subject to write upon.

Of course this is only a stopgap—no sort of proper poem is likely to emerge from it at all. I'm going to begin by reading one such poem that I wrote on a subject not of my choosing: gloves. Now gloves is not by any means a subject that could ever turn me on, but it was the subject given and I thought I'd better see what I could do with it. So I took a large piece of paper and wrote on it all the things that I could think of to do with the subject of gloves, and then in a very cold and calculated sort of fashion—using lots of little arrows and drawings and so on—I assembled a piece of verse. I took the subject of my father's gloves, largely because you never see him wearing them, and this was the poem:

Father's gloves

Not garments. A craftsman's armour
Worn to blunt the hooks of pain.
Massive, white asbestos mitts
He brought back from the shipyard
Hang cool by his blowlamp
And his sailmaker's palm.
In his hearth, treasured still,
Scored by remembered cinders,
Lie gauntlets from his dirt-track days
That sometimes, when his fire is dull,
He wears to prod the embers.
Keeping them rekindles him.

He keeps them all, the pairs
We give him on his birthdays,
Crammed in drawers too full to shut.
Some of them may have a use
At family ceremonial:
But, christening or funeral,
Pigskin, suede, kid or calf,
We'd have him carry them, because
His hands are warmer with them off.

Well, as I say, that's a piece of verse; it's not a proper poem, in my estimation at any rate, because I knew before I wrote the first line, so to speak, what this poem was going to say. Writing it was not what writing a poem ought to be, a voyage of discovery. I knew what the last line was going to be, I knew what sort of images I was going to put in, they were all there assembled, numbered, ready and waiting.

Also, it was written with the intellect entirely; I could make up points to say. For example, those gauntlets in the second stanza: my father did in fact spend part of his youth riding dirt-track motor-cycle and he did still have these old gauntlets, so I used them to make up the conceit that when he put them on to stir his fire, keeping them re-kindled him—not only his fire but him. Now, that was a made-up idea, using the intellect rather than those other areas within oneself that one calls upon to write a proper poem. And I finished up in a rather sentimental sort of way which I don't entirely approve of; it seemed to be a slick sort of ending. So there is an example of a non-poem, something which was written to order, something which I don't in fact think very highly of. One poet whose autobiography I read confessed once to sitting down on a wall in Spain, trying to think of an image to explain what he had to say. I think this gave him away because true poets, it seems to me, don't look for images; images are there and happen to be seen.

Sometimes, though, being asked to write a poem on a given subject can prompt something which one didn't know about. I was asked at one point to write on the subject of Rome. Well, I'd never been to Rome—the nearest I'd been was Milan—I didn't have any great feelings about it and I felt a sort of wry despair as I looked at the word written down on a blank sheet of paper. I didn't really think that I could do it—incidentally, the friend who'd set the subject was just going to Rome and it seemed to me that he was playing very unfairly! Anyway, a few days elapsed and I bothered myself with it and one night, unable to sleep, I started to think back to when I was a very small boy and I remembered how one afternoon in the infants' school our ordinary teacher was away and we were sent a supply-teacher just for that afternoon. And she came into the classroom and said that she was going to tell us the story of Romulus and Remus. Well, we weren't too happy about this, but it was better than doing a lot of other things. But then it turned out that this teacher was an absolute genius; by God, she could tell a story! And as I lay in bed, thirty years later maybe, trying to think of what to say about Rome, I suddenly found that as a little boy once again, I was actually crawling about on the hills of Rome; because that teacher managed to tell us so much about the place, calling upon her imagination and our imagination, that it was as though I had actually been in Rome.

So I tackled this subject from the point of view of the Romulus and Remus story. It was cheating a bit, but there it is, poets do cheat, and I found that a proper poem came out of it, just as a proper poem did not come out of the subject of gloves. I wrote this poem from the point of view of Romulus; he is telling the story in his words, looking back on how he did it:

Founder

I awoke as rushes hissed,
brushing my dream. The stem
fouled the roots of a fig tree.
A day, a night and a day
went by. Nobody came.
We waited. My runt twin wept.

Then there were fangs at my nape.
I was trailed through fallen figs,
meadow-marsh, and up to stone
that, moonlit, I crawled upon
till she brought him and her dugs:
all the strength I had to sap.

He had to be kept alive
long enough to be of use;
when our foster-mother died
I let the woodpecker feed
him, and the shepherds, sometimes.
He worked; cleared an olive grove,

hewed great stones and trimmed them;
laid them as I commanded.

He leaped my wall— but *Romule*,
noli, noli, Romule,
he moaned before I murdered
him. I looked over Latium,

alone, and saw above my hills
an eagle rising like a sun
to burn upon Liguria,
Picenum and Calabria,
turn, and glide superbly down
to strut along my city walls.

Now the point I'm making here is that with this attempt to write about Rome I was doing something more than what I did with the subject of gloves. If I'd tried to do the same as I did with the subject of gloves, I suppose I would have taken down the *Encyclopaedia Brittanica* and one or two books of travel, a few photographs or picture-postcards, and written a whole sheet of paper of that sort of observation. But in fact the way it came about was just by accident; I didn't deliberately try to remember being back at school. It just suddenly occurred to me by reliving a childhood experience in my imagination; for it's in the imagination that poems begin, go on, and finish for me.

What happened was that my choice of the word "runt"—"My runt twin wept"—indicated that Romulus was talking in a tough sort of way, and I realised in that moment that my poem wasn't just about the founding of Rome and the traditional Romulus and Remus story. It was about something else, the notion that dictators are ruthless men. So, having seen an accident occur, what I had to do then was to capitalise upon it, so I had to go on using the same tough sort of style, and by the time I'd finished what was a fairly short poem I seemed to have made a statement about the ruthlessness of dictators in general. It seems to me that that's what I expect from a poem, that it ought to say something beyond its literal meaning.

The next poem I'm going to talk about came about in a very haphazard, accidental fashion. At the time I was teaching in a school in Middlesex, in an industrial area where the boys I taught seldom saw a green tree or a green field. One of the things I used to was to take out parties for hikes during the Saturdays and Sundays. We'd catch a train into the Buckinghamshire or Berkshire countryside and in their clumsy shoes they would walk about, their eyes opening to all sorts of things. Pigs, cows, of course they'd seen them before, but they hadn't seen them closely. And somehow or other I myself, having been brought up in the countryside, saw a lot of these things through their eyes, afresh; I could see their delight in investigating these things close to.

Well, there came a day when we walked through a farmyard and there, nailed up on an out-building, was the body of a fox. Now, I'd seen hundreds of foxes, and I'd also seen, not hundreds but certainly a couple of dozen or so, dead, nailed up on a farm building, and I knew what this was all about. It was the farmer's superstition that by nailing up the body of a dead fox he would warn off other foxes from coming to steal his chickens. But most of the boys who were with me had not only never seen a fox in the flesh, but had certainly never seen such a horrific image, and they investigated this strange phenomenon with great wonder and amazement.

When I got home that evening I was somehow bothered about it. I didn't know what it was that troubled me; it may have been, I thought, that I was bothered by the boys being bothered about it, but in the end it wasn't that, it was something else. The image kept nagging at my mind, it meant something, I didn't know what. So what I began to do—as I always do—was to write down just a factual, detailed description of what I'd seen, the small details as well as the big ones. And what I got down was a picture of a fox nailed up on the door of a barn; it was still not the poem by any means, nothing more than descriptive writing.

At this point I still didn't realise what was bothering me. And then happened the accident—I keep coming back to that word—the accident which made this piece of writing start to be a poem. By giving the hard, concrete, factual detail, I revealed for myself what the poem was to be about. I'd written down the fact that the fur of the fox had some seeds of burdock in it at the head, and as I thought about these seeds of burdock I realised that what I had on my hands was a Crucifixion poem. The burdock was the crown of thorns.

Now we're on the way to having a poem: an image first bothering one, and then becoming an image which reminds one of something else. But it still wouldn't really be a poem unless the crucified Christ meant something to me as I was writing about it, and this is where the third point of the poem, the important point, came up. I was, in fact, going through a sort of spiritual crisis myself: the Christian faith, which I had held very firmly for many years was, though I wasn't admitting it, slipping away from me. And suddenly all these things came together. There were these boys looking at the fox and the image bothering me though I didn't know why. Then I tried to write about it and saw the fox as a crucifixion piece, and then it became a problem for me: what did Christianity mean to me, was I just hanging on to it, or what?

On the page in front of me I already had quite a number of lines written down of pure description; I don't like pure descriptive writing myself because it seems to me that it doesn't say all that much. I had to turn the poem into the way I wanted it to go, and so this is what I finished with, this is the finished poem:

Easter Poem

I had gone on Easter Day
early and alone to be
beyond insidious bells
(that any other Sunday
I'd not hear) up to the hills
where are winds to blow away

commination. In the frail
first light I saw him, unreal
and sudden through lifting mist,
a fox on a barn door, nailed
like a coloured plaster Christ
in a Spanish shrine, his tail

coiled around his loins. Sideways
his head hung limply, his ears
snagged with burdock, his dry nose
plugged with black blood. For two days
he'd held the orthodox pose.
The endemic English noise

of Easter Sunday morning
was mixed in the mist swirling
and might have moved his stiff head.
Under the hill the ringing
had begun: and the sun rose red
on the stains of his bleeding.

I walked the length of the day's
obsession. At dusk I was
swallowed by the misted barn,
sucked by the peristalsis

of my fear that he had gone,
leaving nails for souvenirs.

But he was there still. I saw
no sign. He hung as before.
Only the wind had risen
to comb the thorns from his fur.
I left my superstition
stretched on the banging barn door.

As you see, the poem is a good example of how a poet may lie in order to tell a bigger truth. This shocks some people but, of course, art is a question of selection: it's not what you put in but what you leave out that counts. The facts of the matter are that on that afternoon I had a crowd of about thirty yelling teenage boys with me, and that it was autumn, but this poem is about one man's spiritual crisis and so it would be quite inappropriate to have all those boys hanging about, so to speak, on the sidelines. The poem is about a problem which a man must face alone, so one of the very first words is the word "alone". And secondly, because the whole point of Christianity is the risen Christ, it suited my purpose to have this occur on Easter Day, the focus of the Christian year.

So there are two lies that I had to tell—let's call them fibs—to suit my ends, and there are other things too. I find in writing a poem that what I say had better mean something apart from the literal or superficial meaning. For example, later on in the poem I say,

I saw
no sign. He hung as before.
Only the wind had risen
to comb the thorns from his fur.

He wasn't a risen Christ, I wasn't given a sign. Then there is a flat statement about the weather, but the use of the word "risen" reminds us again of Christ. The wind clears away the mist of the previous two stanzas, which is a way of talking about one's confusion and bewilderment; and it combs the thorns from his fur, meaning that the crown of thorns has gone; in other words, yet another symbol of Christianity has been blown away.

I also intended a further meaning in the banging door in the last lines—"I left my superstition/stretched on the banging barn door". This had in fact happened on that afternoon, but the point is that here banging suggests something else: that although Christianity has gone and gone for good maybe the door is still half open, and if so then it keeps banging me and reminding me of something there that bothers me. So as this poem got written I was aware of the fact that I was turning it to my own purpose all the time, but I've got to believe it myself as I'm writing it. It was the same with the image which occurred to me quite early on, the fact that the fox did look like one of those little wayside shrines that you see in Catholic countries. I'd been in Spain that year and these images were still very much alive in my mind—when you have a proper poem going all sorts of recent images come to your aid, they seem to be there in the wings, ready to be used as you want them.

Once the poem has the sort of texture that I'm after, then really it is finished. What I don't do is go back a year after to a younger man's poem and mess about with it; this seems to me to be a kind of dishonesty. Once I've finished with a poem I like to feel that I've done my best for it, that at the time there's nothing else that I know to do with it. I know that years on I will have learnt a bit more; I know now, talking about "Easter Poem" ten years after I wrote it, that there are things in it so bad that I shudder—"peristalsis" is all wrong, and that bit about walking the length of the day's obsession. If I wrote that poem now I could do something with it, but it would be dishonest because it was the poem of a young man trying in his own way to look for truth, and somehow his very clumsiness is part and parcel of the poem.

Further Reading

Books about writing poetry:

W.H. Auden, *The Enchafed Flood* (Faber, 1951)
Marjorie Boulton, *The Anatomy of Poetry* (Routledge, 1953)
James Dickey, *Metaphor as Pure Adventure* (Washington Library of Congress, 1968)
Roy Fuller, *Owls and Artificers* (Deutsch, 1971)
Helen Gardner, *Poems in the Making* (University of Southampton, 1972)
Brewster Ghiselin (ed.), *The Creative Process* (University of California, 1952)
Arthur Koestler, *The Act of Creation* (Hutchinson, 1964)
C. Day Lewis, *The Poetic Image* (Cape, 1947)
Winifred Nowottny, *The Language Poets Use* (Athlone, 1962)
Robin Skelton, *The Poetic Pattern* (Heinemann, 1956)
The Practice of Poetry (Heinemann, 1971)

Stephen Spender, *The Making of a Poem* (Hamilton, 1955)

Books about modern poetry:

Calvin Bedient, *Eight Contemporary Poets* (Oxford, 1974)
Martin Dodsworth (ed.), *The Survival of Poetry* (Faber, 1970)
Elizabeth Jennings, *Poetry Today* (Longmans, 1961)
John Press, *Rule and Energy* (Oxford, 1963)
A Map of Modern English Verse (Oxford, 1969)
Michael Schmidt and Greval Lindop, *British Poetry since 1960* (Carcanet, 1972)
David Timms, *Philip Larkin* (Oliver, 1973)